THE MASTER BUILDERS

LE CORBUSIER
MIES VAN DER ROHE
FRANK LLOYD WRIGHT

LE CORBUSIER

MIES VAN DER ROHE

FRANK LLOYD WRIGHT

THE
MASTER
BUILDERS

by PETER BLAKE

W · W · NORTON & COMPANY

New York · London

W. W. Norton & Company, Inc.
500 Fifth Avenue, New York, N.Y. 10110
www.wwnorton.com

W. W. Norton & Company Ltd.
Castle House, 75/76 Wells Street, London W1T 3QT

Printed in the United States of America.

First published as a Norton paperback 1976 by arrangement with
Alfred A. Knopf, Inc.; reissued 1996

Library of Congress Cataloging in Publication Data

Blake. Peter, 1920–
    The master builders.

    Includes index.
    1. Jeanneret-Gris, Charles Edouard, 1887-1965.
2. Mies van der Rohe, Ludwig, 1886--1969. 3. Wright,
Frank Lloyd, 1867-1959. 4. Architecture, Modern—
20th century. I. Title.
NA680.B52 1976   724.9   76-7067

ISBN 0-393-31504-5

67890

Acknowledgments

A GREAT DEAL has been written about modern architecture; a great deal has been written, too, about the three men who are the central figures in this book; and a great deal has been written both by Le Corbusier and by the late Frank Lloyd Wright about their own work and principles. (Mies van der Rohe has always left the business of words to others.) No one attempting a critical evaluation of the work of Le Corbusier, Mies van der Rohe, and Frank Lloyd Wright can help being indebted to all these sources.

I am indebted, in particular, to the complete record of Le Corbusier's work published over the years by the Swiss architect Willy Boesiger; to the biography of Mies van der Rohe by my friend Philip C.

Johnson (and to Mr. Johnson's frequent, stimulating, irreverent, and penetrating comments on the present architectural scene); and to the books on Frank Lloyd Wright by Grant Manson and Henry-Russell Hitchcock. My own interpretation of the work of the three architects represented in this book does not always coincide with the interpretations offered by earlier writers. But much factual, biographical material was gathered by others long before this book was conceived, and I gratefully acknowledge the contribution these critics have made to my education. Needless to say, none of the three architects dealt with in this book assisted me in any way in the writing of his biography, or authorized the book's publication.

P. B.

Preface to the Paperback Edition

THE BULK of this book was written in the 1950s, and published in the United States, Europe, South America, and Asia in 1960. At that time, both Le Corbusier and Mies van der Rohe were still alive and extremely active; Frank Lloyd Wright had just died, in 1959, but some of his most interesting works, such as the Guggenheim Museum in New York, and the Marin County Civic Center in the San Francisco Bay Area, were still under construction.

Le Corbusier died in August 1965, having completed at least a dozen buildings and projects of considerable importance during the final years of his life. For obvious reasons, these were not covered in the 1960 edition of *The Master Builders*. Mies van der Rohe died in August 1969, shortly after the dedication of his National Gallery in West Berlin, which is considered, by some of his admirers, to have been his most beautiful building. Between 1960 and 1969, he designed and built a number of other large and impressive projects—both in Canada and in the United States. They were largely elaborations and refinements of the Lake Shore Drive Apartments in Chicago, and of the Seagram Building in New York.

To make this book a reasonably complete record of the work of these three Heroes of the Modern Movement, I have added new chapters to my original discussion of the work of Le Corbusier and of Mies van der Rohe, as well as numerous illustrations. Nothing has been changed in the wording of the original text (except for one or two corrections of minor factual errors, which had slipped into the first several editions). As a result the tense employed in the first twenty chapters on Le Corbusier, and in the first fourteen on Mies van der Rohe, is in conflict with that employed in the new chapters written after their deaths and for this edition. Revising and resetting the type for every other sentence in those earlier chapters would have been an expensive and pointless exercise. My apologies to the reader, and my publisher's apologies as well.

Since the main body of this book was written, many things have changed in our perception of the Modern Movement. The "Ideal Cities" sketched out by the men whose work is recorded in this book have been built (more or less) and lived in, and the experience has at times been sobering. Frank Lloyd Wright's "Broadacre City"—or a caricature thereof—was constructed, on millions of acres, in the U.S. and elsewhere, after World War II; it is known to all of us as suburbia, and most of it is a crashing bore. Mies van der Rohe's, or his friend Ludwig Hilberseimer's, "Rational Cities"—or another caricature thereof—were built both in the capitalist world, in monotonous, curtain-walled office parks along beltways and elsewhere, and in the communist world, in even more monotonous precast concrete diagrams from Moscow to Warsaw to East Berlin. And Le Corbusier's "Radiant Cities"—or still another caricature thereof—were built in Brasilia, in Chandigarh, and in many European "New Towns." They were not quite as monotonous as those curtain-walled utopias, but they invariably seemed devoid of what is often referred to as "human scale": the pedestrian scale that continues to attract so many of us to certain beautiful cities of the past, like Florence, Bologna, Paris, and Prague. The "Ideal Cities" proposed at various times by the Masters of the Modern Movement were scaled, almost invariably, to the automobile rather than to the human frame—a profound misunderstanding of what life in cities will always be about so long as the human race inhabits them.

Much of this has been made clear to us by Jane Jacobs, whose book *The Death and Life of Great American Cities* (1963) generated much rethinking on the part of architects and urban designers—a very healthy exercise, leading many of us to look at cities once again as pedestrian environments inhabited by human beings.

But her book also generated some grotesque exercises in populist kitsch, better known as "Postmodernism." These exercises were supposed to show respect for and memories of things past—the past, in the case of the U.S., being one that never really was.

Although postmodern theory was dressed up in deceptively sophisticated prose, it was successful largely because it offered respectability to "marketing"—the motivating force in more and more human enterprises. Buildings were designed not to reflect some human or rational or artistic concerns (God forbid!), but to sell the owners' products, or to sell the architect's name. In fact, "name architecture" became a way of identifying the work of the most widely publicized practitioners—and incidentally the names of their publicists and clients.

This architectural fashion business continued in full swing for about twenty-five years, and by 1995 it seemed to some of us that it had run its course.

Alas, it was just about then that Walt Disney Enterprises decided to build a City of the Future near Orlando, Florida, to be known as "Celebration"—the "Sparkling Cider" of Mickeyland. All the predictable "name" architects in the U.S. were commissioned to design the landmarks for the new Capital of Mickeyland, and one or two architects who had been known, earlier, for their more serious work were signed up as well.

Postmodernism had never caught on in Europe or in Asia or in other parts of the world where the past was real and architecture was taken more seriously. And so the center of gravity, as it were, of the Modern Movement began to shift back to areas where architecture was still thought to be an art rather than a marketing gimmick: the most convincing second- or third-generation modernists were architects like Tadao Ando, Norman Foster, Herman Hertzberger, and others similar to them in Europe, Japan, India, and elsewhere, who had never been corrupted by postmodernism. Some of the best U.S. architects, like Paul Rudolph, Kevin Roche, I. M. Pei, and others of their caliber were doing more and more of their best work outside the U.S.

Well, the future may not be what it used to be, to paraphrase the late French poet Paul Valéry, but I doubt very much that the future is going to be anything like Mickeyland.

The three architects whose work I tried to describe in this book had a rather more serious and more beautiful vision of the future. Their age is sometimes called Heroic. However that may be, they were possessed by a clear and pure vision of an Ideal World—a peaceful, humane, and decent world, anyway—and they pursued that vision honestly and without significant compromise. They may have been wrong some of the time, but they were always beautifully and honestly wrong. And in their own work, over the years, they reviewed and revised many of their original versions, and offered even more impressive alternatives.

Le Corbusier, Mies van der Rohe, and Frank Lloyd Wright set a standard for the rest of us against which we will be judged in the years to come. I offer no apologies for having paid homage to them in the late 1950s, and, despite certain reservations advanced since then by Jane Jacobs and others—including myself—I offer no apologies for paying additional homage to them in the 1990s. We may not see the likes of them again for some time to come.

Peter Blake
Branford, Connecticut, 1996

Preface

AT NO TIME in the recorded history of architecture has the manner in which men build undergone changes as radical as those that have occurred during the past century. Under the pressure of the tremendous growth in the earth's population, new developments took place in almost every field of human endeavor; but these developments were nowhere more spectacular than in the field of architecture.

Because more and more people had to be housed and employed in large urban centers, builders had to learn to build vertically. Technology provided two essential tools: the steel-framed building that could rise to great heights without requiring enormously thick walls at ground level; and the mechanical elevator. Because more and more goods had to be manufactured by mass-production methods on large assembly lines, builders had to learn to roof over very large spaces with uninterrupted spans, and technology again produced the answers in terms of great iron-and-glass halls and, later, in terms of large, reinforced concrete vaults. And because transportation and communication became essential tools without which a mass society could not hope to function properly, builders had to learn to construct great bridges and viaducts, great railroad sheds, canals, and harbors.

Indeed, most of the building types that are now a part of our daily lives did not even exist before 1850. The modern factory, the modern skyscraper, the shopping center, the modern school, and the modern hospital—all these are completely new inventions, with almost no antecedents prior to the middle of the nineteenth century. When architects first developed some of the new building types, they had a very hard time finding the right "style" for these new-fangled structures. For the nineteenth century was entirely eclectic, and every respectable building (the architects thought) had to follow stylistic precedent—whether medieval-romantic, or renaissance-classical.

But where in the Middle Ages or in the Renaissance was there a precedent for a skyscraper? Where was there a precedent for a steel mill or a railroad shed? Some architects evaded the issue by deciding, quite simply, that these new building types belonged in the realm of engineering rather than polite architecture. Others tried to stretch the eclectic patterns to fit the new façades—and failed. And there were a few—a very few—who faced the new problems squarely and saw in them a great challenge to their creative abilities. These few architects and engineers displayed an inventiveness unmatched in any other period of building: within the span of a single generation, this handful of pioneers in effect created an entirely new vocabulary of building types, and gave each of these building types a distinctive and expressive face of its own.

These early pioneers are now a part of architectural history: Louis Sullivan, the architect who, almost single-handedly, turned the skyscraper into architecture; Joseph Paxton, the landscape designer who built the London Crystal Palace in 1851—an exhibition hall covering some eighteen acres of ground; and others before and after him, in

England, France, Germany, and the United States, men who created the first great structures of iron and glass. And, finally, the theorists and practitioners who, in metal, glass, and stone, reasserted certain qualities of unaffected structure and unadorned form. All of them laid the foundations for what we know today as modern architecture.

Yet, regardless of the spirit of the times, regardless of the daring of engineers and the vision of those architects who broke with the past, modern architecture could not have gone far beyond purely utilitarian solutions without the appearance, around the turn of the century and in the decade following it, of half a dozen great individual artists who knew, instinctively, what they must do with the new tools at hand.

This book is concerned with three of this small group: Charles-Edouard Jeanneret, better known as Le Corbusier, native of Switzerland and citizen of France; Ludwig Mies van der Rohe, native of the German Rhineland and now a citizen of the United States; and Frank Lloyd Wright, an American largely of Welsh ancestry. These three did not do it alone; indeed, there were others who may have contributed a great deal more in certain areas of modern architecture: Walter Gropius certainly did more toward the establishment of a modern *rationale*—in architectural education, in the industrialization of building, and in the analysis of social problems—than any of these three masters; Eric Mendelsohn, Alvar Aalto, Richard Neutra, and others produced many solutions of a much more practical nature than the three men we have singled out; and there were engineers like Robert Maillart, Eugéne Freyssinet, and Pier Luigi Nervi who understood much better than these three men the potentialities of all the new structural techniques which the masters discussed so airily and sometimes experimented with so primitively.

Still, Le Corbusier, Mies, and Wright will ultimately appear more important than their contemporaries because they were greater as artists. All three had a sort of poetic vision of the world they lived in, and, in trying to give form to this poetic vision, they often advanced farther and more daringly than their more rational fellows, who were handicapped by the more prosaic limitations of the moment. Many of Frank Lloyd Wright's early flat roofs leaked; so, presumably, did

Chartres. Much of Le Corbusier's concrete has cracked; so has the Parthenon. Mies van der Rohe's buildings, it is said, are not always comfortable; neither, one suspects, was Hadrian's Villa. Great buildings tend to have several lives: Life One begins as the building is completed; its success or failure is then judged according to whether or not the building works. Life Two begins a generation or two later, when everyone has forgotten whether the building worked out particularly well in terms of budget, comfort, or planning; by that time it is looked upon simply as a work of art—good, bad, or indifferent. Sometimes there is a Life Three that begins much, much later; any building that lasts until Life Three gets a real break, for in Life Three the mere fact that a building is very old makes it valuable—even though it may be as ugly as sin.

Most of the buildings designed and constructed by Le Corbusier, Mies, and Wright have yet to complete their Life One existence. People still look at them in terms of how much they cost, how well they function, whether they are too hot or too cold—in short, whether the roof leaks or doesn't. To select these three men and call them outstanding architects of their epoch is taking something of a risk. Yet there is one measure that can be applied to gauge the greatness of an artist even during his lifetime: that is to ask how strongly he has influenced his contemporaries, how visible an imprint he has left upon his time.

The fact is that virtually no modern building constructed today would look the way it does if it had not been for the work of one or more of these three men. Lever House in Manhattan? The stilts are by Le Corbusier and the glass walls by Mies. The United Nations Headquarters? Inconceivable without Le Corbusier—even if he had not had a direct hand in their initial design. The General Motors Technical Center near Detroit? Clearly an elaboration of Mies van der Rohe's work. The curvilinear, shell-formed structures going up all around us? Obviously a new interpretation of Frank Lloyd Wright's concepts of "plasticity" and "continuity"—i.e., the development of fluid spaces and fluid structures. The rambling, one-story house with deep roof overhangs and large areas of glass? This, too, is a by-product of Wright's work.

Le Corbusier, Mies, and Wright, in their very different personalities and cultural origins, represent among them all the great traditions of the western world: Le Corbusier is the heir to the classic tradition of the Mediterranean; Mies likes to refer to the structural poetry of the Gothic tradition; and Wright was the eternal anarchist, the defender of absolute freedom, the heir to the ideal of the America of the Revolution.

What personal traits shaped these men and what their traditions and ideals did to shape their work goes far beyond architecture; for to them architecture is simply the language they used to express their ideals of a better world. All three have, at one time or another, been touched by the political issues of the twentieth century; but, somehow, these issues seem insignificant in the light of the broader vision that animates the work of these architects. All three have been attacked, reviled, ignored—until years later their fellow men suddenly began to understand what these three had tried to say against the din of professional noise-makers.

This book is a tribute to them by one architect whose generation owes most of what it knows about architecture to Le Corbusier, Mies, and Wright. It is also an affirmation of a fading belief: that the history of art is written by artists, not by "forces." There is no "force"—economic, sociological, technological—that could have created Ronchamp, the Barcelona Pavilion, or Taliesin West. And there would be no modern architecture as we know it without individual, creative acts of the sort represented by these great buildings.

Contents

LE CORBUSIER

and the Mastery of Form

WHEN THE LATE abstract painter Fernand Léger first met Le Corbusier in 1921, the occasion turned out to be something to remember. Léger was standing on the terrace of the Rotonde, in Montparnasse, when a friend said to him: "Just wait, you are about to see a very odd specimen. He goes bicycling in a derby hat." A few minutes later, Léger recalled, there was a strange apparition, a creature, very stiff, completely in silhouette, "an extraordinarily mobile object under a derby hat, with spectacles and wearing a dark suit." To Léger, this creature looked more like a clergyman or, better still, like an English clergyman, than a visionary pamphleteer on architecture, painting, and the world in general. "He advanced quietly," Léger said, "scrupulously obeying the laws of perspective."

Le Corbusier at Marseilles (Photo: Fenno Jacobs)

Charles-Edouard Jeanneret—the "extraordinarily mobile object under the derby hat"—was born on October 6, 1887, in the small watch-making town of La Chaux-de-Fonds, near Neuchatel, in Switzerland. His family, like just about everyone else in the town, had been connected for generations with the manufacture of watches; both his father and mother were professional engravers of watch cases. By ancestry Jeanneret is French; some of his forebears were Albigensians—fanatical French heretics of the fourteenth century who fled into the Alps to escape persecution in their homeland. Most of them were peasants, and their harsh fate made them reserved, cold, and suspicious of the world around them. One of Jeanneret's southern French ancestors was called Le Corbusier, and he assumed that name in 1923 to distinguish between two of his multiple personalities—those of painter and of architect.

Le Corbusier has not been known to wear a derby hat in quite some time, yet his appearance is almost as baffling as it must have been in the twenties. His face has the flat, almost monumental cast of an Easter Island head. It looks dead white, much whiter than it really is, because Le Corbusier has, for many years, worn the blackest, most exactly circular, and thickest-edged horn-rimmed glasses known to the optical trade. These glasses, his personal emblem, appear in photographs of his early houses, casually left lying on a kitchen table or a mantelpiece. Together with the razor-edged features of his face, the black-rimmed spectacles soon brought Le Corbusier the nickname of "Corbu"—a variation on the word *corbeau*, or "raven." He is now known as Corbu among architects all over the world. (In recent years, some of them have donned similar black-edged glasses, presumably to show their solidarity with Corbu. As a result, a typical meeting of the *avant-garde* nowadays tends to look like a convocation of owls, ravens, or giant pandas—depending upon the *avant-gardist's* other physical characteristics.)

Although Corbu has many admirers, he has very few close friends; for the personality he presents to much of the outside world is almost a caricature of all the ancestral and geographical influences one might expect to have shaped him. On casual acquaintance he appears cold, suspicious, pugnacious, sarcastic (but quite humorless about himself), and arrogant. Most of his admirers have learned to put up with this rather unappealing image, explaining it by referring to the bitter fight for recognition which Le Corbusier has had to wage most of his life. But, to the few people who know him well, Corbu is an entirely different sort of person: a man of tremendous charm, wit, and great warmth; of scholarship, vision, and superb taste. All these qualities are evident in his work and in his extensive writings. Yet, because the world, to him, seems almost always to have been populated with real or, at least, potential enemies, Corbu wears the mask of a suspicious Swiss peasant, or, worse still, of a suspicious Swiss *petit-bourgeois*.

Under these circumstances, it is not surprising that Corbu evokes only extreme responses in those who have worked with him. Some of the architects who were associated with him on the initial planning of the United Nations Headquarters in New York have said, more or less publicly, that they would never again touch a project in which Le Corbusier had any part. On the other hand, Oscar Niemeyer, the brilliant young Brazilian architect who played a major role in that same collaborative effort, will state without the slightest hesitation that he considers Le Corbusier the Leonardo da Vinci of our epoch, and that Corbu deserves all the respect, honor, and affection due to an artist of such caliber. Many of Corbu's contemporaries in architecture agree. Walter Gropius, the most important educator and theoretician of the modern movement, who first met Le Corbusier in 1910, has said that it will take an entire generation of architects to realize all the visionary concepts Corbu has outlined in his innumerable sketches and projects. And Mies van der Rohe, an architect whom many consider on a par with Le Corbusier, recalled recently that when he was Director of the famous Weissenhof development in Stuttgart, in 1927—a full-scale architectural exposition in which most of the leading modernists of the day contributed one or two important buildings—he started out by inviting Corbu and giving him first choice of a site for his buildings. "Naturally, he picked the best one," Mies van der Rohe commented with a grin. "He has quite an eye! And I would give him first choice again under similar circumstances, any time!"

Corbu's extraordinary talent and his insatiable capacity for absorbing visual experiences everywhere and in all periods of art became evi-

dent at a very early age. When he was only fourteen years old he quali-
fied for the Ecole d'Art at La Chaux-de-Fonds, a kind of technical high
school set up for the express purpose of training engravers for the watch-
making industries in the town. There he became the student of Professor L'Eplattenier. Several years later Corbu described L'Eplattenier
as "a fascinating teacher . . . a master who opened to me the gateways
to the world of art. With him, we lost ourselves in the art of all ages
and of all lands." L'Eplattenier encouraged his young student to concentrate on architecture, as well as to participate in the work of a newly
formed department for sculpture and for mural painting.

The Art School in his home town became a major influence in
Corbu's life throughout his younger years—in fact until he moved to
Paris for good at the age of thirty. As its most promising student, Corbu
was commissioned, when he was only eighteen, to design and build a
villa for one of the Art School's trustees. Although this first building is
not considered particularly significant in the light of his later work, it
did enable Corbu to take the first of a series of major trips that carried
him beyond the borders of Switzerland—trips that proved to be of considerable importance in his future development. The year was 1906, and
Corbu spent much of it in Italy and Austria. Italy was his first introduction to the plasticity of white stucco forms in the bright sun, seen
against a Mediterranean sky. Austria was his first introduction to the
Art Nouveau movement in general, and to the architect Josef Hoffmann
in particular.

Art Nouveau was a short-lived but enormously important movement, world wide in scope. It had its protagonists in England, Germany,
France, Belgium, Spain, the United States, and elsewhere. In the history
of art there are occasional movements whose actual output is highly
questionable, but whose impact upon what went on before them (and
what was to come later) is tremendous. Art Nouveau was such a movement; it began as a protest against nineteenth-century eclecticism—
neoclassicism in particular—and it ended by destroying not only eclecticism, but itself as well. It attempted to substitute a new kind of honesty
in design for the sham of classical imitation, and it looked for this new
kind of honesty in forms that could be found in nature—in trees,

flowers, swirling clouds, and craggy rocks. For a rather short period—thirty or forty years—Art Nouveau dominated all forms of creative expression, from the poster art of Toulouse-Lautrec to the furniture of Guimard. Before long, however, its influence began to pall: the premise upon which it had been based (i.e., that forms in nature were more valid sources of inspiration than forms in the Renaissance or in the Gothic) seemed to collapse; yet the movement did not fade away until it had completely destroyed both neoclassicism and the Gothic Revival as serious, creative points of view. And when Art Nouveau finally died, it had opened the gates to something Corbu was to call, in later years, the New Vision—the style of a new industrial epoch.

Josef Hoffmann's Wiener Werkstaette (Viennese Workshops) were a highly sophisticated offspring of the Art Nouveau movement. Unlike Art Nouveau designers such as Louis Tiffany in the United States, who found "honesty" in the tulip form and turned it into a vase, Hoffmann never quite succumbed to the purely decorative aspects of the Art Nouveau—the "enervating atmosphere" of the movement, as the historian Nikolaus Pevsner calls it. Certainly Hoffmann, being Viennese, was playful; but he was also "modern" in the sense that he looked for inspiration in things that were characteristic of the time in which he lived, such as the forms of machines. Corbu worked for Hoffmann very briefly in 1908; but when the latter suggested a more permanent arrangement, Corbu made his excuses. Although he was still in his early twenties, it was clear to him that the fondness for decorative panels in the Art Nouveau manner, which characterized most of Hoffmann's work, was not for him. Still, he had seen the outlines of a new and exciting discipline beyond Hoffmann's playful details, and he appreciated this underlying discipline while rejecting the surface décor.

Here, perhaps, is the first important manifestation of a quality that sets Le Corbusier apart from most of his contemporaries. That quality is his faultless taste. Frank Lloyd Wright, whose fundamental contributions to architecture may someday be considered more important than those of Le Corbusier, possessed the taste of a Victorian embroiderer. His sense of color, of decoration, often even of form was, to put it mildly, disconcerting. Mies van der Rohe's taste is as impeccable as a fine Savile Row suit, yet it is so perfect for pecisely the same reason that a fine Savile Row suit is perfect: because Mies, as he is generally referred to, takes no chances. But Corbu not only takes a new chance with every new building; he also manages, generally, to win his gamble. Even the outrageously "primitive" architecture he began to produce after World War II—at a time when everyone expected him to lead the way toward a new world of luminous plastics and shining metal—even this "new brutalism" (as an English magazine called it) had a splendor, an absence of grossness combined with sheer guts—in short, a perfection of taste which no one, not even Corbu's many imitators, was able to copy.

So, when he saw Hoffmann's doilies stuck on Machine Art buildings, Corbu politely said no. Yet he did see the Machine Art—as, indeed, he saw everything else around him. On every trip he was to take, on every visit to a new Greek Island or a new American metropolis, Le Corbusier would store away impressions, ideas, forms, colors that might not turn up again in his work for decades to come. He generally carried his sketchbooks with him, filling them with quick, dramatic, incisive drawings of a casual object here or a whole city there. These sketches in themselves reveal more about Le Corbusier's clear vision than the thousands of words he has put on paper. They reveal, above all, that he is not primarily a technician or a social philosopher or a city planner—as his books sometimes make him appear—but a plastic artist of supreme authority.

I I

I N 1908 Le Corbusier went to Paris for his first extended visit. Although he was only twenty years old, he knew precisely what he was looking for: like the adherents of Art Nouveau, he was looking for a new kind of honesty; but, unlike them, he was looking for it in the geometry of the machine forms that seemed to typify his time.

No artist, however creative, can avoid being influenced by the spirit of his time; Le Corbusier has not only been influenced, he has consistently pictured himself as a sort of spokesman for that spirit. To re-create, for a moment, the spirit of Paris in 1908, it is important to recall a number of significant events: the year before, Picasso had painted his Les Demoiselles D'Avignon, "the first cubist picture," according to Alfred Barr. The naturalism of Picasso's earlier work had been replaced by a painting resolved into flat, geometric elements. Braque, too, was painting his first cubist pictures; his *Houses at L'Estaque*, done in 1908, was a composition of cubes and pyramids, very precisely rendered. Meanwhile, Cézanne's rather questionable assertion that "everything in nature is formed according to the sphere, the cone and the cylinder" was widely quoted among painters and sculptors, partly because it was still fashionable to pay homage to nature (in the Art Nouveau tradition), even while you were patently trying to get away from the Art Nouveau *mystique*.

But the people who really understood the new spirit Le Corbusier was seeking were not the painters or the sculptors, but a small band of engineer-architects—a group of rather unsophisticated men who, believing in "honesty," had decided that architectural expression needed to be completely overhauled if it was even to begin to reflect the new technology of our time. And the greatest of these honest men was Auguste Perret—the master of reinforced-concrete construction.

Le Corbusier went to work for Perret and stayed for fifteen months. "I wonder whether anyone realizes today what a heroic part Perret played in those years," Corbu wrote in 1929. "Perret had the temerity to build in [exposed] reinforced concrete, and he insisted that this new structural method was destined to revolutionize our achitecture." Perret had the temerity, and the instinct, to do much more: he took a plastic material at a time when plasticity to excess was the mode, and forced it into a classical discipline of restraint which, he knew, offered the only rational solution to the most urgent problems of his time—the building of tall structures, lightly framed and infinitely flexible in plan.

Although Perret is today admired largely for what he did, he should be praised as much for what he did not do. In the mud-building countries around the edge of the Mediterranean, highly plastic, almost sculptural architecture—whether in clay, stucco, or concrete—is the tradition. These pliant materials present a tremendous temptation to the architect, and few outside the classical tradition were able to resist that temptation when Art Nouveau came along and made plasticity respectable by relating it to forms in nature. Most of the great Art Nouveau architects, from Antonio Gaudi, in Barcelona, to Victor

Horta, in Brussels, surrendered to the voluptuous plasticity of concrete or the malleability of wrought iron. Auguste Perret and Tony Garnier, his contemporary, were among the very few important architects of their region and their time to insist upon architectural logic in disciplining their concrete frames.

In wood-building countries like the United States the straight stick and the equally straight board are the tradition; and the challenge is to bend these straight sticks and boards into plastic forms. The great Finnish architect Alvar Aalto met that challenge in his own wood-building country in the 1930's, and Frank Lloyd Wright, in the United States, made plasticity and continuity the twin principles of his life's work. But, in France and in all the other countries of the Mediterranean basin, the challenge is to discipline plasticity into order. Where the excitement of a Wright house is in the degree to which Wright succeeded in bending the stick, the excitement of a concrete building by Perret was in the degree to which he succeeded in straightening out and disciplining mud.

Le Corbusier was enormously lucky to meet and work for Perret when he did. For Perret was destined, in his later years, to see in classical discipline an end in itself, and in his final work—especially in the vast reconstruction of the port of Le Havre, after World War II—Perret had become an elegant and somewhat dry classicist. But in 1908 Perret was at the very peak of his career. His own office was located in the building at 22 bis rue Franklin, the first tall, exposed, reinforced concrete frame structure he had built half a dozen years earlier. In this building Perret had managed to realize a number of major principles of structure and plan which his talented pupil could take as points of departure toward his own objectives.

The apartment house at 22 bis rue Franklin is nine stories high. Its frame is unfinished reinforced concrete, clearly expressed on the façade and left completely undecorated. The grid of columns and beams is filled in almost entirely with glass, except for a few areas that are enclosed with panels of brickwork to meet special building-code restrictions in the area. In plan the building is quite open: the only fixed elements are the slender reinforced concrete columns and certain stairwells. Everything else is nonstructural and, hence, entirely flexible. On the ground floor, for example, which contained Perret's office, Le Corbusier could see before his eyes the astonishing spectacle of a tall building apparently held up on nothing except a very few slim posts; all walls, all interior partitions, were large sheets of glass, some transparent, others translucent. Here, in all likelihood, was Corbu's first encounter with the concept of *pilotis*, or stilts holding up a tall building and liberating the space beneath it—a concept Corbu was to develop into a revolutionary principle of city planning, as well as civic art.

Several other aspects of this building fascinated Le Corbusier and influenced his later work: first was the manner in which Perret had recessed the ground floor behind the plane of the main façade and, conversely, cantilevered or projected the upper floors out beyond the glassy face of the street floor. By today's standards, Perret's effort in this respect seems a little timid; we are accustomed to seeing tall slab buildings, like Lever House, in New York, supported on a smaller, receding base. But, in 1902, when Perret designed this structure, the accepted way of arranging the masses of a building was not unlike that of building a pyramid: start with a broad base at the bottom, and taper off to a fine point as the building rises to its full height. Perret's understanding of reinforced concrete—a material composed in exact proportions of steel strands that can resist enormous tension, and concrete bulk that can resist enormous compression—led him to realize that a homogeneous and organic framework of this sort could be arranged to stand like a tree: its foundations rooted in the ground, its trunk slender and strong, projecting out of the ground, and its greatest mass, the branches and the foliage, spreading out in all directions at the top. 22 bis rue Franklin was the first tall building constructed on this tree principle—the precise opposite of the pyramidal structure derived from massive stone-building. Again Le Corbusier took note of the principle and determined to explore its potentialities still further.

Another aspect of the apartment house which intrigued Corbu was its roof garden. The two top floors were stepped back to form small terraces, on which Perret placed evergreen poplars planted in boxes. Again the Perret experiment seems timid by comparison with Corbu's later, grandiose roof structures. Yet the germ of the idea was there;

Perret, being a sober, if brilliant, engineer, could not be expected to develop it much further. Le Corbusier could and did.

But the most daring aspect of this simple and modest apartment structure was the manner in which Perret had exposed its brute concrete frame. "Decoration," Perret used to say, "always hides an error in construction." (Adolf Loos, one of Perret's Viennese contemporaries, was even more vehement on the subject; according to *him*, decoration was "a crime!") In any event, Perret's honesty of structural expression was almost unprecedented among designers in concrete, and most architects considered the approach beneath their dignity. Le Corbusier recalls that one day in 1909 the professor in charge of structural theory at the conservative Beaux Arts Academy was indisposed, and his place was taken by the chief engineer of the Paris Métro. "Gentlemen," the chief engineer began, "I intend to devote this lecture to a description of a new method of construction known as reinforced concrete. . . ." He was unable to proceed further, for his voice was drowned out by catcalls. One student asked whether the Métro engineer took them "for a lot of contractors," whereupon the lecturer retreated into a timid discourse on wood-frame structures of the Middle Ages.

The Beaux Arts did make Perret a professor in the early thirties, by which time Perret and reinforced concrete had both become quite respectable. Yet Perret's brand of honest radicalism was a rare sight in the first decade of the century, both in France and elsewhere. It is true that in 1908, when Corbu went to work for Perret, a warehouse of exposed reinforced concrete was built for Montgomery Ward & Co. in Chicago, and that other "honest" work was being done in Vienna, Berlin, and other cities. But, by and large, these structures were not considered polite architecture; they were part of the inventory of purely utilitarian buildings demanded by industry and commerce. Because this was so, Le Corbusier and others found themselves more and more attracted to utilitarian buildings, like factories, as they seemed to provide the only outlet for their energies and convictions. One of the great architects who had found this to be the case was the German Peter Behrens; and Behrens's studio in Berlin was, therefore, a natural next stop in Corbu's educational development.

S EVERAL FACTORS made Peter Behrens important and attractive to the new generation of dreamers to which Corbu belonged: first, Behrens had started as a painter and craftsman in the Art Nouveau manner, and had gone on to reject it. That placed him several steps ahead of men like Josef Hoffmann, who never quite succeeded in shaking off the decorative urge of the Art Nouveau. Second, Behrens had turned to the classical tradition for some of the discipline he found lacking in Art Nouveau. Finally, and most importantly, Behrens had concentrated more and more upon industrial work—factories and the like—and upon the design of the industrial products made in those factories.

For Behrens had become the chief architect for the A.E.G.—a sort of German equivalent of our General Electric. It was his job not only to design A.E.G.'s factories, but also many of A.E.G.'s lighting fixtures, the typography for use on stationery and signs, and many other details that today go under the broad heading of "industrial design." Behrens was, indeed, the first modern industrial designer, and he gave A.E.G.'s buildings and products the sort of "corporate identity" through total design which is admired so much today in firms like Italy's Olivetti and our own Container Corporation.

Behrens was a classicist—or a semiclassicist—only in his "important" work, such as his Art Building at an exhibition in Oldenburg in 1905 (which consisted of a series of cubic pavilions symmetrically grouped upon a formal pedestal), and in his monumental German embassy in St. Petersburg, done in 1913. This was still polite architecture and seemed to call for a polite expression; Behrens's industrial work for A.E.G. was considered by most of his contemporaries as the sort of thing you had to do to meet the office overhead. Yet it is Behrens's steel-and-glass Turbine factory for A.E.G., in particular, which has assured him a permanent place in architectural history.

Because of Behrens's preoccupation with utilitarian building, his studio became the center of much advanced work and thinking in the years immediately preceding World War I. To become a Behrens apprentice was the ambition of many young, would-be architects of Corbu's inclinations and convictions; and so, when Le Corbusier obtained a special fellowship from his former Academy at La Chaux-de-Fonds to study advanced arts and crafts in Germany, he left Perret's office and proceeded to Berlin to meet Behrens and to work in his studio.

During the five months Corbu spent in Behrens's studio, there occurred one of the most remarkable coincidences in the story of architecture. While Corbu was working there, two other young men turned out to be fellow apprentices; one was the young Ludwig Mies van der Rohe, son of a modest masonry contractor in Aix-La-Chapelle (Aachen); the other was Walter Gropius, the elegant scion of a well-to-do North German family of professionals and businessmen. Corbu was twenty-three; Mies was twenty-four; and Gropius was twenty-seven years old. Each of the young apprentices was to learn something very special from Behrens: Corbu was to learn about technical organization and about Machine Art; Mies was to learn about classicism; and Gropius was to learn about the potentialities of an industrial civilization—a lesson he was to apply with tremendous success at his Bauhaus school ten years later.

Both Gropius and Mies had started with Behrens several years earlier, and remained in his studio after Corbu moved on to his next stop—another brief stint with Hoffmann in Vienna. But for all three the period in Behrens's office was tremendously significant. Le Corbusier saw something in Behrens's product design, in particular, which he had vaguely understood for some time, and which was now being confirmed. "Nobody today can deny the esthetic which is disengaging itself from the creations of modern industry," he announced several years later, undoubtedly thinking of some of the things he had first seen in Behrens's studio. "It is in general artistic production that the style of an epoch is found and not, as is too often supposed, in certain productions of an ornamental kind. . . ."

It is almost impossible to exaggerate the depth and profundity of the change this new faith in the man-made object represented in architectural thought and, especially, in Le Corbusier's fundamental approach. Corbu and others were driven into utilitarianism in building because the doors to polite architecture were closed to them. Yet Corbu and Mies and Gropius were and are artists, first and foremost; the functioning of a lighting fixture or a power station was not of *primary* interest to them; it was something that must be taken for granted, just as one takes for granted that a writer knows how to use a pen. The important thing to these men was the development of a new aesthetic language, and specifically a language that could be used to deal with the problems of today. In utilitarian buildings and products they found the aesthetic vocabulary—cubes, spheres, cylinders, cones, and so forth. In their purity and precision, these objects (which might happen to be salt shakers, meat grinders, or racing cars) represented a "new look"—the look of what was later termed Machine Art. It was an exhilarating experience, the discovery of this vast new world of form. Amédée Ozenfant, the painter who was associated with Le Corbusier for several years after World War I, once pointed out that it was much better to be a first-class engineer than a second-class artist, and added that Ettore Bugatti, who designed the most beautiful sports cars ever built, was obviously a much greater artist than his brother, the rather indifferent sculptor Rembrandt Bugatti!

Le Corbusier, Léger, and many other painters and sculptors were carried away by this same enthusiasm for Machine Art. They saw no need to justify among themselves this new vocabulary of forms: the forms were beautiful, they belonged to an orderly and coherent system, and that was all that really mattered. But vis-à-vis the lay public, they took a different position. Just as the Art Nouveau designers had justified their point of view by suggesting that (a) nature is "honest" (whatever that may mean) and therefore (b) forms taken from nature must be "honest," too, so Corbu and his fellow enthusiasts felt compelled to argue that (a) machines are efficient and therefore (b) forms borrowed from machines must be efficient, too. Nobody except, perhaps, the nineteenth-century American sculptor Horatio Greenough (Emerson's friend) ever really believed this; but the notion caught on like wildfire, and "functionalism" in architecture was born. Almost everyone was willing to accept buildings they considered ugly if those "ugly" buildings were indeed less expensive to build and more efficient to operate. The functionalists were stuck with their machine analogy—and are stuck with it to this day.

The discovery of a new world of geometric forms affected Corbu in another profound way. He and his contemporaries considered themselves in revolt, not only against eclecticism, but against the pseudonaturalism of Art Nouveau as well. Specifically, Le Corbusier—now a firm believer in the man-made object—became something of an anti-naturalist. "The city," he said, "is man's grip upon nature. It is a human operation directed against nature." To him the idea of integrating architecture and nature, in the manner of Art Nouveau and, later, of

1 7

Frank Lloyd Wright, became anathema. A building must be a clear, sophisticated statement, he felt, and it should stand in contrast to nature, rather than appear as an outgrowth of some natural formation. Nature and architecture could enhance one another in this manner and create a sort of harmony by contrast. The concept, of course, was not new: the Greeks believed in it and made their Acropolis a man-made crown to top off a mountain. To Corbu this approach to nature seemed somehow more truly respectful than the emulation of natural forms as practiced by Gaudi or Guimard.

By the time Corbu left Behrens's studio late in 1910, he had made certain clear-cut decisions for himself—decisions that changed very little during the decades that followed. First, he was committed, completely and irrevocably, to the new world of form which the cubists had begun to paint and which the architect-engineers of Perret's and Behrens's stripe had begun to manipulate. Second, he was committed to a *laissez faire* attitude toward nature: he believed that nature should be left to her natural devices, and that architecture should be the prerogative of men. Third, he was committed to reinforced concrete, not only because this seemed the obvious modern material of France, but also because it appeared to possess a certain amount of plain "guts," which he, being of the Mediterranean tradition, preferred to the impersonal slickness and precision of steel. And, finally, he was committed to the tradition of the Mediterranean—not the rehashed tradition as interpreted by the Beaux Arts, but the strength and vigor and grandeur of Greece and Rome and the Renaissance. After his stay in Germany, he said that there was a great deal the French could learn from German technology, but that there was an absence among the Germans of certain traditions. Their hands, he said, seemed to be rather clumsy, unlike (he might have added) the hands of the fishermen-builders of the coasts of Greece and Italy and Spain.

In the years that remained before the outbreak of World War I Corbu increased his knowledge of the traditions of the Mediterranean basin. For more than a year he traveled through the Balkans, in Asia Minor, in the Greek Islands (including especially Mykonos), and in

Italy. His sketchbooks of this trip—like those of his earlier travels—contain not only the obvious, though beautifully rendered impressions of Pisa, Pompeii, the Acropolis, the Piazza San Marco, but also some fascinating details of a stone wall, a cluster of trees in a Middle East market place, a plan of a Roman house, the distant silhouette of a small Italian hill town. When he returned to La Chaux-de-Fonds, Le Corbusier's basic education was complete.

I V

THREE EVENTS of major importance in the history of modern architecture took place in Europe during the years immediately preceding World War I. The most important of these, in all likelihood, was the publication of a book—or, rather, of two books: the 1910 and 1911 editions of the Berlin publisher Wasmuth's *Executed Buildings and Projects by Frank Lloyd Wright*. In connection with the first of the two Wasmuth publications, an exhibition of Wright's work came to Berlin also. Mies van der Rohe remembers the occasion well: "Wright's work presented an architectural world of unexpected force, clarity of language and disconcerting richness of form," Mies has said. It is easy to see what Mies and his contemporaries found disconcerting; for, unlike them, Wright had never been won over to the pure geometry of machine forms. Instead, his architecture contained, from the start, a certain exuberance that was typically Art Nouveau—or, perhaps, even more typically American. This richness of detail and of form was all the more disconcerting to the Machine Art men because they had just discovered another sort of American building which seemed to strengthen their own purist position: the great silos, bridges, and docks constructed by American engineers. They fully expected that any "modern" American architect would inevitably be a Machine Art man, too. Certainly Wright's monumentally simple Larkin building of 1904 must have appealed to any disciple of Peter Behrens; but Wright's decorative detail in such buildings as the Coonley house of 1908 ran directly counter to all Machine Art thought.

A second event of tremendous importance was the design and construction of two buildings, in 1911 and 1914 respectively, by Walter Gropius in association with Adolph Meyer. These two structures were the only completely "modern" buildings (in our sense today) erected in Europe before 1914. In their over-all concept and in many details these buildings seem so advanced that a layman, coming upon them unprepared today, would almost certainly date them in the middle 1930's or even later. Unfortunately, of the two buildings only one has survived the wars.

The first of these extraordinary structures was the Fagus factory, built for a manufacturer of shoe lasts. It was Gropius's first large commission, and he left Behrens's office to undertake it. The main portion of this building was a three-story cage of exposed steel and glass, as completely and uncompromisingly "modern" as Mies van der Rohe's glass-and-steel campus for the Illinois Institute of Technology, started in 1940, almost thirty years later. The glass façades of the Fagus factory were among the first completely modern "curtain walls"—skins or membranes stretched tautly over the structural framework of the building behind the glass. Not even Behrens, in his Turbine factory, had so completely expressed the separation of the glass skin from the steel skeleton; in the Turbine factory the corners were still massively of concrete, whereas in Gropius's structure the corners had, in effect, been dissolved in a knife-edged line of two planes of glass meeting on a thin steel edge-strip. The Fagus factory has now been made a "historic monument," protected by the laws of the Bonn Republic.

The 1914 building was Gropius's contribution to the Cologne exhibition of the Deutsche Werkbund, an association of artists, workers, and industrialists dedicated to the production of objects of high aesthetic quality. His administrative office building for the exhibition again presented a sheer, seemingly weightless "curtain wall" of glass, hung from the structural framework; in addition, the building contained two glass-enclosed, spiral staircases of reinforced concrete—a device that was much admired and imitated by modern architects for decades to come. Oddly enough, the Werkbund building also betrayed certain touches of Wrightian detail, particularly in the sweeping roof overhangs. No such influence was evident in the Fagus factory; but whether Gropius was indeed influenced by Wright in the design of this exhibition building is questionable. There is no question, however, that Gropius was still somewhat under the influence of Behrens's classicism when he designed the Fagus and the Werkbund buildings: both have a rather classical base; both retain certain semiclassical details around entrances; and both are largely symmetrical—as, indeed, were most of Frank Lloyd Wright's early buildings. Still, even with these few, somewhat traditional touches, Gropius's two buildings represented so radical, so complete a break with the past that their construction must have had the effect of a violent explosion in the world of architecture. So great was their impact that several architects of considerable reputation built a large part of their life's work upon further development of the Fagus and Werkbund themes. The Werkbund building, incidentally, was destroyed in World War I.

The third event that shaped the development of modern architecture in general, and of Le Corbusier in particular, took place in painting and sculpture in the years before World War I. In their Cubist paintings both Picasso and Braque had begun to portray people and objects in such a way that several sides of the model, animate or inanimate, were visible simultaneously. In Futurist sculpture and painting —a school particularly strong in Italy—the concept of movement became paramount: objects and figures were shown not in a single, static position, but while in motion. Marcel Duchamp, though not a Futurist himself, expressed the idea in his famous *Nude Descending the Staircase*

—a figure shown actually in motion, much as it might appear if several successive movie frames had been projected simultaneously upon the same screen.

What all this meant to architecture was the possibility of exploring a new and different kind of space—a space not bottled up in cubicles, not statically contained within four walls, a floor, and a roof, but a space experienced simultaneously from without and within, seen by the observer in passing through, rather than frozen to a single spot in the total composition. In a different sort of way Frank Lloyd Wright had made a similar discovery of space-in-motion a few years earlier, but his kind of space was, fundamentally, horizontal. The spatial discoveries made by the Cubists and the Futurists were both more formalized and more all-enveloping—up, down, sideways, back, and front, all at the same time.

Gropius's glass-sheathed buildings, in which there was, in effect, no visual separation between the indoors and the outdoors, paralleled the space-in-motion theories developed by the painters and sculptors. But Corbu was to advance the theme still further in architecture: he would hollow out parts of the cube to create outdoor space within his buildings, and, at the same time, enclose parts of the outdoors to create clearly defined "rooms" *outside* his buildings; moreover, he would make his buildings not only objects to be seen in a horizontal plane, but objects in the round, meant to be seen from underneath and from above, from all sides and from inside—and let each view suggest all the other views.

Meanwhile, the painters and sculptors taught Corbu something rather obvious: that it was much easier, in certain ways, to conduct experiments in spatial and formal organization by means of painting and sculpture than by means of full-scale architecture. For one thing, it was certainly cheaper; for another, there was no client and there were no functional limitations. So, when the war came, Le Corbusier returned to La Chaux-de-Fonds to paint, to teach, and to think. "Today painting has outsped the other arts," Corbu said. "It is the first to have become attuned with our epoch. . . . Far removed from a distracting realism, it lends itself to meditation. . . . After the day's work it is good to meditate."

EING SWISS by nationality, Corbu was not directly involved in World War I; but, being French by inclination, Corbu tended to "meditate" in ways that are characteristic of the French.

Compare what happened to Machine Art in the hands of the German pioneers—and what happened to Machine Art in the hands of Le Corbusier. In Germany, needless to say, the argument that because the machine was efficient, any architecture derived from Machine Art must therefore be functional in the extreme, found ready adherents everywhere. But in France the basic premise of this argument was immediately recognized for the fallacy it contained: as every Frenchman knows, machines hardly ever work; as every Frenchman also knows, French machines, while particularly ineffective, are invariably much more beautiful than machines produced in any other country. The French, being the most humorous nation on earth, never really took their machines as seriously as did the Germans (or, for that matter, the English, the Americans, or the Russians). Machines were beautiful toys: only in France could one expect to find as lovely a piece of madness as the famous Pont Transbordeur, which spanned the entrance to the Vieux Port of Marseilles.

This fantastic suspension bridge consisted of two tall towers with an elevated roadway between them; the roadway was used by small trolleys that shuttled back and forth between the ends of the bridge; and, suspended from these trolleys by cables, were little ferry boats that, in turn, shuttled back and forth from one side of the Vieux Port to the other as the trolleys moved back and forth high above them. Now, to a German engineer, it might have seemed a little simpler to operate an ordinary ferry service between the two sides of the harbor without benefit of superstructure; and, indeed, the German commandant of Marseilles, in World War II, was so infuriated by this delightful piece of nonsense that he had the Pont Transbordeur melted down for scrap. Yet, to the French, it was equally obvious that the *poetic* solution to this engineering problem demanded exactly the lovely sort of structure erected at Marseilles.

The important thing about Le Corbusier's conception of Machine Art was that the emphasis was on the word *Art*. All his talk about functionalism, his later and oft-quoted insistence that "a house is a machine for living in"—means only two things: first, that he felt compelled to "sell" his ideas to an unsympathetic public in terms other than those of pure art; and, second, that he was primarily saying that "a house should be as *beautiful* as a machine," not necessarily as efficient as an A.E.G. generator.

This does not mean that Corbu was or is against functionalism; it only means that functionalism has never interested him as much as his so-called humanist critics have alleged. Undoubtedly a painter needs to know something about the chemistry of pigments; but, knowing this does not make him a good painter. As a matter of fact, Corbu's buildings, generally, have been very well built; in many of them he has introduced technical innovations of major importance. For example, the grilles of sun-control devices now so fashionable in certain kinds of modern architecture were pioneered by Corbu several decades before others were able to turn them into a personal "trademark" or publicity stunt. But, by and large, Corbu has been less concerned with the technology of architecture than with its art. The confusion about Corbu's true objectives stems from the single, simple fact that he found his major sources of *aesthetic* inspiration in the *technology* of our time.

In his own way Le Corbusier tried to make this point quite clear in his paintings done during the war years and afterward. Like the Cubists, Corbu chose the most uninteresting objects he could find—bottles, pipes, violins, cups, and saucers—so as to avoid distraction from the basic theme of the painting, which was the arrangement of pure, geometric, Machine Art forms like cylinders, cubes, cones, and spheres. The literary images in the painting were decidedly incidental; it was the formal quality of each object which interested Corbu. When Gertrude Stein said that "a rose is a rose is a rose," she meant that a rose was an object of beauty with inherent qualities of its own, not a symbol of something else, like love, or sentiment, or early summer. In his paintings Le Corbusier said, in effect, that "a cube is a cube is a cube"—and never mind what the cube (or cylinder or sphere) might happen to represent. "Eyes that do not see" became one of Corbu's most insistent laments about his contemporaries; what he was trying to recreate in his paintings and drawings was the appreciation of forms for their own sake, and specifically, the appreciation of a new order of forms.

Le Corbusier returned to Paris in 1917, to stay. He moved into a studio at 20 rue Jacob, where he was to remain for the next seventeen years. Shortly thereafter he met the painter Amédée Ozenfant. It was one of Corbu's many partnerships with men and women of creative vision, and it lasted until 1925, when the two broke up their association—as, indeed, most of Corbu's later associations were to break up.

Still life painted by Le Corbusier in 1920. **Geometric forms are similar to those found in elements of the Villa Savoye.** *(Courtesy, Museum of Modern Art)*

Ozenfant, a Cubist, possessed something Le Corbusier had great difficulty in finding elsewhere: he had eyes that *did* see! Corbu wrote to him: "Of those I know, you are the one who seems to be carrying out most clearly what is stirring within me. . . ." Several months later Corbu and Ozenfant jointly signed a manifesto entitled *Après le cub-*

isme, which suggested that while Cubism had cleared the air by removing the most distracting elements of realism from painting, it had now degenerated into a sort of playful, romantic, decorative movement. Corbu and Ozenfant proposed to return to the rational, geometric foundations of Cubism, and began a new movement within the Cubist tradition which they named Purism. Their first joint exhibition of paintings took place in 1918, at the Galerie Thomas, and from that time on, for the next several years, Corbu (known then by his original name, Jeanneret) and Ozenfant were more or less inseparable. Together with the poet Paul Dermée they began, in October 1920, to publish a magazine they called *L'Esprit nouveau*, devoted to all the plastic arts, to architecture, engineering, music, writing, industrial design, and *"l'esthétique de la vie moderne."* That just about covered everything, and *L'Esprit nouveau* was, indeed, an extraordinarily lively and broad review, whose influence could hardly be exaggerated. The magazine itself folded three years and twenty-eight issues after it was founded, but the term *L'Esprit nouveau* continued as a kind of trademark for much of Corbu's later work. And most of his books in the twenties and thirties were published under the *L'Esprit nouveau* imprint.

A collection of statements on architecture which had appeared in *L'Esprit nouveau* were republished in 1923 by Le Corbusier in a book entitled *Vers une architecture*—the most important book produced by this prolific writer and one of the most influential books to have been produced by a Europeon architect since the inception of the modern movement. Ozenfant has claimed that *Vers une architecture* was largely a rewrite of articles jointly produced for *L'Esprit nouveau* by himself and Corbu; however that may be, the book came out under Corbu's name alone, and its publication was the beginning of a certain coolness between Corbu and Ozenfant. The book is primarily concerned with architecture; it lays down, with almost frightening prescience, certain principles according to which Le Corbusier has lived and worked ever since; and whether or not he was responsible for every word of the text, he has, in his life's work, given substance to each word of that text, and thus made the book one of the great manifestos in the history of art.

The publication of *Vers une architecture* marked a milestone both in the development of modern architecture and in Corbu's own life. As of that date, Le Corbusier stopped exhibiting his paintings (he was tired of being known as a painter and a sort of "dilettante architect") and stopped using the name Jeanneret. He continued to paint, of course; but he wanted to be known primarily—even exclusively—as an architect, and he refused to show any of his other work until many years later, in 1937. By that time Corbu had radically altered the architectural face of the twentieth century, and no one could possibly accuse him of dilettantism.

V I

A GREAT EPOCH has begun! There exists a new spirit!" That is how Le Corbusier opened his *Vers une architecture*. No one but the French should be permitted to make revolutions; only they know how to compose the necessary manifestos. Throughout *Vers une architecture* there is this same revolutionary fervor—the emotional appeal, the audible rolling of drums. This was heady stuff. It was the beginning of Corbu's poetic vision of architecture.

Never has architecture been more beautifully defined. *"L'architecture est le jeu savant, correct et magnifique des volumes assemblés sous la lumière,"* Corbu wrote. In the English translation, published four years after *Vers une architecture* appeared in France, his words lose some of their passion. "Architecture is the masterly, correct and magnificent play of masses brought together in light." And Corbu continued: "Our eyes are made to see forms in light: cubes, cones, spheres, cylinders or pyramids are the great primary forms." The statement was, of course, accompanied by the now standard photographs of American grain elevators and silos, bridges, docks, ships, and airplanes. "The engineer, inspired by the laws of economy and governed by mathematical calculation, puts us in accord with universal law," Corbu wrote. But, almost in the same breath, he made it absolutely clear that to him, at least, functionalism was *not* architecture. "Architecture goes beyond utilitarian needs," he said. And then: "*Passion can create drama out of inert stone.*"

It is hard to understand how so many of Corbu's critics could fail to see Corbu for what he was and is: a hopeless romantic, a dreamer, a passionate lover of architecture as man's most noble form of self-expression. Naturally Corbu's romanticism is of an order very different from that of Wright or of the latter-day Arts-and-Crafts enthusiasts in California and elsewhere. For his is a romanticism born not out of the American prairie or out of the Japanese garden, but out of the greatness of the Mediterranean—out of the greatness of its particular and fabulous tradition. To Corbu the silo is today's Luxor, today's temple at Thebes, today's Parthenon. The "masses brought together in light" are the cylinders and spheres of Ancient Egypt, Greece, and Rome, of the Renaissance, as much as the cylinders and spheres of today's power stations and ocean liners. And if he believes in a "spirit of order, a unity of intention," then he is not speaking as a modern totalitarian (as certain American critics have stated), but as the heir to a tradition of laws without which democracy would never have had a chance to function in the first place.

Vers une architecture was not only a tract on aesthetics, it was a statement about the all-encompassing role of architecture as Corbu saw it. Although it started with a denunciation of eclecticism—of the revived "styles"—and went on to offer a modern alternative, this was merely the beginning of an extraordinarily broad definition of architecture. For here, in his first major book, Corbu showed himself not just as another partisan of modern art and modern architecture, but as an impressive social commentator, critic, and philosopher of his time.

The new "machine aesthetic" led him, naturally, to a rationalization of the effect of the machine upon the production of architecture. With supreme clarity he discussed the problems and opportunities of mass production in building, recognizing that such mass production would mean adherence to certain dimensional standards. This fact had, of course, been understood by others before Corbu, but he went beyond the then widely accepted need for standardization by making two significant points: first, Corbu suggested that the objective of standardization imposed upon every architect a sort of moral obligation to design *only* in a vocabulary that might, some day, fit into a mass-production grammar. In other words, he made it quite clear that the time for individual, egocentric expression in architecture had passed, and that the only architectural statement of any validity or significance was one that pointed directly toward a broader solution. And, second, Corbu went back to the traditional Renaissance rules of measure and proportion for a guide to some sort of modern unit system. Specifically, he analyzed the "Golden Section"—the famous proportional system of old—and suggested that it was as valid today as it was when used in the design of Notre-Dame.

The significance of Le Corbusier's insistence upon a *proportional* system of measurement has been widely overlooked. While others recognized the need for what is now called a modular system of design— i.e., a system based upon the repetition of *identically* dimensioned units —Corbu realized from the very start that a system based upon a 1 plus 1 plus 1 plus 1 rhythm (ad infinitum) could only lead to monotony. (Every New Yorker looking at the 1 plus 1 plus 1 plus 1 glass-and-metal "wallpaper" that has sprung up around him since 1945 knows exactly what Corbu had in mind.) To avoid this deadly sort of monotony, Corbu felt that a system not of identical units but *of related proportions* was the answer to the mass production of building parts. The Greeks' "Golden Section" represented a possible approach; it took him twenty years to develop a more refined system—a system he has called the Modulor—to serve the needs of mass production today. Those needs, as he saw them from the start, were to facilitate prefabrication while avoiding repetitive monotony. The Modulor, with its proportionate scale, makes possible an infinite number of variations within a unit system of construction. In 1958, when Corbu began to build the Dominican monastery of La Tourette near Lyon, he used the Modulor to determine the spacing of his window divisions, and the result was a façade that was vibrant with movement, and ever changing in the light. *"Le jeu savant, correct et magnifique . . . sous la lumière . . ."*

But Corbu went far beyond his aesthetic analyses, far beyond the analysis of function, of plan, of structure, of prefabrication. To him it was clear that architecture in the twentieth century could no longer be the isolated building, the individual house (or even the individual skyscraper). *The city as a whole was architecture:* its basic organization, its spatial relationships, its forms, its levels of activity, its heart—all these seemed to Corbu of supreme significance, of much greater importance even than the development (or absence) of a style.

It is very likely that Corbu was influenced, in his concepts of city planning, by two earlier visionary ideas: the Cité Industrielle, suggested as early as 1901 by Tony Garnier, the enthusiastic exponent of reinforced concrete; and a somewhat similar notion developed by Corbu's old master, Auguste Perret, in an interview with a correspondent from the Paris *L'Intransigeant*. Garnier's ideal city of 35,000 inhabitants was based upon a network of transportation arteries, with each type of transport separately provided for. The core of Garnier's city was a large civic center, and there were separate areas for industry, commerce, residential use, health, etc. Perret's idea was to build a city of isolated towers spaced far apart. In certain ways Perret had turned the principles embodied in his apartment building on the rue Franklin into a city pattern: the street level was to be open to through traffic, the residential areas were to be located in the tower floors above, and the roof was to be a garden space.

Le Corbusier took these two concepts and made them rational, modern, and beautiful. A year before *Vers une architecture* was published, he designed a "City for 3 Million Inhabitants," which was exhibited in November 1922 at the Salon d'Automne in Paris. This project, in almost every detail, laid down the principles of city planning to which Corbu has subscribed ever since. It has been widely (and ignorantly) attacked ever since it was first publicized; and yet no city planner in Europe, the Americas, or Asia has come up with a clearer, more rational, more "human," or more beautiful proposal for a large metropolis in the thirty or forty years since Corbu first developed his scheme.

The 1922 Ville Contemporaine was, of course, a diagram, and never intended to be anything but a diagram. Its most important features were these: all fast automobile traffic was to be handled by a few elevated highways, never crossed by a pedestrian. These elevated highways crisscrossed the city, made its center easily and quickly accessible, and were joined at their ends by a peripheral highway system that bypassed the city altogether. (By 1956 Philadelphia, Fort Worth, and other cities had finally decided to adopt substantially the same system to solve their apparently insoluble downtown traffic congestion.) Meanwhile, all pedestrian traffic was to take place on the normal ground level, on streets and walks threaded through open parks and gardens. As most of the buildings were to be elevated on stilts, or *pilotis*, pedestrians were free to walk anywhere, everywhere, and without the slightest danger.

The center of Corbu's Ville Contemporaine was to be a group of skyscrapers, cruciform in plan, fifty or sixty stories in height, and spaced very far apart to permit the development of generous park spaces between them. The cruciform towers were to contain offices for the administration of the city, for business, and the professions. A civic center was to be located nearby.

The next "ring" in this pattern—the Ville Contemporaine actually consisted of a series of concentric, rectangular belts—was a development of apartment houses, each of them six "double stories" in height. These apartment houses were to be built in the form of long, continuous "walls," wandering in and out, changing direction, and thus creating spacious garden courts and parks for the use of the apartment dwellers. As these buildings were to be raised on *pilotis* as well, there was free movement between adjoining courts underneath and through the various structures.

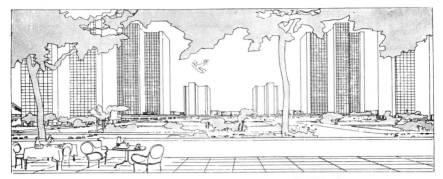

View from a terrace restaurant into the Ville Contemporaine, 1922. (From Oeuvre Complète)

Plan for a city of 3 million inhabitants, 1922. The street pattern combines the American gridiron system with the radial plan of Paris. (From Oeuvre Complète)

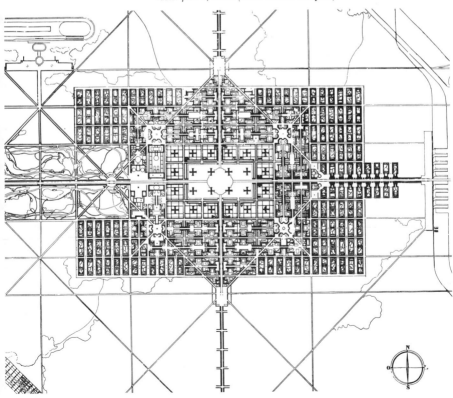

Finally, there was to be an outer ring of garden apartments of a very special sort—Corbu called them *villas superimposées*—which were to be grouped around inner courts laid out as recreation areas. These villas will be described in some detail later on; it is enough to say now that here again Le Corbusier anticipated our very latest housing concepts by more than a generation.

The Ville Contemporaine was to be protected by a massive belt of greenery, several miles thick, beyond which would be located industrial districts, perhaps a port, a great sports arena, or a small suburb of individual houses.

Two aspects of this project seem particularly impressive today: first, that this is in essence the basis for every radical "new" city plan being discussed seriously anywhere in the world today; and, second, that in this one project Le Corbusier, with a precision of mind rarely equaled by artists in any field, outlined exactly what he planned to do during the years ahead. Since 1922 Corbu has given life—bones, muscles, flesh, blood, and, above all, heart—to the exquisite and delicate drawings prepared in that year; but he has never deviated very far from the basic principles established in the Ville Contemporaine and in *Vers une architecture*.

V I I

I N RETROSPECT today, it seems odd that Corbu's *Vers une architecture* attracted as much attention as it did when it appeared. The fact is that before 1923 Le Corbusier had built almost nothing: apart from the early villa at La Chaux-de-Fonds, a commission that enabled him to take his first series of trips outside Switzerland, he had barely completed two small houses: one at Vaucresson; the other—a studio for Ozenfant—in Paris. Although they were exciting for their time in their simplicity, in the use of the "open plan" and of rectangular, as well as more plastic, forms, these two houses do not measure up to the standards he was soon to set in more mature buildings.

Nor did these houses measure up, entirely, to the quality of Le Corbusier's many proposals developed during the war years and after. It was these proposals (of which the Ville Contemporaine was the most important) that attracted people's attention to Le Corbusier and gave him the audience he deserved when his book appeared.

Among the projects of the war and postwar years, there were two that stood out, in addition to the City Plan: his design for the Dom-ino houses in 1914, and his project for the Citrohan house in 1920. Dom-ino was a simple statement about the possibilities of reinforced-concrete construction: a frame of six columns, supporting all floor and roof slabs, with a cantilevered concrete stair linking the different levels to the ground and the roof. These structural elements were the only fixed parts of the house; everything else was nonstructural and, hence, entirely flexible. It was a clear and convincing statement of the "open plan"—a plan freed from the need of load-bearing walls and, hence, capable of infinite variation within the same structural system.

The Citrohan house was a much more sophisticated affair. Here was the first development of one of Corbu's major spatial ideas: the creation of interlocking spaces of different but related heights. The house was two stories high. It had two floor levels on one side, with the kitchen and the dining area on the lower level, and bedrooms on the upper floor. The living area, however, was a double-story room, its floor on the same level as the kitchen and dining areas, its ceiling an extension of the bedroom ceilings upstairs. A spiral stair connected the living level to the sleeping areas and formed a sculptural counterpoint to the severe, rectilinear geometry of the hollow cube that was the interior. The flat roof was treated as an elaborate garden, with guest rooms located in a small penthouse superstructure.

This basic idea—the two-to-one interior space—has been a recurrent theme in all of Le Corbusier's work ever since Citrohan. In keeping with his conviction that every design, however small, must make a contribution to the solution of a wider, more general problem of architecture, he used the Citrohan two-to-one scheme as a kind of laboratory for an apartment prototype he was to develop further in his Ville Contemporaine a couple of years later, and still further in years to come. It is an exciting spatial concept, giving each apartment (or row-house unit) a tall, studiolike living area contrasted with service rooms of lower ceiling height. In the *villas superimposées* for his Ville Contemporaine,

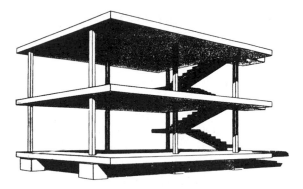

Column-and-slab structure for Dom-ino houses, 1914. (From Oeuvre Complète)

One version of the Citrohan house concepts, developed by Le Corbusier between 1922 and 1927. Each house is on stilts and has a roof patio. (From Oeuvre Complète)

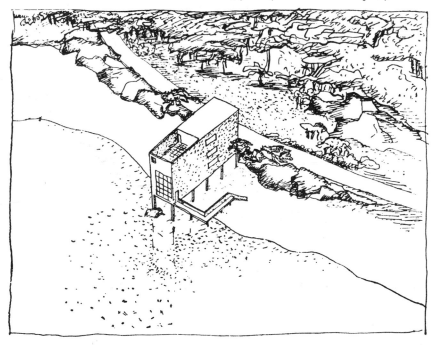

Corbu extended this spatial idea to the outdoors as well and provided each of the "superimposed houses" not only with a two-story living room *but also with a two-story garden terrace punched out of the building at regular intervals.* Here is a truly radical concept of urban living— a concept that is only just being accepted by a very few architects in this country: the idea that a private garden-in-the-sky can be provided for every family even in a so-called high-rise apartment unit. In aesthetic terms this creation of hollow outdoor cubes within the building volume exactly parallels the Cubist attempt to make objects visible simultaneously from several sides and directions. Corbu's two-to-one, indoor-outdoor spaces suggested a spatial advance beyond that of the "open plan" developed by Wright and others—an advance beyond the horizontal movement of space and into the vertical dimension.

Citrohan's roof garden, as well as the roof gardens on the apartment buildings in his Ville Contemporaine, are steps beyond Perret's somewhat timid indication in the apartment house on rue Franklin. The roof garden (as opposed to the punched-out private garden next to each apartment) was conceived of as a communal space, a kind of elevated piazza for the use of all the inhabitants of the building. And Corbu began, almost immediately, to treat the roof garden as an architectural space: a plaza animated by forms (both of architecture and of plantings) which would give its space light and shade, life and scale. At Citrohan the penthouse was merely a smaller cube placed upon the larger cube of the house proper; but before long he carried the Citrohan concept beyond its initial stage and gave the roof garden a distinct visual enclosure —the form of an outdoor room open to the sky.

In these sketches Corbu had, in effect, developed almost all of his tall-building concepts—developed them in microcosm, as it were. The best way to understand what he had done is to think of a typical small French street, the sort of street Maurice Utrillo loved to paint. The street is the public circulation artery; it is lined with high walls that, in turn, are punctured at regular intervals by doorways and gates. Behind these walls is a series of enclosed, very private patios, one for each family. And within each patio stands a house, an enclosed living space. At the far end of the street there is, generally, a small public plaza, a place where the inhabitants of the street may gather and conduct what-

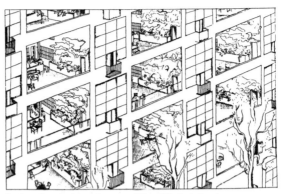

Portion of an apartment house consisting of "superimposed villas," 1922. Each living unit has a two-story "garden-in-the-sky." (From Oeuvre Complète)

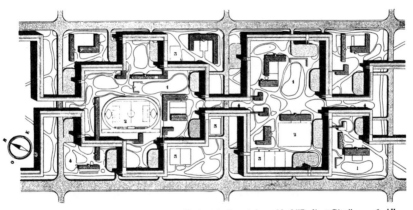

Garden apartments in an ideal "Radiant City," 1930-6. All buildings are to be on stilts so that pedestrians can circulate freely at ground level. Automobile traffic is on elevated highways. The architectural pattern is geometric, but the pattern of pedestrian paths and landscaping is very free. (From Oeuvre Complète)

Sketch for an ideal apartment was produced by Le Corbusier in the 1930's. Its use of two interlocking levels was prophetic of his Marseilles apartments and those that followed. (From Oeuvre Complète) ever social functions are conducted outdoors. This is the communal outdoor space, as differentiated from the private outdoor space represented by each of the small patios.

What Corbu proposed was, in essence, to stand this traditional French street up on its end: the street was now a vertical circulation shaft (elevators, fire stairs,· and so forth). At each level there were entrance doors into single-family "houses," the patio being the garden-in-the-sky, the house being the enclosed living space available to each family. And, at the end of the circulation shaft, on the roof, there was the public plaza, the outdoor space within which the inhabitants along the vertical street could meet to talk and to watch their children play.

Le Corbusier realized from the start that he had to go up, and that the only way to preserve any park spaces worth talking about was to go up very high, and to locate his towers very far apart. One result of this was bound to be a rather detached attitude toward nature—detached in fact as well as in spirit. While Frank Lloyd Wright was trying to dig in and, literally, get under nature's skin, Corbu tried to divorce his buildings from the ground as much as possible to keep that ground free from man-made obstacles, and to use some of the elements of nature, such as trees and shrubs, as architectural forms lifted out of their natural habitat and plunked down on terraces and roof gardens where they might form a pleasant diversion.

As Le Corbusier refined the basic idea of a vertical street, he included shops along the street as well; these became shopping levels halfway up the building, as in the apartment building he completed in 1952, at Marseilles. And he incorporated in his public plaza certain enclosed communal spaces, such as nursery schools, gymnasiums, movie theaters, and restaurants. The public plaza on the roof became a social and cultural center of major importance.

In plastic expression, he began to differentiate between the repetitive patterns of the "street" and the unique structures required by the public plaza. The "street" and its "houses"—i.e., the apartments—tended to form a tall, rectangular slab subdivided more or less regularly into apartment units; but the "plaza" on the roof became an increasingly free composition of curvilinear forms, a huge sculpture garden designed as a counterpoint to the simplicity of the slab, just as his interior spiral stairs and sculptural fireplaces were designed to provide counterpoints to the geometry of the cubic space in which they stood.

Although most of this did not become reality until much later, Corbu rarely designed or built anything in the twenties that did not in some manner contribute to his central idea of a vertical city. It is almost incredible today to see Le Corbusier's singleness of purpose throughout these years: however small the project, however far removed it may have appeared from what he considered to be his central mission, there was hardly a line drawn in his office which did not elaborate upon that mission. In the double house for La Roche and Albert Jeanneret (a cousin), designed in 1923, there is the first actual use of the *pilotis* to elevate a portion of the building and thus permit a continuous garden space at ground level; there are several interlocking one- and two-story high spaces, connected again by means of sculptural stairs and bridges; there is the first actual execution of a roof garden treated as a plastic counterpoint; and there is an attempt to rationalize the entire building by subordinating its design to some sort of proportionate scale.

In 1925 Le Corbusier and his cousin, Pierre Jeanneret, with whom he had become associated in all his architectural work, were commissioned to design and build an advanced housing development in Pessac, near Bordeaux. As this was to be located in a suburban area, there was no reason to use vertical structures; but Corbu's solution of row houses with completely developed roof gardens, patios, and open ground floors was simply a horizontal variation upon the same theme.

Here at Pessac, as in many other places, Le Corbusier was to run head-on into violent opposition on the part of various authorities, and his buildings stood vacant for more than three years after they were completed because some benighted local bureaucrats, who objected to the uncompromising geometry of Corbu's open and closed cubes, refused to issue the necessary occupancy permits. Le Corbusier noted wryly that it took less than one year to construct the Pessac buildings, but that it took more than three years, plus the intervention of two high government officials from Paris, to get the necessary occupancy documents signed!

V I I I

Throughout the 1920's Le Corbusier concentrated upon the further development of this one basic theme: the hollowed-out cube (which he called a "pure prism"), generally raised on *pilotis* and topped with a roof garden whose forms were suggestive of sculpture. In the course of this development, he built half a dozen houses of great beauty and strength.

The first of these was not, strictly speaking, a house at all. It was a pavilion—the Pavillon de L'Esprit Nouveau—designed by him and Jeanneret for the International Exposition of Decorative Arts, held in Paris in 1925. The pavilion was a full-size model of one of the two-story "superimposed villas" Corbu had developed a couple of years earlier for his

Pavillon de L'Esprit Nouveau, 1925. This exhibition structure is actually an apartment unit similar to one of the "superimposed villas" designed in 1922. (Courtesy, Museum of Modern Art)

Ville Contemporaine. There was a two-story garden space (a hollow, outdoor cube), closed off on two sides by a typical two-story apartment, complete with a two-story living room.

Here, as at Pessac, Corbu was to meet a degree of hostility hard to imagine today. While there is still, of course, a good deal of opposition to the sort of work done by Le Corbusier and others, most of this opposition nowadays is confined to mortgage bankers or editors of ladies' magazines. At the Paris exposition the hatred for Corbu's pavilion was passionate and vitriolic; indeed, it is difficult to understand why he was asked to participate in the first place, as the authorities did everything possible to sabotage his efforts. They began by giving him the worst site in the entire exposition, a spot practically outside the exhibition grounds. Next, they erected a fence some eighteen feet high all around Corbu's pavilion to keep out visitors altogether. It took the intervention of a cabinet minister to have the fence torn down! Finally, when an international jury decided to award the first prize to Corbu's pavilion, the French member of the jury succeeded in vetoing the proposal on the grounds that the structure "contained no architecture."

Corbu has often been criticized for his lack of tact and his belligerence; but he has usually had just cause; virtually every single building put up or proposed by him in the 1920's and 1930's was treated with the same sort of contempt by the critics of the moment. As a matter of fact, it would be very difficult to find anyone who remembers another exhibit at the 1925 exposition; only Corbu's pavilion has really survived the test of time.

It has survived that acid test not only because it was the first, clear statement of his notion of the "superimposed villa," but also because it contained two further contributions for which the modern movement is indebted to Le Corbusier: first, a collection of exceedingly handsome modern furniture, some of it designed by him; and, second, a proposal for the reconstruction of the center of Paris, which advanced Le Corbusier's city-planning ideas still further.

The committee that ran the Decorative Arts exhibit does, perhaps, deserve some sympathy for its opposition to Le Corbusier's proposals. For Corbu made no secret whatever of his own contempt for "decorative arts" as such, as he believed "that the sphere of architecture embraces every detail of household furnishing, the street as well as the house, and a wider world still beyond both. My intention," he explained, "is to illustrate how, by virtue of . . . standardization . . . industry creates pure forms, and to stress the intrinsic value of this pure form of art that is the result." Proceeding on this premise, Corbu furnished his pavilion with chromium-plated, tubular-steel furniture heretofore seen only in offices, and with standardized unit furniture (now generally referred to, in America, as "storage walls") also very similar to utilitarian office furniture. In addition to these pieces, which Corbu redesigned to fit his own needs and taste, he used some of the most beautiful bent wood chairs produced before or since: the circular Thonet dining chairs of bent "sticks" of wood. The chairs had been designed during the Art Nouveau era of the late nineteenth century, and had been mass produced ever since by their Austrian designer-manufacturer. Corbu, with his unfailing, selective eye, rediscovered them and made them famous again all over the world. As a direct result of Le Corbusier's rediscovery of the Thonet line of bent-wood furniture, these nineteenth-century pieces are now treated as precious antiques and incorporated in the permanent collections of such institutions as New York's Museum of Modern Art. Indeed, the pressure for the revival of some of the designs has been so heavy that several manufacturers, including Thonet, have recently gone back to making one or two early chairs!

More will be said about Le Corbusier's furniture design in a moment; meanwhile, this exhibition pavilion, with its collection of "useful objects," as well as examples of Cubist and post-Cubist painting and sculpture, was a convincing statement of the *aesthetic* position of the Machine Art men. Again, as on previous occasions, Corbu confused the issues by talking about "practical machines for living in." But by this time, with paintings by Léger and sculpture by Lipchitz displayed in his pavilion, no one had any excuse for failing to understand that Corbu was talking about a new world of *form*, rather than a new world of function.

The Plan Voisin for the center of Paris was exhibited in an annex to the two-story pavilion proper. It was an application of his Ville Contemporaine principles to an area of Paris roughly to the northeast of the Louvre. It is curious how close in spirit this radical plan was to the Tuileries and the Invalides!

Next to Corbu's pavilion in 1925, his most important small-scale experiments were five houses done between 1926 and 1929: the Cook house in Boulogne-sur-Seine (1926); the Villa Stein at Garches (1927); the two structures, also in 1927, for the Weissenhof exposition in Stuttgart; and the Villa Savoye, at Poissy-sur-Seine, designed in 1929 and completed two years later. Several other buildings were done by Le

Stein house, 1927. Another unit designed much like one of the "superimposed villas" of 1922. The house has a two-story "hollow cube" and a roof garden. (Courtesy, Museum of Modern Art)

Portion of Plan Voisin for Paris, 1925. This model was exhibited in the Pavillon de L'Esprit Nouveau. (Courtesy, Museum of Modern Art)

Cook house, 1926. Prototype for a row house on stilts, with parking space below and roof patio above. (Courtesy, Museum of Modern Art)

Corbusier and Pierre Jeanneret during this period, but these five stand out in retrospect.

The Cook house was a row house about twenty-five feet wide, an almost perfect prototype for a small, single-family urban dwelling using several of Le Corbusier's pet planning ideas. For example, the ground floor was almost entirely open; all it contained was a parking space for a car, a small enclosed entry and stair hall, and a paved and planted open terrace. The upper floors were supported on a very few concrete *pilotis*. The second floor contained all the bedrooms and baths, and the third and fourth floors contained all living areas.

As at Citrohan, Corbu made the most of the living areas upstairs by extending the living room proper upward through two stories, and by using a portion of the roof as a spacious garden terrace. But the most interesting fact about the Cook house was the extremely free handling of partitions: on every floor level Corbu made a point of curving his partitions to make it quite clear that they were entirely independent of all structural supports, and could be bent into any shape that might be required by function or composition. (One of Corbu's favorite tricks was to enclose his lozenge-shaped bathtubs within form-fitting walls, and to suggest a possible location for a grand piano by bending one living-room wall into the shape of an elongated S. Some of his imitators later borrowed the shapes created by Corbu, and applied them indiscriminately

4 9

to almost any interior and exterior element that could be bent out of shape without too much trouble. A nice example of this sort of nonsense is the curved entrance canopy at New York's Museum of Modern Art. Unless its designers planned to use this canopy to support a grand piano and to conduct recitals on West Fifty-third Street, there does not seem to be much justification for its shape.) In any event, the Cook house was a forerunner of Corbu's later exercises in a sort of controlled plasticity—a direction that occupied him more and more in the years after World War II.

Even more convincing than the Cook house was the Villa Stein (for Gertrude's brother), which he built at Garches during the following year. Again: *pilotis* supporting a part of the ground floor; a hollowed-out, two-story *outdoor* cube; freely curved partitions on every floor; a "Golden Section" system of façade design; and a handsome sculptured roof garden on top. The villa, in short, is another contribution toward Le Corbusier's central objective—to create prototypes for a vertical city.

The villa at Garches—recently restored though also, unhappily, altered—is so full of details that have influenced architects all over the world that it is difficult to list them all. Among them are the eloquently sculptured stairs and suspended entrance canopies, the long, uninterrupted ribbon windows, the interplay of levels and of forms. But Garches has another characteristic that has become a trademark of cer-

Roof garden of Stein house. (Courtesy, Museum of Modern Art)

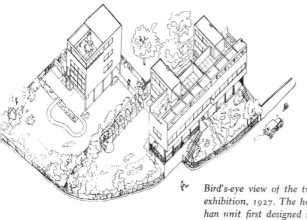

Bird's-eye view of the two units built at the Weissenhof exhibition, 1927. The house on the left is a typical Citrohan unit first designed in 1922; it is on stilts and has a roof patio. The building at the right is an apartment house, also on stilts and with a roof garden. (From Oeuvre Complète)

tain kinds of modern architecture: both its short end walls are blank, or almost blank. For Garches was designed again as a unit in a repetitive block of "superimposed villas," and built on a rather narrow lot. (In the Cook house the end walls were blank, too, for the simple reason that they were party walls in a strip of row houses.)

In all likelihood, the device of leaving the short end walls of his buildings blank grew out of Corbu's conviction that he was designing and building "vertical slices" of some bigger unit, rather than independent houses in the landscape. Soon, however, the short, blank end walls became a kind of mannerism in much of his work, and only in very recent buildings has he opened up the short ends of his slablike buildings, as well as the long façades. Actually, the contrast between a long, open, and glassy façade and a short, blank end façade turned out to be a very satisfactory aesthetic solution—especially in Corbu's Swiss Pavilion, built in 1932. But the origins of the idea, undoubtedly, are in Corbu's feeling that he was building units of a bigger whole, rather than complete, independent entities.

Perhaps the most sharply defined statements by Le Corbusier during these years are contained in the two houses he built at the Weissenhof exposition in Stuttgart, also in 1927. He and a dozen other leading modernists from all over Europe had been invited by the exposition's director, Mies van der Rohe, to contribute an experimental building to this modern suburb. Le Corbusier and Pierre Jeanneret were asked to design two. As the sponsors of the exposition, the Werkbund (for which Gropius had designed his famous glass-faced administration building in 1914), believed strongly in the integration of art and modern industry, Corbu felt fully justified in making his Weissenhof buildings a kind of summary of all his convictions concerning an industrialized architecture.

Characteristically, he began with a statement of several hundred well-chosen words; and, just as characteristically, he began that statement with a highly self-conscious, chip-on-the-shoulder defense of his own position as an architect. "This is by no means an esthetic fantasy or a search for fashionable effects," he informed his potential critics with ill-concealed contempt. "We are dealing with architectural facts which call for an absolutely new way of building." He then listed these facts, in this order: first, the *pilotis*, designed to raise the building off the ground and thus free the site and permit the garden to continue under and through the building; second, the *roof garden*, which, Corbu pointed out, meant in effect that all the ground covered by the buildings in a city could be recaptured in terms of parks up in the sky; third, the *open plan*, the result of a structural system of a very few widely spaced columns that permitted the utmost freedom in the arrangement of partitions and other space divisions; fourth, the *ribbon window* extending from one structural column all the way over to the next one, and thus allowing for uniform day lighting inside the building—unlike the traditional window (a hole punched into a structural wall), which, according to Corbu, creates pockets of gloomy darkness inside, next to rectangles of glaring light. And, finally, the *free façade*, as Corbu called it, by which he meant exterior walls that were no longer load-bearing and could, as a result, be opened up or closed at will, to satisfy functional or aesthetic requirements. And he concluded: "The above five basic points add up to a fundamentally new esthetic. Nothing remains for us of the architecture of earlier epochs. . . ." Great men should certainly be permitted their quota of silly remarks, and Corbu—whose quota has been astonishly small—was to reverse himself on this one in very short order. The first of Le Corbusier's and Pierre Jeanneret's Weissenhof buildings was a precise and beautifully proportioned version of Corbu's Citrohan project of 1922: a white cube on stilts, with a two-to-one apartment on the second and third floors, and a clearly defined roof garden on top. Again the "house" was really a slice of a city; but even when looked upon as a single, free-standing villa, the building had tremendous elegance. The free façade was treated somewhat like an abstract painting, with large rectangles of glass, vertical slot windows, and a single, boldly projecting balcony composed in the manner of a post-Mondrian painting.

The second building was an actual apartment house—or, rather, a portion of what we might call a garden-apartment unit. Again on stilts, the building had single-level apartments on the second floor, and a roof garden on top. The stair towers were treated as separate elements, projecting out from the "pure prism" of the apartment block. A ribbon of glass consisting of horizontally sliding windows of a design pioneered by Corbu extended across the full length of the building. All partitions inside consisted of prefabricated storage walls, and all furniture, other than chairs and an occasional table, was built in also. While this may seem fairly routine today, it was anything but routine in 1927. Corbu's built-in cabinets were so handsome that few furniture designers of the past thirty years have been able to improve on their proportions and details.

The Weissenhof buildings, in a sense, concluded one particular phase in Corbu's work. With their construction, he had in effect solved the problem of the vertical city building to his own satisfaction. While he has since gone far beyond Weissenhof in other city structures, his advances have been primarily aesthetic; the practical problem he had set himself was solved by 1927. His next and, possibly, his most important house, the Villa Savoye, revealed Corbu not only as a rational analyst of modern urban life, but as an architect in the finest traditions of the western world.

*Apartment house at Weissenhof exhibition. Smooth and
flat finish of façades is typical of Le Corbusier's work of
this period. (Courtesy, Museum of Modern Art)*

I X

P OISSY-SUR-SEINE is a small town about an hour's ride from Paris. The Villa Savoye, in turn, is located in the center of an estate of about a dozen acres, up in the hills overlooking Poissy and the valley of the Seine. Today the somewhat forbidding walls that surround the estate have begun to crumble, and the single gate, with the inevitable sign warning of a *chien méchant*, has rusted. No sight-seers may enter the estate: Mme Savoye's instructions on that point are quite specific.

As a matter of fact, there is nothing very secret or private behind these walls. It is just that the owner would rather not have people see what is left of the house she was forced to abandon at the time of the German invasion, in 1940. For the famous Villa Savoye that Corbu de-

Villa Savoye, 1929-30. Entrance hall and garage are at ground floor; living areas and patio are on upper level; and a penthouse structure forms the roof. (Courtesy, Museum of Modern Art)

signed in 1929—one of the two or three most famous houses built anywhere in the past hundred years—is now a strange and rather tragic ruin.

Like all of Corbu's work, the Villa Savoye was not an isolated event in his creative life. It is part and parcel of the central concept he first developed in the Citrohan house in 1922 and brought to full flower in the apartment structure in Marseilles exactly thirty years later. More specifically, the Villa was not even designed for the Savoye family or for that particular site: as early as 1925 Corbu had produced a poetic version of his favorite trinity—the stilt, the cube, and the sculptured roof —for the Villa Meyer to be built near Paris, a project that was never realized except in a set of charming drawings. But regardless of the historical origins of the Villa Savoye, *it*—at least—was built; and *it*—rather than its predecessors—influenced perhaps half the modern houses built anywhere in the world during the past twenty-five or thirty years.

The Villa Savoye was the most complete, the most self-assured, the most convincing statement of Corbu's beliefs that he was able to produce in concrete and glass before he stopped being a young radical and started being a "mature master." Indeed, it might be said that most of his completed work before 1929 could, theoretically, have been built by other talented men of the younger generation. But the Villa Savoye could have been built only by a master.

What remains of the Villa Savoye today is, briefly, this: a streaky, gray, rectangular box of reinforced concrete, measuring about sixty feet square, raised up in the air and supported on a dozen round, concrete *pilotis.* Deeply recessed under this concrete box, where the entrance foyer and garage used to be, there is now a hideously ugly pile of junk that looks, more or less, like the local village dump. Among the items in this junk pile, there are two old easy chairs of rattan; a coiled-up garden hose; several broken crates; an ancient Citroen sedan converted, at one time in its life, into a vegetable delivery truck; the remains of an old dining table; and, depending upon the season of the year, a few dozen bales of hay. From inside this junk pile there emerge occasional muffled sounds; these suggest that the once elegant foyer of the Villa Savoye now serves as a stable for an asthmatic horse.

Upstairs, inside the great concrete box, things are not very different; most of the windows are boarded up; much of the floor area serves as a hayloft. The living room contains an old workbench and a dilapidated tea-serving cart. A single, torn, U.S. army issue boot stands on the mantelpiece. Most of the paint has flaked off the walls; white splotches of plaster have appeared next to the original pastel blue. The patio, in the center of this upper floor, is part hayloft, part weed garden.

Finally, the roof structure, one flight farther up by a long ramp: this is a composition of straight and curved concrete screens and forms, now as pale and flat and desolate as the rest—flaking paint, streaked concrete, rusty railings, weeds everywhere.

Suddenly, out of a gray sky, there may flash a brief hint of the sun, and the ruin comes to life. The weeds become flowers, the flaking paint becomes an abstract mural, the great concrete shapes become plastic again, the few remaining walls of glass shine in the light. The Villa Savoye is as beautiful as it was in 1931, when Corbu completed it.

At Poissy, Le Corbusier made a series of fundamental declarations about architecture as he saw it: for example, he declared that he was a classicist about form and a classicist about nature. The Villa Savoye is divorced from the ground and raised up against the sky in a precise, geometric silhouette—raised up as if by some giant hand. (It is fascinat-

Spiral stair in Villa Savoye, after World War II. Wall at right was painted a pastel blue; most other surfaces were white. (Photo: Peter Blake)

Penthouse for M. de Beistegui, 1930-1. The hedges that form the roof parapet were set on elevators and could be made to drop out of sight. (Courtesy, Museum of Modern Art)

ing to see this recurrent theme of the giant hand raised against the sky in Corbu's sculpture from that time on: for example, the great symbol of his civic center at Chandigarh, in India, some thirty years later, was a huge hand sculptured in wood and iron, held up to the winds!) The precise, geometric silhouette of the Villa Savoye permitted no confusion of architecture with nature. This was meant to be a man-made object, the product of man's one great distinguishing characteristic— pure reason. Frank Lloyd Wright, of course, would never, under any circumstances, have divorced a house from its natural setting. His houses don't just grow out of the land; they are *part* of the land, part of the mysticism that has always governed northern man's relationship to nature. They hark back to the mounds that conceal the ancient graves of Vikings, to Harlech Castle growing out of a Welsh hilltop, to Mont St. Michel; whereas Corbu's pure prism is the symbol of Mediterranean man's conquest of nature—the determination of sophisticated builders to shape their own habitat.

Corbu made this point even more clearly in another project built while the Villa Savoye was under construction. This was the penthouse apartment for Charles de Beistegui, on the Champs-Elysées. Here, as in Perret's first apartment tower, the "natural environment" consisted of neatly clipped boxwood hedges in classic, geometric forms and carefully planted in rectangular boxes so placed as to enclose the roof terraces and screen them against the Paris skyline. Should M. de Beistegui wish to take a quick look at that skyline—well, then, all he had to do was push a button and one entire section of boxwood hedge would disappear on an electric elevator. "The complicated electrical installations required in this apartment," Corbu remarked at the time (and, presumably, with a straight face) "required 4,000 metres of cable." It is not likely that Frank Lloyd Wright would ever have put a plant on an elevator platform, to have it pop up or down at will, and it is perhaps even less likely that *anyone* except a Frenchman in love with modern machinery would ever describe a landscaping project in terms of the length of electric cable required to make it function.

At Poissy, a country house, the manipulation of nature is not nearly so mechanized, though it is no less sophisticated. The second-floor patio, upon which all living spaces are centered, is the real garden: a paved

Roof structure of Villa Savoye. Patio and living room are visible at lower left. (Courtesy, Museum of Modern Art)

courtyard with carefully controlled planting in boxes. Moreover, the views of the surrounding fields and trees are just as carefully controlled: on all four sides of the concrete box there are horizontal viewing slots through which sections of the landscape appear like naturalistic murals painted, between pilasters, in some great room of a Renaissance *palazzo*. Only the roof of this patio, this outdoor room, is entirely open—to the sky.

This, of course, is in the best tradition of Mediterranean building. Around the crowded basin of that sea, men have been forced for centuries to build vertically, and to enclose what they built with walls that could guarantee privacy from close-by neighbors. On the wide and spacious American prairie, where Wright grew up and learned to build with nature, men lived few and far between. They could build horizontally, parallel to the contours of the land, rather than up and away from them. The resulting differences were almost inevitable: as the Italian architect, Ernesto Rogers, has pointed out, Corbu's Mediterranean houses are patio houses, walled in, open only to the sky; Wright's prairie houses are like tents, with the walls rolled up. They are sheltered against the threatening sky with heavy, low-slung roof planes; and the visual limits of Wright's houses are those prairie horizons he learned to love in his youth.

The traditional Mediterranean separation of house and land lead Corbu into another conflict with Wright's philosophy. While Wright made a great point of using natural materials, preferably unfinished, to help him merge the house with its natural setting, Corbu gloried in making his building materials look as man-made as possible. The Villa Savoye was a reinforced concrete structure finished smoothly and precisely with painted stucco. Its exteriors and interiors were largely white —the white that can look so plastic under a Mediterranean sky—but there were a few accents of color on an occasional wall or partition. These colors came straight out of Corbu's painting: they were never the pure, primary colors of the bright and entirely flat sort used by Mondrian, but, rather, pastel shades that suggested three-dimensionality. Alfred Roth, the Swiss architect, pointed out some years ago that Le Corbusier's concept of color was intimately related to his concept of space. Corbu's spaces are hollow cubes animated by contrasting geometric volumes like spiral stairs, cylindrical chimney flues, columns, and other objects of applied as well as fine art; these spaces are intensely plastic, vigorous, sculptural in the manner in which the white stucco houses on Greek islands, like Mykonos, are sculptural. And his sparing use of pastel shades, especially his pastel blues and charcoal grays, was designed to stress this plasticity of form. To a good many modern painters, the idea of making a flat, two-dimensional canvas look three-dimensional (or, for that matter, of making a flat wall look "plastic") is sheer heresy; and when the De Stijl painters—Mondrian, van Doesburg, and others—wanted to be three-dimensional, they became sculptors. But Corbu was never bothered by such rationalizations, and his color does what color has been used to do from the beginning of time: it helps manipulate space and form.

There is another aspect to the finishes in the Villa Savoye and in Corbu's work prior to it which is worth mentioning. The Villa Savoye's exterior surfaces are a tautly stretched skin of stucco and glass, absolutely flush and finished as smoothly as Corbu knew how. The effect was that of a precise membrane stretched over a skeleton of concrete, and, indeed, inside the elevated patio the concrete skeleton is exposed and clearly differentiated from the outer membrane. This was a very popular façade treatment in Cubist and post-Cubist architecture, and it looked wonderfully machine-made—at least for the first month or so after the building was completed. Unfortunately the weather started to take its toll before very long, and cracks and streaks appeared on the stucco surfaces. The harsh facts of practical building began to conflict with the intellectual concept. Frank Lloyd Wright, a country boy, always understood those facts and never failed to see a building in terms of time—to see how it would weather. But men like Corbu, who were and are city slickers at heart, went through some major disappointments before they were forced, in the end, to give up the flush stucco-and-glass membrane.

When they finally did give it up, some of the Machine Art men found themselves in real trouble because it became more and more difficult for them to produce buildings with sharply defined silhouettes. As soon as you begin to have roof overhangs, recessed panes of glass, projecting window sills, the silhouette of your "pure prism" becomes considerably less pure and considerably less prism-like. So that today much of the Machine Art architecture that really works in terms of withstanding the test of time does not look very pure or simple.

Only Le Corbusier, and possibly Mies van der Rohe, made the transition from the pure prism of buildings like the Villa Savoye to the three-dimensional façade without the slightest apparent difficulty. Corbu stuck to the taut membrane a little longer; but after World War II, when his work suddenly took on a rough and almost brutally virile cast, the taut membrane was discarded. In its place appeared a façade developed in depth, with receding voids and an occasional projection breaking up the (imaginary) surface of the prism, without ever really destroying its visual integrity. The basic, over-all form remained strong, simple, and geometric; indeed, it continued to look very plain and flat-sided from a distance. But at close quarters the pure prism became a many-faceted crystal, full of intriguing changes in light and shadow, color and texture. If Corbu had built his Villa Savoye thirty years later, it would have been a "rough," rather than a "pure," prism.

That is one reason why the Villa has become one of the great historic monuments of modern architecture—one of its "period pieces" —and why there was such a storm of protest when the building was threatened with destruction in 1959. In the spring of that year the town council of Poissy suddenly decided that the Savoye estate would make a fine site for a new high school; and plans were made to expropriate the estate, destroy the Villa and the little gate house, and erect a new school in their places. Almost within hours of the publication of this decision, André Malraux, De Gaulle's Minister for Cultural Affairs, found himself bombarded with letters, telegrams, and resolutions from architects all over the world demanding that the Villa be preserved. The question arose immediately—"preserved for what?" In all likelihood it would cost tens of thousands of dollars to fix up the Villa, and Mme Savoye simply could not afford to spend such amounts. There were suggestions that the place be turned into a sort of retreat for young architects, in which they might continue their studies or, simply, continue their arguments. In any event, Malraux, who showed himself intensely conscious of the importance of Corbu's work, immediately intervened to save the buildings from further destruction. Whether or not a wealthy patron will be found to repair and endow the estate remains to be seen.

Meanwhile, as soon as the storm had subsided, the Villa returned to its lovely, surrealist dream existence—a delightful ruin, perhaps much better left that way. The war and the weather could destroy much of the original polish and sophistication of this building, but they could not destroy the great passion Corbu once poured into this little prism on stilts. Five years after the Villa Savoye was completed, he wrote this about architecture: "When the cathedrals were white . . . the new world was opening up like a flower among the ruins. Let us bring this joyful spectacle to life in our imaginations . . . and put clearly before our eyes those white cathedrals against the blue sky. We must get that image into our hearts. . . ." When the Villa Savoye was white against the blue sky, it, too, was a "joyful spectacle." It is not that today. But the image remains in our hearts.

Note: Since this was written, the Villa Savoye has been restored. Unfortunately, much of the original estate is now occupied by a rather banal building that houses a public school. It forms an unfortunate backdrop to one of the century's architectural masterpieces. —P.B.

X

W HILE THE PLANS for the Villa Savoye were being drawn up,
Corbu and Pierre Jeanneret were also at work remodeling an old house
at Ville d'Avray, which was to contain the first group of chairs, tables,
and cabinets completely designed by the architects. The year was 1928,
and their collaborator on the interiors was Charlotte Perriand, one of
the few great original furniture designers of recent times.

The pieces at Ville d'Avray consisted of, among other things, three
types of chairs which have spawned entire schools of furniture design
since they first appeared. There was, to begin with, a long, form-fitting
reclining chair or lounge; next, a modern version of the traditional
"British Officer's Chair"; and, finally, a heavily upholstered easy chair.

Interior at Ville d'Avray, 1928-9. All the furniture is by Le Corbusier and Charlotte Perriand. It includes the steel-and-leather version of the traditional "British Officers' Chair," the form-fitting lounge chair, and the heavily padded easy chair to the rear. All storage was built in. (Courtesy, Museum of Modern Art)

All three were framed in tubular steel either chromium-plated or enameled, and the upholstery was of leather or black-and-white cowhide.

The reclining chair and the "British Officer's Chair" were completely delightful and revealed much about Corbu's taste. Tubular steel furniture, of course, was nothing very new: men like Marcel Breuer had designed tubular steel chairs and tables at the Bauhaus in Weimar and Dessau from 1923 on, and Breuer's designs had been taken over by Thonet and other manufacturers to become almost standard items in most modern interiors. The quality that distinguished Corbu's designs from those of the Bauhaus was exactly the same that distinguished German functionalism from Corbu's rather special brand: while Breuer's chairs were entirely rational, technically impeccable, and, incidentally, very handsome, Corbu's were neither particularly rational, nor especially easy to manufacture. All they were, in fact, was ravishingly beautiful.

The reclining chair consisted of two entirely separate parts: an H-shaped cradle constructed, as Corbu remarked, *en tubes d'avion* (a characteristic reference to another technology: all it meant was that the tubes were oval in cross section!) This cradle in turn supported a long, form-fitting, sled-shaped contraption of tubular steel and leather, whose angle could be freely adjusted. A good many designers have tried their hands at producing a simplified version of this chair, and a vulgar, massive copy of it is currently on the American market. Few of the copyists seemed to realize that the very complexity of this chair's structure was the ingredient that made it so wonderfully elegant.

This reclining chair and, to an even greater extent, the Corbu version of the smaller "British Officer's Chair" looks like the complicated, beautifully articulated chassis of a Bugatti racing car. In the latter chair, for example, there are two chromium tubes that connect the front legs to the rear legs. In a Bauhaus chair these tubes would, quite obviously and soberly, have been straight. But in the Corbu chair the tubes start out straight and then, for no particular reason at all, suddenly leap up in a quarter-circle before they join the rear legs. This and other little details—such as the cylindrical pillow strapped to the head of the reclining chair—make these just about the wittiest, sexiest chairs designed in modern times. The fact is, of course, that much modern steel furniture does tend to look a little grim; all of us who solemnly assert that we like it do so because we think we *ought* to like it because it "makes sense." To a Frenchman this is a perfectly silly argument; he would never think of making love to a "nice, sensible girl" as an Englishman might, or to a potentially "good mother" as a German would. Corbu's chairs are rather like expensive tarts: elegant, funny, sexy, and not particularly sensible. Nobody has improved upon them to date.

The heavily upholstered easy chair was perhaps a little more practical: a rectilinear frame of tubular steel making a sort of square basket that, in turn, held squared-off leather pillows that formed the very comfortable seat. Eero Saarinen's easy chairs designed for the General Motors Technical Center, and some recent pieces by the Danish architect Arne Jacobsen, are based on Corbu's development, but few other

Easy chair by Le Corbusier and Charlotte Perriand, 1928.
(Courtesy, Museum of Modern Art)

designers of the younger generation have tried to do anything further with this promising concept.

Corbu's dining and working tables of that year, however, have been copied by every furniture designer west of the Yangtze River. Basically there were two: a type with a recessed base of four legs joined by an H-shaped frame and made again of *tubes d'avion*; and another type with a square frame of angular, chromium-plated steel sections, with the legs at the corners of the table. The table tops were generally of glass to keep the furniture from obstructing visually the free flow of space; occasionally they might be of polished marble.

Corbu's chairs and tables are masterpieces of proportion and detail to any connoisseur, though they may look pretty much like a lot of other modern steel furniture to the layman. Apart from the conscious use of simple, geometric forms in these tables and chairs, such as prisms, cylinders, and cones, these chairs and tables reveal one other trademark of functionalism: the separation of functionally different parts of the same object. Corbu went to great lengths to differentiate in form and material between the thing you sit on in a chair, and the thing that does the hard work of supporting your weight (soft leather versus hard steel); the thing you work on in a table, and the thing that supports the table top (glass or marble versus *tubes d'avion*). This basic law of functionalism had been clearly established in Gropius's Bauhaus, but Corbu carried it even further—and, one suspects, sometimes with tongue in cheek. One of his dining tables, for example, has the standard H-frame for support plus the marble slab for the top; but nowhere does the slab touch the supporting frame. Instead, there are very thin pins of steel that grow out of the supporting frame and, in turn, support the table top.

These chairs and tables, together with some beautiful storage-wall units, were exhibited in 1929 in a modern apartment designed by Corbu, Jeanneret, and Charlotte Perriand for the Salon d'Automne. The storage walls were particularly elegant, being framed in delicate sections of chromium-plated steel which formed a modular grid into which Corbu inserted units of shelving, storage drawers, glass-fronted display boxes, and mirrored sliding-door cabinets. The kitchen and bathroom designed as part of this apartment look as modern in almost every detail as the very latest built-in equipment being made by American manufacturers today. These same manufacturers and the industrial designers in their employ have spent years denouncing the "angularity" and "aridity" of Corbu's designs, only to come out with second-rate copies of the Salon d'Automne designs thirty years later (needless to say, without offering any financial reward to those who first conceived the ideas).

That many modern architects like Corbu, Breuer, Aalto, and Mies van der Rohe have devoted so much time to furniture design may be puzzling. The reasons are twofold: first, no modern architect believes that interior design can be separated from exterior design. The inside and the outside of a modern structure are regarded as one, thanks to the technological development of building with large sheets of glass, and the aesthetic development of sensing objects simultaneously from many vantage points. And, second, most modern architects have found chairs and tables to be excellent guinea pigs on which to experiment, simply and directly, with certain aesthetic and technical concepts. In a chair, for example, just as in a skyscraper, there are problems of function, of proportion, and of manufacture. Yet in a chair these problems can be studied much more readily (and economically) and their interaction observed much more rapidly than in a skyscraper. For this reason a piece of furniture has often taken the place of a small-scale sketch by means of which an architect was able to crystallize some new philosophic concept without going to any great expense.

With the exception of an occasional table or an occasional storage unit for a specific house, Corbu has not designed any furniture worth speaking of since 1929. Yet in this small group of chairs, tables, and cabinets, he produced a sufficient number of ideas, both of detail and of over-all form, to inspire a dozen or more furniture designers for many years to come.

Model room designed for the Salon D'Automne, 1929. Free-standing and built-in furniture by Le Corbusier and Charlotte Perriand. (Courtesy, Museum of Modern Art)

X I

B Y 1930, or thereabouts, Corbu had built only about a dozen relatively small villas, a housing development, and a couple of exhibition pavilions. He had also fixed up a river boat and turned it into a Salvation Army hostel, designed half a dozen pieces of furniture, written a similar number of books and propaganda tracts, and added a wing on stilts to another Salvation Army structure. In short, his architectural practice had been something less than a world-shaking success; yet his office was as busy as an ant heap, turning out projects and proposals for all sorts of buildings and new plans for cities. Many of his assistants were young European, Asian, and North and South American volunteers who had been drawn to Corbu's studio on the rue de Sèvres by his books and published projects. There was a spirit of tremendous excitement in his office at all times; yet the world outside continued to reject, denounce, and ridicule Corbu's ideas.

During the twenties an incident occurred which more than any other was to be responsible for Corbu's bitterness and coldness toward the world at large. Of course, he had already run into considerable trouble at the Exposition of Decorative Arts, where his pavilion was surrounded by a gigantic fence to keep it out of sight; he had run into opposition at Pessac, where his housing units stood unoccupied for three years before local bureaucrats would issue the necessary occupancy permits; and almost every house built by him had run into criticism and violent attacks. But the hardest blow came to Corbu in 1927.

In that year an international competition was held for the design of the headquarters for the new League of Nations at Geneva. Le Corbusier and Pierre Jeanneret were among the 377 contestants, and their design was one of the few serious "modern" projects submitted. To a large segment of the international jury Corbu's proposal seemed outstanding; there was no question in their minds that it should receive first prize. Historians, with the admitted advantage of hindsight, agree with that view. However, politics, narrow-mindedness, and sheer stupidity triumphed, and a compromise was reached which was, in effect, no compromise at all, as it removed Corbu's project from all serious consideration.

The story is complex and has been reported in detail by Corbu's friend, the Swiss art historian Dr. Sigfried Giedion. It is a pretty sordid story, of interest primarily because it tells something about the grim struggle Corbu and others had to wage before modern architecture became widely accepted.

Corbu's proposal for a site overlooking Lake Geneva consisted of four elements: a secretariat or office building for the day-to-day activities of the League; a large library; a wing containing meeting rooms for various League of Nations commissions; and a great wedge-shaped Assembly Hall for the annual meetings of the foreign ministers. The four elements were extremely well integrated; the growing problems of automobile traffic had been clearly understood and met in a practical way; the symbolic requirements of the building had been solved by the use of impressive approaches to the main Assembly Hall, by the suggestion of sculpture in a grand, though entirely modern, manner, and by a massing of forms that clearly expressed the purpose of the buildings and their relationship to one another; the existing landscape had been respected as much as possible by the characteristic use of *pilotis*, which permitted the informal gardens to continue beneath and beyond most of the new structures; and the roof gardens proposed for the top of the Assembly Hall building formed a series of "piazzas" with magnificent distant views across Lake Geneva. All these qualities were evident in Corbu's delicate and eloquent drawings for the project.

The importance of this design, however, went far beyond its inherent qualities. This was the first great challenge flung at the "official" academicians by those who stood for the new architecture in Europe. It was an important event—the most important, international design competition of the twentieth century. And though there were other modern submissions, only Corbu's represented an entirely serious, entirely practical proposal.

The jury consisted of six men: three "modernists"—H. P. Berlage (Holland), Josef Hoffmann (Austria), Karl Moser (Switzerland); one Art Nouveau man—Baron Victor Horta (Belgium); and two traditionalists— Sir John Burnett (Great Britain), and M. Lemaresquier (France), a leading spirit of the Beaux Arts Academy, one of whose great contributions to the jury's sessions consisted of proving that Corbu's drawings were rendered in printer's ink rather than Chinese ink—a serious violation of the program! The three modernists settled on Corbu's proposal, and there was some hope that Horta might be willing to join them, as his own early work seemed to have much in common with the anti-eclectic approach of the modernists. After sixty-five jury meetings, however, Horta decided to vote with the traditionalists, and a tie resulted. The jury thereupon did two things: it decided to award nine first prizes, including one to Corbu; and it asked the political heads of the League to select from among the winners an architect who should get the actual job of building the League's headquarters. That left the problem just about where it had been before the start of the competition.

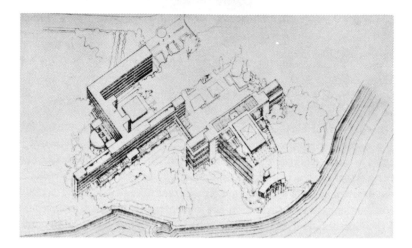

First project for the League of Nations palace, 1927-8. The wedge-shaped auditorium was here developed for the first time. (Courtesy, Museum of Modern Art)

During the following two years, there was much public and private agitation about the character of the proposed structures. Corbu describes one typical incident in his own book of collected projects and buildings of the period. "A small paper, *La Suisse libérale* of Neuchâtel published . . . in 1927 a series of articles by a Herr von Senger. These articles were put together in book form, published very quietly . . . and distributed gratis to municipalities and federal offices, to create hostility to our endeavors at the exact moment when the final decision was about

League of Nations palace at pedestrian eye level. Because the buildings are on stilts, there is an unobstructed view of Lake Geneva in the distance. (Courtesy, Museum of Modern Art)

to be made on who was to build the Palace of the League of Nations. . . . What stuff for the journalists! Two years later, *Le Figaro*, in Paris, ran a series of articles from the talented pen of Camille Mauclair, with a sharpness bordering on the ridiculous. The attacks were based on the 'heroic' pieces that had appeared in 1927 in the 'heroic' *La Suisse liberale*. . . . And finally, in 1933, there appears a book by Camille Mauclair, entitled '*L'Architecture, va-t-elle mourir?*' . . . Mauclair certainly needs to be consoled: Camille, have you lost your head? . . . Architecture is far from dying, it enjoys the best of health. The new architecture is just being born!"

No degree of sarcasm could gloss over the bitterness Corbu felt about the result of the League of Nations competition. The politicians had decided to select four traditionalists from among the nine winners; these four spent two years trying to arrive at a solution for the building complex. During those two years the site for the headquarters was changed, and Corbu and Jeanneret submitted a second design, even more open in its organization than the first, to fit the new site. When the League officials finally accepted the design agreed upon by the four traditionalists, the world (of architecture, at least) discovered to its amazement that the over-all plan proposed by the four men was remarkably similar to that suggested by Corbu, and entirely different in spirit and in detail from the designs originally submitted by the traditionalists in 1927. (The style, of course, was neoclassical.) Corbu and Jeanneret thereupon instructed their attorney to submit a detailed thirty-six-page brief to the League of Nations indicating that they felt their design had been pirated. The sole acknowledgment of this brief on the part of the League was a five-line letter stating that the organization could not concern itself with complaints submitted by individuals.

A dozen years later the original competition drawings by Le Corbusier and Pierre Jeanneret were purchased by the University of Zurich, and the bird's eye view of the project now hangs near the University's Department of Mathematics. Not too far away, on the shores of Lake Geneva, stands the empty neoclassic palace that was actually built to house the League. It proved to be inadequate from the day it was finally opened, in 1937.

X I I

THE LEAGUE OF NATIONS fiasco was only one of several major disappointments Corbu had to suffer in the late twenties and early thirties. The blows came with the monotonous regularity of a twenty-one-gun salute. There was, for example, the rejection of Corbu's proposal for a new Palace of the Soviets, in 1931; there were the city plans for Algiers from 1930 to 1934, with their fluid forms and their mile-long curvilinear buildings; and there were the plans for Paris, for Antwerp, for Stockholm, and for many other large cities—all painstakingly worked out in great detail, all rejected, sometimes by juries after competitions, at other times by local authorities without benefit of jury advice.

To say that all this work was in vain is obviously not true. Throughout the world younger (and more tactful) architects avidly studied every line drawn and published by Corbu, and began to "sell" the ideas to more receptive clients. To Corbu there was, perhaps, some sense of satisfaction in seeing his ideas so widely accepted elsewhere; but he would have been less than human if he had not grown increasingly bitter at seeing his work copied without any benefit whatever to himself.

For the record, it is perhaps worth listing some of Corbu's brilliant innovations of these years. Many of these innovations finally bore fruit in the hands of younger architects, who have never denied their debt to Le Corbusier, and who have made it clear that Corbu developed certain solutions that simply cannot be improved upon at the moment. Such men as Eero Saarinen, who regards Corbu as one of the great "form givers" of modern architecture, would be the last to deny that he has been enormously influenced by the forms Corbu gave to modern architecture; the same holds true of Corbu's Brazilian disciple, Oscar Niemeyer, whose work would be completely unthinkable without Le Corbusier's tutelage; and of the late, brilliant, Polish-born architect Matthew Novicki, killed in 1950 in an airplane crash in the Egyptian desert, who had received his apprenticeship in Corbu's studio in Paris before World War II. These men Le Corbusier accepts as worthy followers; and though he can hardly be blamed for wishing that he had had some of the opportunities available to the generation that followed him, he recognizes the hardships of his life as part of the price you must pay for being the first.

For Corbu was first with an astonishing number of ideas that seem startling even today when imitated by his many admirers: the huge parabolic arch from which was hung the roof of the Great Hall of the Palace of the Soviets, for example, was a brilliant piece of structural exhibitionism, scaled to the monumental occasion. Here was to be an assembly hall for 15,000 spectators and 1,500 "performers"—a fantastic political circus. And Corbu developed a scheme that was a spectacle in itself, yet so carefully thought through in terms of human progression on different levels and by different means that somehow an understandable scale was preserved. Since that competition (to which Corbu had been in-

Project for the Palace of the Soviets, 1931. Part of the great assembly hall at left was to have been suspended from the parabolic arch. (From Oeuvre Complète)

vited by Soviet authorities as a sop to Western "progressives" disappointed by the League of Nations fiasco), the great parabolic arch has fascinated many other architects: Saarinen used the device for his prize-winning Jefferson Memorial design for St. Louis (as yet unbuilt), and Mussolini had a much smaller parabolic arch built for himself as a war memorial to celebrate his dreams of empire. Corbu's design, however, did not get off the paper it was drawn on. "Out of considerations which I must recognize," he stated, "the jury of this competition decided that the Palace of the Soviets should be built in the Italian Renaissance style. It must be admitted," he added, almost audibly gnashing his teeth, "that a Palace which in form as well as technique should be an expression of the new age, can only be the result of a social development that has reached a high point—and not of one at the beginning."

In 1933, two years after the Soviet Palace, Corbu entered another competition—this one for the headquarters building of a life-insurance company, to be erected in Zurich. He explained that the program, as written for that competition, simply did not take cognizance of the possibilities offered by new techniques in planning and construction: hence he ignored the program (which had envisaged a low structure with a central court) and produced a ten-story office building whose organization in terms of structure, heating, air conditioning, functional relationships, and so on was explained in his drawings in the most meticulous way possible. The result of that competition for Corbu and his cousin, Jeanneret, was just as expected: their entry was immediately

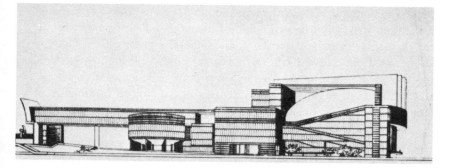

disqualified, as it did not satisfy the traditional preconceptions held by the client. Yet here again Corbu presented a series of ideas that have come to life in other buildings by other architects in the years since the Rentenanstalt project was first presented. For example, here was the first office tower with a lozenge-shaped plan, the shape having been arrived at by the simple rationalization that the elevator core in the center of a slablike building required extra space, and that such a slab should, therefore, be fattened up in the middle. Today three such lozenge-shaped towers are built or projected: the B. C. Electric building in Vancouver, completed in 1956; the Pirelli building in Milan, completed in 1959; and the great tower near Grand Central Station in New York, first projected in that same year. Like the Salvation Army hostel in Paris, built in 1932-3, the Rentenanstalt was to have been sheathed in glass and equipped with window-washing platforms suspended from trolleys on the roof—a standard American practice today. And, like so many of today's most distinguished tall buildings, the Rentenanstalt was to have had a penthouse of curved and vaulted planes, housing (among other things) a theater.

The various projects for the rebuilding of Algiers (all of them bogged down in a bureaucratic morass) represent modern solutions to the typical crowded Mediterranean town, which had first introduced Corbu to certain concepts of architecture—especially to the image of the white-walled patio open to the brilliant blue sky. Somehow the plastic coastline of Algiers, covered with clusters of walled buildings, kept Corbu intrigued for many years; and in responding to its landscape and townscape, Corbu created some of his most brilliant projects for row houses, terraced apartments, and multilevel highways that effectively sorted out different kinds of traffic and made all of them work together separately. One of his most interesting solutions for Algiers was a tall hillside apartment house, designed to be built in continuous strips, and entered on the uphill side on a floor halfway up the building. This entrance floor was to be open, so that pedestrians on the uphill side of the building could enjoy a continuous view of the Mediterranean, framed between horizontal slabs of concrete. At this entrance level and just below it, there was to be parking space for cars. With characteristic thoroughness, and with his characteristically French delight in the complexities of machinery, Corbu even laid out the ducts for an air-conditioning system, although his building was designed as a complete breezeway, with apartments extending right through the structure from north to south. (This principle has become common practice in all tropical hotels built since the end of World War II.) Toward the north and the view of the Mediterranean, Corbu placed his double-story living areas.

The city plan for Antwerp, produced in 1933 as a competition entry, fared no better than Corbu's other projects. "Crazy stuff," the jury called it, and passed on to more "practical" submissions. Yet the Antwerp plan does not look very different today from such eminently sound proposals as those made by the architect Victor Gruen for Fort Worth: the creation of a largely pedestrian city core ringed by superhighways. Even more impressive in terms of today's best city-planning practice is Corbu's proposal for Stockholm, also done in 1933; here, at least, the jury paid Corbu the compliment of studying his proposals for all of ten months—only to reject them in the end. Yet there is literally nothing in these proposals which would not seem entirely reasonable today to the city planning commissions of Philadelphia, New Haven, Chicago, Los Angeles, or Cleveland. In fact, Corbu may, if anything, have *under*estimated the problems raised by interlocking automobile and pedestrian traffic; today's American planners would probably feel that the separation should be even more complete than Corbu suggested in the early thirties.

"The defeats of these past years represent so many victories," Corbu said in 1934. "Our rejected plans will become public accusers, for the public will judge the bureaucrats according to these plans; and the day will come when these plans will force a change." To many of his contemporaries, Corbu may have seemed to be whistling in the dark; but his faith was real enough—a Frenchman's passionate faith in the eventual triumph of reason.

X I I I

DESPITE THE DISAPPOINTING outcome of the League of Nations competition and of many of his other projects, the furor they created helped advance the cause of modern architecture in general and Corbu's career in particular. In the summer of 1928 Corbu, Giedion, and other leading architects of the modern movement banded together to form CIAM (Congrès International d'Architecture Moderne). One of the prime movers of CIAM in its early days was Mme de Mandrot de la Sarraz; she offered her family's old Château de la Sarraz for the first meeting of the group and helped it in numerous other ways. (Incidentally, she also commissioned Corbu to design a house for her a couple of years later.) At this first CIAM meeting, Corbu outlined a program for discussion which ranged from subjects like "modern technology and its consequences" to "city planning" and "the education of young architects." CIAM was to become a powerful force in the modern movement, and its influence can be felt to this day, particularly through certain schools of architecture. In 1928, however, it was in effect a sort of defensive alliance of architects and planners who believed that the League of Nations competition and other fiascos required them to stick together and form their own pressure group.

Even though Corbu lost the League of Nations job, he was soon busy designing his first large structures: the Centrosoyus for Moscow (1928), headquarters for the Soviet Co-operative Unions, and now the Soviet Ministry for Light Industry; a multistory apartment building for Geneva (1930-2); a smaller one in Boulogne-sur-Seine with an apartment for the architect on top (1932); a large Salvation Army hostel in Paris (1932-3); and the Swiss Pavilion—a student dormitory building—in the University City in the south of Paris (1930-2).

Of these five buildings the Centrosoyus, a huge complex for some 2,800 office workers, is by far the largest. Apart from this, the Centrosoyus is interesting primarily because in it some of the concepts originally projected for the League of Nations were finally executed; and because its multilevel public areas, with their great, sweeping ramps, showed Corbu at his sculptural best. The structure was probably the last "modern" building of any consequence erected in the USSR before the party line swung to wedding-cake architecture. Although the Centrosoyus was built without Corbu's supervision, it was still the most modern and self-assured building in Moscow more that twenty-five years after its completion.

The Salvation Army hostel, whose glass façade was badly damaged during World War II (and even more badly repaired), was a fantastic piece of planning, with elaborate interior automobile and pedestrian ramps, a library, dining and sleeping facilities, etc., all contained within a narrow, slablike building on a rather complicated site. The air-tight glass façade, designed to simplify air conditioning, could be washed by men standing on a platform that was suspended from a trolley that traveled back and forth along the edge of the roof garden—a forerunner

8 3

of a similar mechanism installed at New York's Lever House when it was built after World War II.

The Salvation Army hostel is much more glassy, much more metallic in detail than most of Corbu's buildings before or since. In addition to plate glass, Corbu sparingly used a glass block—one of the few instances in recorded history when that hideous material was used well. (One reason was that French glass block, unlike that produced in the United States, was small and rather handsomely patterned.) Although the Salvation Army building was full of elegant detail, it suggests, in retrospect, that Corbu is at his best when he stresses reinforced concrete in all its plastic possibilities.

The Swiss Pavilion, which was indeed supported on a reinforced concrete substructure, is not as large as the Salvation Army hostel, or as complex in terms of planning. But in the history of modern architecture this little five-story building is one of the most important "vertical slabs" built before World War II, and it is one of the three or four most beautiful "vertical slabs" built at any time during the past few decades.

This is so for several reasons: first, and most importantly, the Swiss Pavilion is a building of disarming simplicity and purity—a precise, four-story vertical slab, free-standing and raised one story above the ground on *pilotis*. Secondly, the Swiss Pavilion is a wonderfully effective play of contrasting forms: the pure prism of the steel-framed slab contrasted with the massively sculptured concrete *pilotis*; the smooth and slightly curved shaft of the stair tower contrasted with the free-formed ground-floor structure that contains the entrance foyer, the communal lounge,

Swiss Pavilion, University City, Paris, 1932. The first completely uncompromising slab building constructed by Le Corbusier. (Courtesy, Museum of Modern Art)

Rear of the Swiss Pavilion, showing curved stair tower and the stone-faced communal areas at ground level. The natural stone wall was set into a concrete frame and treated much like a mosaic. (Courtesy, Museum of Modern Art)

and the janitor's apartment. Third, the Swiss Pavilion is full of striking surface contrasts: the curved rubble-stone wall on the ground floor as opposed to the smooth stone-veneer finish on the building proper; the all-glass south façade along three floors as opposed to the stone-veneer finish on the high parapet of the roof patio (the parapet, in turn, being punctured here and there to create the same sort of "viewing slots" Corbu used in the patio of the Villa Savoye); and, similarly, the contrast between the open façade to the south, the blank façades facing east and west, and the punctured façade facing north. Finally, the Swiss Pavilion is an exceptionally clear statement of the aesthetic of functionalism. Its three principal elements—the slab, the ground-floor structure, and the stair shaft—are all clearly articulated, separated, and then linked in a manner that emphasizes, rather than detracts, from their separateness.

During the war a German anti-aircraft unit mounted some twenty mm. Bofors guns on the roof of the Swiss Pavilion, and the recoil shook up the building here and there. However, there was no structural failure of any sort; the Pavilion was repaired at little cost and, by 1950, looked as good as new. Le Corbusier painted a long floor-to-ceiling mural onto the inside of the curved rubble-stone wall in the student lounge, replacing a photo mural he had put there originally.

The Swiss Pavilion has been the forerunner to so many famous slab buildings that it is hard to mention them all. The most obvious one, of course, is the slab of the United Nations Headquarters, for which Corbu himself was one of the architectural consultants. Another is the Ministry of Education building in Rio, designed by Oscar Niemeyer in consultation with Le Corbusier, Lucio Costa, and others in 1936; and there are various and sundry postwar hotels, apartment buildings, and office towers built in the United States, South America, Europe, Asia, Africa, and Australia. All of these buildings have four things in common with Corbu's Swiss Pavilion: they are vertical slabs; they

The Swiss Pavilion after its recent renovation. Aluminum sunshades have been applied to the glass façade, thus compromising the purity of the original form. (Photo: Peter Blake)

Weekend house at Vaucresson, 1935. Traditional and natural materials are used sparingly but with growing frequency. (Courtesy, Museum of Modern Art)

have long, glassy façades, and short, blank façades; they are raised on stilts; and the ground-floor space—whether it be a lobby, assembly hall, or shopping area—is treated as a free-form structure that is "slid" under the raised slab and handled as a separate and contrasting element.

The Swiss Pavilion and one or two houses of the same period reveal another development of major significance in Corbu's work: the use of traditional, natural materials. Corbu's curved rubble-stone wall at the Swiss Pavilion is framed in concrete like an abstract mosaic. There is no intention of making the wall look "natural": like all the rest of his architecture, the wall is meant to look sophisticated and man-made—in fact, rather painterly. The stone looks and is treated almost like a very rich sort of wallpaper, applied to the structure, but not trying to look as if it held up anything whatever.

The vacation house for Mme de Mandrot, built near Toulon while the Swiss Pavilion was under construction in Paris, was of local rubble stone also; but that is where any resemblance ends between it and the Pavilion—or, for that matter, between it and any of Corbu's earlier

Studio in Le Corbusier's apartment, showing some of his paintings and sculpture of the 1930's. The rough brick and concrete block add texture to the space. (Courtesy, Museum of Modern Art)

houses. For here Corbu suddenly began to experiment with something that must have shocked a good many of his Machine Art friends: he took a primitive, local building tradition and transformed it, with infinite sophistication, into an entirely modern statement.

Corbu's interest in traditional and natural materials was not as sudden as it may have appeared. Throughout his trips in southeast Europe, Greece, Italy, and North Africa he had been struck by the virility of simple, native construction. As early as 1923, in *Vers une architecture*, he made references to primitive building. By the late twenties he had started to use an occasional wall of local stone to contrast with the precision of his white cubes. The charming little gate house for the Villa Savoye (a sort of "baby" to the Villa proper) had a base of stone; Corbu's own apartment, in Boulogne-sur-Seine, has party walls of brick and concrete block—left unfinished (in his studio, at least) just as he found them on the site.

But the house for Mme de Mandrot and the later summer house at Mathes were built entirely, or almost entirely, with natural materials. They had bearing walls of native stone supporting floors and roof, with occasional inserts of glass and wood. The de Mandrot house still had reinforced concrete elements (floor slabs and an occasional concrete column where the bearing wall had been replaced with a large expanse of glass); but the summer house at Mathes was all stone and wood, with massive wooden posts, beams, and planks next to equally massive walls of local stone.

As in the Swiss Pavilion, Corbu treated these natural materials in the most elaborately sophisticated way. The stone walls of the house for Mme de Mandrot are framed panels and look almost painted rather than real. On the inside they were whitewashed because, as Corbu observed a long time ago, "white is always powerful and positive." No attempt whatever was made to "merge" the house with the landscape; indeed, it stands on a small platform, built on a sort of promontory from which there is a beautiful view of a plain. Yet, despite its antinaturalism, the house looks just "right" in a formal French landscape.

The summer house at Mathes was built in 1935. It is two stories high, has a "butterfly roof" (V-shaped in cross section), and a simple, rectangular plan. Both floors have their circulation along an outside "corridor"—a terrace and a balcony; the wooden structure is quite traditional in principle and clearly expressed. It is a house that explains itself without any trouble, inside and out.

These two houses, together with a couple of other projects of the same period, are the forerunners of many of the modern stone, wood, and glass houses we see all around us in the United States. Of course, Frank Lloyd Wright had used these materials in their natural state for many years, long before the house for Mme de Mandrot was built. But Wright used them in a naturalistic way—i.e., in a way that was anathema to all believers in a machine aesthetic. Now Le Corbusier, the greatest Machine Art apostle of them all, had found a way of using traditional materials in an entirely modern, almost abstract manner. He had made natural materials respectable in terms of the Machine Art idiom.

As usual, Corbu developed innumerable details in these stone-and-wood houses that have inspired his admirers: in the stone-and-wood Errazuris house in Chile, designed in 1930, there is the first dramatic, modern use of the unequal butterfly roof, bridging a house that is part two stories, part one story in height. Ramps that connect the levels are parallel in slope to the pitch of the roof—a very handsome spatial organization, quite different from the more common butterfly roof used so often today without the slightest relationship to the interior. In the house at Mathes the fenestration is worked out as part of a panel system, part glass, part plywood, painted in brightly contrasting pastel colors—all inserted in a grid of wooden vertical and horizontal divisions. This idea, too, has been copied again and again ever since. In that same house there are post-and-beam connections that have been more or less standard for centuries, but were never used in Machine Art architecture until Corbu rediscovered their beauty and strength.

However much Le Corbusier might shy away from naturalism in architecture, his rediscovery of natural materials brought with it a revival of interest in natural forms per se. In a letter to a group of young South African architects, dated 1936, Corbu wrote: "How are we to enrich our creative powers? Not by subscribing to architectural reviews, but by undertaking voyages of discovery into the inexhaustible domain of Nature! . . . I wish that architects would sometimes take up their pencils to draw a plant or a leaf—or to express the significance of a tree, the essential harmony of a shell, the stratifications of the clouds, the ever-changing ebb and flow of waves at play upon the sands . . ." This, of course, is precisely what Frank Lloyd Wright had been saying to disciples at Taliesin for quite some time, between acid cracks at that "pamphleteer and painter," Le Corbusier, who seemed to think that architecture was just a matter of piling boxes upon more boxes. Whether Corbu realized it or not, this rediscovery of the "inexhaustible domain of Nature" was the beginning of a new phase entirely in his own work—a phase that, as time went on, he was to call "organic."

X I V

I N THE LATE FALL of 1935 Corbu made his first trip to the United States. The Museum of Modern Art was arranging for an exhibition of his work, and invited him to come to New York for a series of lectures in connection with that show.

New York struck Corbu like a bombshell—and vice versa. "New York, clothed in pearly haze and stretching its distant towers to the sky, appeared before me in the morning mist like the promised city," Corbu said about his arrival. "This was the land of modern times and this was that fantastic and mystic city—the temple of the New World!" Le Corbusier, the man who had designed the best skyscrapers and skyscraper cities ever put on paper, had never seen a real skyscraper before in his life! "When I first saw the Empire State Building," he told a friend in India, several years later, "I wanted to lie down on my back right there on the sidewalk, and gaze toward its top for ever." He was completely stunned by the sheer size of the thing. "A thousand feet high!" he said. "That is an event in the history of architecture!"

Yet Corbu was not entirely dazzled by New York, Chicago, or Detroit. Granted, the technical skill that produced the skyscraper was one thing; but the aesthetic ignorance that adorned it with massive gimcrack was another. And still another consideration—the *most* important consideration in Corbu's mind—was this: the fact that the architects and planners of the United States had not the foggiest idea of what to do with the skyscraper *as a tool of city planning!* With his usual perceptiveness, Corbu pointed out that a skyscraper without a city plan was sheer nonsense.

His trips around the United States in late 1935 and early 1936 were peppered with speeches, interviews, and debates. To Corbu, this was a stimulating time: at long last he was in the land of Machine Art and in the land of the Ville Radieuse—the twin subjects that had fascinated him for years. But what was the reality? He told one successful New York architect, while standing at the window of that man's office and looking at Manhattan's skyline, that all those skyscrapers were a disgrace to the engineering skill that produced them. "And here I was," his host complained later, "with this man tearing down everything I had been doing all my life!" He told the New York *Herald* that "New York's skyscrapers are too small," and the *Herald* made it an incredulous headline. He told a dazed New York police official, Harold Fowler, over a breakfast conference, that Manhattan would have to be rebuilt from the ground up. He told a Chicago audience that "as a result of indifference and the all-consuming power of money, irresponsible enterprise has been the controlling influence on [U.S.] townplanning. . . . The great inefficiency of America," he continued, "has enabled me to see more clearly the nature and inevitable end of our present city development. . . ."

In short, Corbu was not particularly tactful; unlike the stereotype of the "European visitor on his first trip to the United States," Corbu was by no means starry- and dewy-eyed. He decided, quite simply, to tell the truth, and the truth turned out to be quite painful.

The most painful truth Corbu decided to tell had to do with the American skyscraper city and its chaotic approach to planning. In a letter addressed to Kenneth Stowell, then editor of the *American Architect*, Corbu gave one of the most brilliant analyses ever produced of what plagued the U.S. city—and what would plague it in days to come unless certain specific measures were taken immediately. This letter was written by Corbu in 1936, almost a quarter of a century ago; if much of Corbu's criticism sounds familiar to us today, it has become so only because the highest American planning authorities, from the mayors of great cities down to New York's chief planners (who often like to deprecate those from whom they have acquired their wisdom), have now come to understand what Corbu saw so clearly in 1936.

"The New York skyscraper is only negative," Corbu wrote. "It has destroyed the street and brought traffic to a standstill. It consumes the very life of the population and eats up whole districts around itself, emptying them and bringing ruin. Build the skyscraper bigger and more really useful, [place it in a park] and it will reclaim a vast amount of land, will compensate for depreciated properties, will provide a perfect system of circulation, and will bring trees and open spaces into the city. The pedestrians will have freedom of parks over the whole ground area and the cars will travel from skyscraper to skyscraper at a hundred miles an hour on one-way elevated roads placed at wide distances apart. . . . Notice how the great hotels and apartment houses [around Central Park] have naturally come to be built here so as to have the advantage of looking out on space. But Central Park is too big; it is an island in a sea of buildings. Crossing it is like traversing no-man's land. The trees, grass and . . . space of Central Park ought to be multiplied and spread over the whole of Manhattan. . . .

"The suburb is the great problem of the U.S.A. . . . I give a lot of thought to those crowds who have to return by subway in the evening to a home which is anything but paradise. Those millions who are condemned to a life without hope, without a resting place . . . Manhattan [as it is now] is so antagonistic to the fundamental needs of the human heart that the one idea of everybody is to escape. To get out. To avoid wasting one's own life and that of one's family in that hard, implacable atmosphere. To see the sky. To live where there are trees and to look out on grass. To escape for ever from the noise and racket of the city.

"Millions of city dwellers have moved out to the country. They arrive and settle down and in so doing they cause the destruction of the country. The result is a vast, sprawling built-up area encircling the city— the suburbs. All that remains is the dream. . . .

"This suburban development makes necessary the hours spent daily on subways, buses and commuter trains; it causes the destruction of that communal life which is the very marrow of the nation."

What Corbu predicted during his first American trip has now become a nightmare reality. Today's city planners in New York and elsewhere are trying, desperately and almost hopelessly, to create zoning patterns that will eventually force the kind of space distribution which, Le Corbusier realized, could still turn Manhattan or downtown Chicago into garden cities punctuated with glistening skyscrapers, spaced far apart and linked by ribbons of expressways. Legislation passed by federal and state governments in recent years tries to achieve the same results— and tries to break through the stranglehold of thick belts of grim suburbia built since World War II. As so often happens, the poet has been vindicated, and his "practical" and "hardheaded" critics have been exposed for their lack of vision.

But shortsighted officials were not the only ones who failed to understand Corbu. The advocates of the horizontal "Garden City" on the English pattern were vehement in their opposition to what they considered to be Corbu's "inhuman" proposals. These planners of villages scaled to the demands of the eighteenth- or nineteenth-century life believed—and some actually still believe—that the American city can be dissolved into low-density patterns of housing (i.e., detached, semidetached, and row houses in garden settings) which will, somehow, be grouped in small satellite communities, each with its own self-supporting industry, commerce, and agriculture, each linked to its neighbor, far away, by highways crisscrossing the countryside. This naïve and romantic notion presupposes several things that simply do not correspond to the facts of modern life: first, it assumes that small-scale industries are economically practicable; second, it assumes that there is enough space in the U.S. to spread out our population horizontally (or, if this is not the assumption, then the Garden City planners evidently believe that either universal birth control or a revival of the bubonic plague will drastically reduce the overpopulation of the globe); and, third, the Garden City planners believe that people don't like to live in big cities. This is simply not true.

Most people like big cities so much that they are willing to put up with them even though the big city has become virtually uninhabitable. This is clearly demonstrated by the increasing flight from the country into towns and cities; only prejudice can obscure it. The problem today, obviously, is not to ship people out of New York, Chicago, Los Angeles, or St. Louis and offer them wholesome living in villagelike satellite communities; it is, quite simply, to create a new kind of city—a city with all the excitement, the stimulation, the glamor, the gregariousness of a big metropolis—and to make that city healthy, efficient, and beautiful.

The principal factors that make Le Corbusier a twentieth-century prophet and Frank Lloyd Wright a nineteenth-century romantic are in their different reactions to the city: Wright hated it, wanted to destroy it, hoped to dissolve it in a horizontal spread of greenery; Corbu loves the city, wants to make it more dramatic, more exciting, more efficient, and, above all, more beautiful. It was quite characteristic for Wright to design his few city buildings—like the Johnson Wax building in Racine, Wisconsin, and the Guggenheim Museum in Manhattan—to look like some foreign object, inexplicably dropped into the urban fabric, but, on the other hand, to design his many country buildings to merge and melt into their natural environment. And it is just as characteristic for Corbu to design his many city buildings to fit perfectly into the angularity of an urban pattern, and to make his few country buildings seem a little out of place in a natural setting. For to Corbu the city is the great challenge, the great contemporary problem. Regardless of whether one regrets this or not, the facts of the world's population statistics support Le Corbusier.

His American trip took Corbu to Detroit, where he saw the Ford assembly line—and immediately wrote an ode to it! Here was the America of Machine Art. "When the cathedrals were white [i.e., when they were first built], everybody worked together in complete unison," Corbu wrote. "In Ford's factory, everyone works to one end, all are in agreement, all have the same objective, and all their thoughts and actions flow along the same channel. In the building industry there is nothing but contradictions, hostility, pulling in opposite directions, differences of opinion, working at cross purposes and marking time. We pay dearly for all this—to build is a luxury and, consequently, society is badly housed. . . . Let the forces which up to now have been pulling in opposite directions mass themselves to march solidly together. . . . Let the ghosts of the past cease to bar the way."

Although Le Corbusier met with a great deal of enthusiasm among students and young architects wherever he went, his public reception, as exemplified by some newspapers and institutions, left something to be desired. Needless to say, certain papers that expect foreign visitors to go through the standard ritual of prostrating themselves before the miracle of America were not charmed by Corbu's acid criticism of the country whose guest he was. He was, of course, quite familiar with this sort of thing from his frequent bouts with the authorities and the press in Europe. What hurt him more were certain misunderstandings that arose during his visit, particularly a misunderstanding with the Museum of Modern Art, which had agreed to pay him a fee for a number of lectures. According to Corbu the fee was too small; moreover, he claimed, the agreement had committed the Museum's directors to much more assistance than they seemed willing to give. Were not the Rockefellers "behind" the Modern Museum? Was it not reasonable to expect them to pay adequately for a visit from the prophet?

Regardless of the merits of his case, Corbu had little to complain about regarding his treatment by the Museum of Modern Art. As early as 1932 Henry-Russell Hitchcock and Philip Johnson had put together an exhibition on "International Architecture" which praised and exhibited Corbu's work as of the greatest importance to his time. (The term *International Style* was coined on the occasion of this exhibition by the Museum's leading spirit, Alfred Barr.) And though the Museum *was* in part supported by the Rockefeller family, it had to pay most of its own way and simply did not possess the sort of funds a European, full of notions about American wealth, might expect. Corbu has had misunderstandings regarding money matters before and since: he feels, quite rightly, that very few of his ideas have ever paid him a financial return; that ideas are, however, the only commodity an intellectual can sell to pay the rent; and that, finally, he should be paid for presenting his ideas whenever possible, particularly as it would seem that others are much more likely than he to turn these ideas into cash. The argument is perfectly reasonable, although it is considered unorthodox in a society that thinks of its intellectuals as nearly worthless, and will pay "idea men" best when their ideas can be made to produce or sell goods. Still, the Museum of Modern Art, a nonprofit organization, can hardly be compared to a big advertising agency; and so Corbu's demands could not be fully met. This was the beginning of a feud between Corbu and America which rages to this day: first he denounced the Modern Museum; then, by indirection, the Rockefellers; next, during the time of the building of the United Nations after World War II, Corbu became convinced that the Rockefellers were again behind some sort of plot to deprive him of the rightful fruits of his labors by promoting Wallace K. Harrison, a Rockefeller relative, rather than Corbu, to be chief architect of the U.N. project; and, finally, he came to believe that most American businessmen were "gangsters" and that one had to be eternally vigilant in one's dealings with them. This just about represents his position today.

In a sense, Corbu has always carried on an unhappy love affair with America. America at first represented all the things he believed in most passionately; after his first trip he realized that America was not, perhaps, all that he had hoped, but that the *possibilities* of achieving his objectives did, at least, exist in the U.S. to a degree found nowhere else; but when Corbu tried—again and again, clumsily, tactlessly, arrogantly, but, in reality, so very desperately—to work in this country and to practice on a great scale what he had preached so long and so ardently, he found himself rejected wherever he turned. That this rejection was due, in large part, to the fact that in a "teamwork age" the individual, eccentric artist is hard to assimilate, Corbu could not be expected to accept.

For one thing, he considers himself to be entirely reasonable—and, of course, he is, within his terms of reference. For another, he does not really believe that committees ever produce great architecture—and in that belief he is entirely correct. Yet, to the Managerial Type, who is generally entrusted with great projects, any man likely to "cause trouble" is anathema. Corbu has caused plenty in his time—and his time is better off for it.

To put it mildly, the love affair between Corbu and America did not get off to a very successful start in 1936. When he returned to France after his stay in the U.S., Corbu wrote a charming and lyrical book—*When the Cathedrals Were White*—which was, in reality, a sort of love letter to America. It is a much more adult love letter than the ones contained in *Vers une architecture* (which praised U.S. technology to the skies); but it was still an affirmation of love for all the great potentialities of the United States. Moreover, it was a touching request for the chance to prove his affection.

X V

T HE LATE THIRTIES were a busy and exciting time for Corbu. Everybody in Europe was, of course, aware of the likelihood of war in the near future, and many artists seemed to feel the need to complete as much of their life's work as possible before the coming of the expected holocaust. After his visit to the U.S., Corbu made a trip to Rio, where a group of architects under the "grand old man" of Brazilian architecture, Lucio Costa, had banded together for the design of the new building for the Ministry of Education and Health. The group asked Corbu to come in as a consultant—possibly a rather reckless gesture on its part, as Corbu has a way of dominating any situation in which he finds himself. At Rio he was soon the dominant influence, designing first a long slab building rather like his Centrosoyus in Moscow, and later, after the site preferred by him turned out to be unavailable, a taller slab for a more confined lot. The Ministry sketched by Corbu was built substantially as proposed by him, and completed in 1945. By that time Costa, an extremely modest and self-effacing man, had virtually withdrawn from active participation in the group's work, as he realized that Corbu was obviously going to be the dominant spirit —whether he was physically present or not. During the development of the project a young Brazilian, Oscar Niemeyer, who had been rather a quiet and reticent participant in the planning of the building prior to Corbu's arrival, suddenly blossomed forth, under the influence of Corbu's stimulating presence, as a brilliant designer in his own right. Today the Ministry of Education building is often referred to as the work, primarily, of this remarkable young Brazilian; indeed, with its completion, Niemeyer suddenly became the outstanding young architect in South America, and he is now in charge of most of the design of Brasilia, the country's fantastic new capital. Interestingly enough, the competition for the site plan of Brasilia was won by none other than Niemeyer's original mentor, Lucio Costa; and Niemeyer, who remained intensely loyal to both Costa and Le Corbusier throughout some trying periods, is again happily working with the former on one of the largest projects to have been entrusted to any architect in the present century. Costa, incidentally, with the magnanimity of true greatness, celebrated the completion of the Ministry building by writing a letter to Corbu which acknowledged, in effect, that Corbu's work on that structure had dramatically changed the direction of Brazilian architecture.

The Ministry of Education represents an important crystallization of several of Corbu's key ideas: in general concept, it is very similar to the Swiss Pavilion—though seventeen stories high, rather than a mere five. Like the Swiss Pavilion, it is a slab building on *pilotis*, with a rather free-shaped assembly and exhibition-hall structure "slid" under the tall, elevated, rectangular prism at ground floor. Like the Swiss Pavilion, the Ministry of Education also has short, blank end walls and long, glassy side walls; but, *unlike* the Swiss Pavilion, the Ministry has a handsome grille of movable *brises-soleil* covering the entire height and width of its

Ministry of Education and Health, Rio de Janiero, 1936-45. The first real skyscraper designed by Le Corbusier (in association with Lucio Costa, Oscar Niemeyer, et al.) This slab building on stilts, with sun-control louvers and a sculptural roof treatment, was the forerunner of hundreds of similar structures built since then in all parts of the world. (Photo: G. E. Kidder Smith) sunny (north) façade. Finally, like the Swiss Pavilion and like the Villa Savoye, the Ministry building has a magnificently plastic superstructure of penthouses containing mechanical equipment, restaurants, and recreation areas—all set in a handsome roof garden.

Although Corbu had been working with the concept of sun-control louvers for several years prior to 1936, the Ministry of Education in Rio was the first large building to make full use of this device. Since that time the combination of a glass "curtain wall" protected by a grille of sun-control devices—vertical, horizontal, circular, or what have you—has become a standard solution for modern buildings. Properly designed, this outside curtain of sun louvers can keep the interior cool without seriously obstructing the view of the outdoors. Even in fully air-conditioned buildings such sun-control devices have helped drastically to reduce the air-conditioning load and cost. Throughout the tropical and semitropical areas of the world Corbu's *brises-soleil* are now an accepted and proven architectural device.

The Ministry of Education was probably the largest building constructed according to Corbu's design in the years immediately preceding World War II. At the same time, he was so busy on so many other projects and structures during those years that it is impossible to mention them all. There were more projects for North Africa, including some designs for a three-winged skyscraper, generally Y-shaped in plan, which suggested a more varied urban silhouette than that offered by slab buildings; and there were several exhibitions, including a steel-and-canvas structure—Le Pavillon des Temps Nouveaux—put up for the Paris World's Fair of 1937.

This light and colorful bit of playfulness was one of the first modern buildings to be based upon the recognition that steel is strongest in tension. The roof—a translucent canvas sheet that permitted diffused light to enter the pavilion—was supported entirely on cables suspended between the uprights and left to assume their natural, catenary curve. The technical principle Corbu demonstrated here in an almost off-hand way is now being applied to tension structures all over the world—by men like the young American architect Paul Rudolph, who has built several such structures in Florida, and by others who feel that the tensile strength of steel strands, demonstrated again and again in our own suspension bridges, has enormous potentialities. In other designs for exhibition pavilions prepared during that period, Corbu and Jeanneret developed systems of so-called space frames of light steel, used both in tension and in compression, which were engineered much like airplane wings. Here again Corbu suggested a new structural form, which has now been further developed, both in concrete and steel, by younger architects in the U.S. and elsewhere. Unfortunately, Corbu was again too early; in 1939 nobody in authority was willing to commission this sort of exhibition structure, despite the fact that exhibitions, from the Crystal Palace Exposition onward, had been traditional proving grounds for experimental architecture.

Throughout the years immediately before World War II, when virtually nothing was being built in a world hypnotized by the gradual build-up of Hitler's attack, Corbu was bursting with ideas, each more challenging than the one preceding it. For Philippeville, in French North Africa, he designed a museum whose plan was like a square snail or square spiral, flattened out and, by its nature, infinite in terms of possible future expansion. This idea has been picked up in different ways by others; even Frank Lloyd Wright's postwar Guggenheim Museum probably owes a good deal to this project or to its predecessor, Corbu's *ascending* spiral museum of 1929. Corbu, the painter, knew more than any other architect of his time about ways and means of lighting a painting; and the Philippeville snail was illuminated entirely by skylights that followed the plan pattern all around the roof. Corbu had to wait for almost twenty years to get a chance to build this museum; finally, in 1958, the structure first designed in 1939 was built by him in Ahmedabad, in India, and another was completed in Tokyo in the same year.

Then there was the sketch for a monument, in 1937, to be erected in the memory of Vaillant-Couturier, the veteran French Communist deputy and first editor of *L'Humanité*. Vaillant-Couturier was the sort of idealistic Communist who vanished from the scene after the Hitler-Stalin pact. A competition was held for the design of a monument to him, to be built at the intersection of two great highways leading into Paris, and Corbu was one of those who submitted an entry to the com-

*Monument for Vaillant-Couturier, 1938. This composition
of geometric and naturalistic forms shows Le Corbusier
taking a dramatically new direction in his work. (Courtesy,
Museum of Modern Art)*

petition jury. His submission was highly sculptural, an entirely plastic,
poetic object of monumental proportions. The composition was quite
abstract, with only two representational elements in it: a giant hand,
palm open to the sky in the manner that seemed to spell "man against
the world"; and a head, also gigantic, that showed the veteran Communist crying out against injustice. These two naturalistic elements
were placed, quite abstractly, into a composition of slabs and frames of
concrete—a composition of violently beautiful contrasts, of brilliant,
searing-white sunlight, and somber, near-black shade. Like all of Corbu's
earlier competition entries, this one was rejected by the jury; yet, in
1945, when the Museum of Modern Art in New York began to face up
to the fact that a new rash of war memorials was about to be visited
upon the U.S., it decided to exhibit Corbu's great monumental project
as an example of what might be done.

Le Corbusier's own apartment, Paris, 1933. This two-story unit occupies the top floors of a building designed by him. The apartment shows his increasing interest in more sculptural forms. (Courtesy, Museum of Modern Art)

The monument to Vaillant-Couturier was particularly significant in this respect: Corbu, who had started as a painter of cubes and spheres and prisms, was now quite evidently determined to bring certain elements of nature—even representational art—back into sculpture, architecture, and, indeed, painting. While the basic composition of the monument was still quite Cubist in feeling, no Cubist who valued his membership in the "club" would have seriously considered including a representation of a human head and a human hand in a composition of this sort. In Corbu's development as a complete artist, this move toward naturalism had been under way for some ten years or so. "Beginning in 1928," he said later, "I threw open a window on the human figure." Some years earlier he had added pebbles, pieces of wood, butcher's bones, and roots of trees—"objects evoking poetic reactions"—to the precise, Cubist forms found earlier in his paintings. Now the human figure was back in his paintings—and in his sculpture as well. Indeed, Corbu could hardly be called an uncompromising Machine Art man any longer: in all his work, from the late twenties on, there were unmistakable signs of a loosening-up process, a growing interest in nature as a source of inspiration. In 1937, for example, when Corbu consented again to show his paintings and sculpture (after an absence from the galleries of a dozen years), the visitors to the Kunsthaus in Zurich were amazed to see a fluidity of line and form, and a preoccupation with the *human* form, which seemed to have nothing in common with the Purist paintings done by Corbu in the early twenties.

This growing fluidity of line and form, coupled with an increasing use of natural materials, should have been apparent to Corbu's admirers for some time: the 1930 plan for Algiers, with its huge, curvilinear apartment and office buildings; the intense plasticity of forms in Corbu's own apartment, built between 1930 and 1933; the free-form patterns that increasingly dominated Corbu's landscape plans for his great urban projects of the 1930's—all these were ample indications that the rigidity of cube, cone, and sphere was being superceded by a much less self-conscious and more varied vocabulary of forms. Indeed, only the outbreak of World War II kept Corbu from entering upon an entirely new phase in his architectural development.

X V I

As HE DID DURING the First World War, Corbu used the years of enforced idleness primarily to paint and to develop new ideas on paper. In a small vacation house at Cap Martin in the Alpes Maritimes, Corbu was at work on a number of murals when World War II came. For several months, to everybody's surprise, the existence of a state of war made relatively little difference to daily life in France. Naturally, nothing was being built, though much was being projected. Yet life continued in a rather placid manner. Corbu was used to painting under almost any conditions and in many kinds of places—on trains, on ships, in hotel rooms—and he had developed a typically orderly method of allocating time to his painting. "For seven years I was able to give only

Saturday afternoons and Sundays to painting," he once explained. "Then, later, until the war, I was able to paint every morning from eight to one." An artist—i.e., presumably a rebel—who paints according to a rigid timetable is, surely, one of the more amusing inventions of the watch-making Swiss! In any event, Corbu continued to paint during the first months of the war, both in the south of France and in Paris, giving more time to this aspect of his work than he had been able to do before.

Then, suddenly, in May 1940 the Germans attacked. Corbu left Paris and went south to the Pyrenees. With the defeat of France, it became more and more difficult to obtain pigments, and his painting began to slow down. Like many others, he hoped that preparatory work for the postwar reconstruction of France could be done in the months and years ahead; but the authorities at Vichy proved to be impossible to work with. Yet, because they were the only authorities potentially interested in postwar reconstruction, Corbu had to deal with them for a while. During this period, particularly while Corbu prepared another of his brilliant and hopeful projects for the redevelopment of Algiers, people outside France heard rumors to the effect that he had become a collaborationist. One architectural magazine in New York actually printed the report, although Corbu's "political history" should have warned everyone that he was highly unlikely to conform to any existing political coloration. In 1928, when he designed the Centrosoyus for Moscow, he had been denounced as a Communist; by 1931, when his project for a Palace of the Soviets was rejected in favor of a neoclassical wedding cake of fantastic proportions, Corbu denounced the Soviets as uncivilized; then, in 1942, when he was about to present his latest plan for Algiers to the Municipal Council of that city, the Vichy authorities decided that he was a Communist and rejected his proposal—at the very moment when so-called liberal architects in the U.S. and Britain decided that Corbu was, in fact, a Fascist collaborator; and when the war was over, Corbu often talked vaguely to visiting Americans about his belief that some sort of "communist" brotherhood of man was the only answer—so there he was a Communist again! But as the Soviet line on architecture had become violently anti-Corbu, the Soviet *New Times*, meanwhile, was denouncing him as a bourgeois reactionary; indeed, the Soviet architect Shkvarikov, who visited Switzerland in 1948, announced that Corbu's apartments at Geneva "looked like an absurd, alien growth," had "nothing in common with the people," and were therefore, "doomed to wither away!" Finally, in the early fifties, Corbu became a Fascist again in the pages of certain American women's magazines (because his architecture was so "inhuman"); he became a Communist again in the pages of *Time*; and he will, undoubtedly, become a good many other things depending upon the prevailing "liberal" or "reactionary" attitudes of magazine editors toward such real or potential clients of Le Corbusier as Nehru, De Gaulle, the Emperor of Japan, or the current dictator of Iraq.

The facts are that Corbu is totally disinterested in politics; that he finds it necessary, at times, to deal with politicians in order to achieve certain important objectives of planning and redevelopment; and that his own "political" philosophy has to do with such issues as the continuity of civilization on earth and the need for assuring such continuity—concerns that are not easily labeled in terms of today's political pressure groups.

Among the many projects of the war years, there was one in particular which represented a powerful new direction in his work. As part of one of his Algiers projects, Corbu designed a skyscraper of fifty-odd stories to serve as a central administration building for the port. This tower was lozenge-shaped in plan, very much like the Rentenanstalt project developed by Corbu in 1933 for Zurich. As in that earlier insurance-company building, the reason for the plan shape was simply that the center of the building was taken up by space-consuming stacks of elevators and other services, so that it seemed reasonable to fatten up the building around its core to accommodate an adequate amount of office space around the entire periphery of the plan.

Apart from the similarity in plan, however, the Algiers tower had very little in common with the Rentenanstalt. The latter was to have been a very slick and glassy building—a volume enclosed by a smooth curtain wall of glass. But the Algiers building was anything but smooth; instead of the slick, glassy skin designed for the Zurich building, this

Projected skyscraper for Algiers, 1938-42. This concrete-grille tower, lozenge-shaped in plan, is Le Corbusier's first major departure from "graph-paper" façades. The interrupted pattern of the concrete grille is determined by a system of identical proportions—*rather than a system of identical* dimensions. (*From* Oeuvre Complète)

monumental tower was to have a deep egg-crate pattern of concrete *brises-soleil* all over its façades. But, even more importantly, the façades were anything but regular, for the egg-crate pattern was full of variations in scale, and it was punctured, more or less at will, with dramatic spaces hollowed out of the mass of the tower, forming great terraces and gardens dozens of stories up in the sky. Corbu's model for this tower suggested something else, which he was to develop in actual buildings after the war: for it seems that the Algiers skyscraper was meant to be built of rough, unfinished concrete, rather than smoothly finished with stucco or stone veneer, as were so many of Corbu's structures in the twenties and thirties.

Because the core of the Algiers tower was a vertical shaft of elevators, and the most important structural element was the load-bearing row of columns surrounding that core, Corbu compared the building to a tree—i.e., a structure with a central trunk, with branches extending out from that trunk (the office floors), and with roots firmly anchored in the ground (the foundations). Obvious as this analogy may seem, it was anything but obvious to have been brought up by someone who had originally reacted against the naturalistic preferences of Art Nouveau. Frank Lloyd Wright, of course, had always used the tree analogy to describe his tall buildings, and he was to use it most effectively in describing two of his postwar projects of the 1950's—the Price tower in Bartlesville, Oklahoma, and the fantastic Mile High building projected for Chicago's Lake Shore. But, then, Wright had never strayed far from Art Nouveau anyway, whereas Corbu had opposed the movement almost as vigorously as he had opposed neoclassicism.

But, as in his paintings and sculpture, the lessons that could be learned from nature were beginning to become increasingly important to his architectural work. His buildings still looked entirely man-made —and they always would. But the principles of continuous structure and of interrelated proportion which Corbu began to see everywhere in nature took over from his earlier infatuation with the machine.

X V I I

WITH THE LIBERATION of Paris, Corbu returned to the capital to try and start again. He found the roof garden outside his apartment overgrown with weeds—an aspect that seemed quite poetic to him. "My garden has been allowed to run wild," he wrote, "the rosebushes have become large eglantines; the wind, the bees have brought seeds; a laburnum has grown; a sycamore; lavender bushes have spread out. The sod has become coarse grass. The wind and sun control the composition, half man, half nature. . . ." There was little coal in Paris, and Corbu would stand in his icy studio, wrapped in a heavily lined, three-quarter length U.S. army Mackinaw, working away on more paintings. Young American and British architects, serving in the Allied armies, would pass through Paris and stop off to pay their respects. Mme Le Corbusier, a wonderfully simple French "peasant" with none of Corbu's sophistication, but all the warmth and humor Corbu sometimes lacked, would occasionally cook for a visiting American soldier and make raucous and irreverent jokes while Corbu was demonstrating, very seriously, some gadget he had designed and put into his apartment years earlier. From all over the world young people inquired as to Corbu's whereabouts: how he had managed to live through the war (he had been seriously sick for a while, but was now back in fairly good shape); how his buildings had survived the bombings and shellings (some very well, others badly); what his plans were for the future.

To Corbu himself, the end of the war was, quite simply, a signal to get going, full blast, with the reconstruction of Europe. There was not a moment to lose. "There are ruins, stones overthrown, frustrated ideas. The universal forge is working at full speed. Give it jobs to do! Work! Let us create the tools of happiness—the equipment for a modern world!" He had a tremendous sense of urgency, yet he also sensed that many opportunities were about to be missed. "France, are you going to withdraw your head and your horns into your shell, like a snail?" he asked. The answer was perhaps not quite as simple as Corbu thought, for there were immediate problems of housing those without any sort of shelter, of fixing up buildings that still could be saved, of simply providing the minimal necessities.

Whatever the problems and delays, Corbu decided that he could not wait, that too much had to be done. The war was hardly over when he began to work on two major projects: the new city plan for Saint-Dié, in the Vosges Mountains of France; and a large apartment project to be built for bombed-out families in the suburbs of Marseilles. These two projects—the first never built, the second completed in 1952—were the culmination of Le Corbusier's work over more than three decades; and they eclipse in importance most of the city planning and housing work done in Europe prior to that time.

To understand what this means, it must be remembered that Corbu was now almost sixty years old; that he was no longer in the best of health; that much of his work of the twenties and thirties had re-

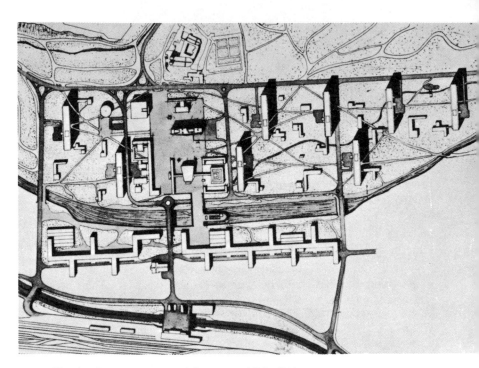

Plan for the reconstruction of the center of Saint-Dié, 1945.
The proposal for the monumental plaza has influenced
every important city plan since 1945. (Courtesy, Museum
of Modern Art)

mained unbuilt, and thus might have simply served as a reservoir, a backlog of existing and well-studied ideas that one could draw upon now at will and rework slightly to fit an immediate situation. In short, Corbu had done his bit—and much more—for modern architecture, and might well be permitted to rest on his laurels.

He did nothing of the sort: at Saint-Dié and at Marseilles he created two concepts of such staggering boldness and beauty that most of his devoted followers in other parts of the world were left far behind, still playing around with the forms of a Ville Contemporaine or a Swiss Pavilion of the twenties and thirties. Corbu, far from settling down to the peaceful role of an Elder Statesman, had opened up several new vistas. Fifteen years later the younger architects of Europe, Asia, and the Americas were only just beginning to grasp the lessons of Saint-Dié and Marseilles.

During the war the historic center of Saint-Dié had been destroyed systematically by the Germans. They had evacuated some 10,000 inhabitants and then, over a period of three days and three nights, had razed the core of the town, block by block, with hand grenades·and mines. After the liberation, officials of the town asked Corbu to work on the reconstruction of its old center.

Corbu's unrealized proposal covered an area approximately one mile square. To the south the area was defined by the river Meurthe, and on all sides, around the periphery of the center, there were highways linking Saint-Dié to Nancy, Strasbourg, and other major cities. Corbu proposed to locate manufacturing plants to the south of the river, and large apartment blocks to the east of the central area. All this was well and reasonably worked out; but it was the civic center itself, along the north bank of the Meurthe, that showed Corbu at his finest.

This center was to have been a magnificent pedestrian plaza, reached from all directions by ramps and bridges, surrounded by parking facilities, and facing the river to the south. The plaza was monumental in scale: its east and west limits were defined by tall apartment slabs, about 1,000 feet apart. Between these tall slabs, which framed the plaza, Corbu proposed to place a series of buildings of varying shape and form, each, in a sense, a huge piece of sculpture set into this paved and landscaped sculpture garden. To the north, impressively tall and robust like some giant Campanile, there was to have been an office tower to contain the administrative functions of city government. This tower was differentiated from the apartment slabs by its lozenge-shaped plan, similar to that of the tower Corbu had designed for Algiers three years earlier. Like the Algiers tower, this one had an irregular egg-crate façade, penetrated here and there by great terraces and other volumes and forms meant to symbolize certain ceremonial functions of civic government. The great administrative tower was on an axis with one of the automobile approaches to the civic center, and visible from every part of town. It was, in a sense, the "cathedral" of a modern town—the central symbol that makes the core of a city also its heart.

Between the great tower and the banks of the river, there were to have been several lower structures: restaurants, stores, a wedge-shaped civic auditorium, and a square museum with Corbu's characteristic snail plan. Beyond these lower structures the plaza extended farther to the south in a broad, pedestrian bridge that spanned the Meurthe and led to a large swimming pool "carved" out of the river. The composition of these different structures, and the composition of landscaping and paving patterns, was entirely asymmetrical. Yet, despite its inherently dynamic qualities, the composition was in monumental repose—a classic outdoor space as serene as any of the great Renaissance piazzas.

Although the plaza for Saint-Dié was formed as carefully as a sculpture-collection, it should not be thought for a moment that it was abstractly conceived, without regard for human scale. Characteristically, Corbu measured his drawings for Saint-Dié not only with the standard metric scale, but, more importantly, with a scale indicating the distance a man might be able to traverse on foot in a quarter of an hour. Moreover, to anyone willing to imagine himself in the position of walking through this great civic center, another extraordinary dimension becomes immediately apparent: this is the dimension of surprise, of changing vistas, of sudden turns around a corner leading toward an entirely unexpected and quite stunning new perspective. This is a center designed entirely in four dimensions, planned to be walked through, to be a delight to the eye of man, whose line of vision might be about sixty-three inches above the ground—not to the eye of a bird or a model-maker, whose perspective has distorted so much urban design in recent decades.

The Saint-Dié plan has served as *the* model for almost every great modern civic center projected since 1945. The elements proposed by Corbu have often been copied too slavishly, too insensitively, too two-dimensionally. Yet in many parts of the world where plans for new "hearts" of cities are drawn, Corbu's vision of a great new piazza for Saint-Dié has dominated all thinking over the past fifteen years.

This is so not only because of the inherent merits of the Saint-Dié proposal; it is so, to a large extent, because Corbu's project for Saint-Dié was a reaffirmation, at exactly the right moment, of his belief—and the belief of many of his contemporaries—that the great city, the metropolis, could be a supremely beautiful thing. Let the Garden City dreamers build their endless rows of detached cottages; let the agrarians rant against the evils of high urban densities. The facts of life, Corbu seemed to feel, would catch up with them soon enough. Meanwhile, let us make a demonstration of how magnificent a modern city can be, how great a heart we can give it, how *human* we can make its scale. Saint-Dié said all this and more; it was the most persuasive argument for urban greatness a modern architect has ever been able to put on paper.

While this city plan was discussed and exhibited in many parts of the world, local politics in the town of Saint-Dié once again intervened —and Corbu's proposal was rejected. He did build a small industrial structure in the town, but no part of his great plan was ever accepted and realized. As so often in the past, Corbu found himself snubbed, his finest ideas rejected by politicians of every stripe. In place of his proposal, a trite, neoclassical plan was finally accepted. Dr. Sigfried Giedion closes this particular chapter in Corbu's life with the flat statement that Corbu's plan for Saint-Dié, "for the first time in our period, would have presented a crystallization of community life . . . [equal to] the Greek meeting place. . . ."

The Marseilles apartment building, however, did get built, though it took much time and much energy to overcome man-made obstacles Corbu's great mentor on this project was the French Minister for Reconstruction, Eugène Claudius-Petit, who fought many a battle for the Marseilles building when every other authority seemed to turn against it.

In a schematic sense, the Marseilles building is a summation of everything Corbu advocated in connection with urban living from 1920 onward. It is a huge slab, 450 feet long, sixty-six feet thick, and about 200 feet tall. It contains almost 340 apartments for some 1,600 people. It has fifteen apartment floors in all, plus a two-story "shopping street" that runs down the length of the building, about one third of the way up. Two rows of Corbu's inevitable *pilotis* hold up the monumental slab; there are the equally inevitable two-story living rooms in each apartment, backed up with two stories of bedrooms and service areas; and above it all is the communal roof garden—the piazza up in the sky—

where the inhabitants of this single, vertical city may meet and talk and watch their children play.

All of this is, of course, simply a crystallization of Corbu's basic beliefs throughout the twenties and thirties. The sole extraordinary fact about the *planning* of the Marseilles building is the proof it again affords of Corbu's almost fanatical single-mindedness over the years—his extraordinarily sharp and precise vision, from the days when he began to sketch out his ideas to the moment when his admirers watched the Marseilles building go up and hailed it as the ultimate revelation of architectural truth. For this building is an absolutely logical extension of Corbu's "superimposed villas" and of his Pavillon de L'Esprit Nouveau—both designed more than twenty years earlier. And every detail in the *planning* of the Marseilles building had, indeed, been clarified by Corbu many years before.

Why, then, is the Marseilles building so much more than a mere summary of Corbu's development over the years? Why is it so startling a departure both for him and for modern architecture as a whole?

To understand the reasons for this, it is necessary for a moment to recall what architects in the West were doing and thinking during World War II. One of the best indices to their thinking are two issues of the American magazine *Architectural Forum*, which invited several dozen U.S. architects in 1943 to project on paper their ideas for a post-war architecture. Their proposals were published under the heading of "Building for 194X," and they covered every conceivable type of structure, from a "disposable house" to a library stocking nothing but micro-film editions and equipped with electronic brains. What all these rather delightful dreams had in common was this: they all assumed that the postwar world would be one of fabulously finished, beautifully manu-factured and engineered synthetics—building components of aluminum, plastics, and glass. Everything was going to be slicker, smoother, more industrialized, more rational—in short, more Machine Art—than ever before.

Well, 194X had come at last, and Le Corbusier, the leading apostle of Machine Art, was surely going to show the world what the machine could *really* achieve in terms of industrial precision.

Instead, Corbu did the exact opposite: he built his first entirely timeless building. The Marseilles structure is all concrete—concrete in its crudest, most brutal form, *béton brut!* Concrete poured into the simplest form work, to come out looking as rough and virile as rock, deliberately chipped and cracked, full of pebble surfaces here and sea-shell surfaces there, as beautifully textured as the now blackened travertine of the great Roman ruins of Italy and southern France. Next to the Marseilles building, Lever House would look like the latest Cadillac—slick, thin-shelled, soon out of date. Next to the Marseilles building, every other modern "curtain wall" structure would look as tinny as an oil can, and sure to rust away just as fast. For this massive piece of brute concrete could be of any time: it could be an Egyptian temple of 2000 B.C., or a vision of the twenty-first century.

Why had Corbu shifted to so earthy, so "organic" a way of building? There were, undoubtedly, a number of practical reasons: he had discovered after the war that many of his earlier buildings, whose finishes had turned out to be something less than permanent, looked depressingly tired after their stucco façades had become streaky and gray. With his intuitive sense of tradition and of historical continuity, Corbu had begun to feel the need for building materials that would age well. Next, there was another purely practical reason—the lower cost of unfinished concrete. And, finally, there was the equally simple and practical fact that the modern materials promised for the postwar world were just not available in France.

Still, all these reasons could have been overcome. Other European architects, faced with similar realizations in the postwar years, simply turned back to traditional materials and details for their building vocabulary. But Corbu, of course, was wedded to concrete. Not only because it was a "modern" material, but because it was the most plastic and expressively sculptural material at hand—and, moreover, the only material that, in the French building economy, could offer the essential city planning device of the *pilotis* and the essential interior planning device of the free and flexible plan. He felt that the potentialities of reinforced concrete had barely been explored: the material was clearly capable of such great variety in texture and color that there was no need whatever of finishing it by applying coats of stucco or paint. And he had found out that the wooden forms into which the concrete must be poured need not be constructed of smoothly finished sheets of plywood, but could be built of rough boards, nailed together with slightly open joints, to leave an imprint of lines and even of wood grain upon the hardened surface of the material.

To many American visitors, in particular, who were used to slick finishes in their buildings, the Marseilles structure seemed to be crude and sloppy. But this is not the case at all; in a sense, this structure is a deliberate affirmation of man in a Machine Art era. The man-made imprint on concrete, according to Corbu, seemed to "shout at one from all parts of the structure." Indeed, he stated at the great ceremonial opening of the building that "it seems to be really possible to consider concrete as a reconstructed stone worthy of being exposed in its natural state."

The gigantic slab rising up behind a row of trees along the boule-

Detail of fire escape on Marseilles apartments. The concrete shows the rough imprint of wooden forms. (Photo: Lucien Hervé)

Apartment block at Marseilles, 1946-52. This gigantic concrete city on sculptured stilts has two shopping streets halfway up, and elaborate communal facilities on the roof. Each apartment has a two-story balcony at one end. Dividing walls between balconies were painted in bright pastel shades. (Photo: G. E. Kidder Smith)

vard Michelet outside Marseilles looks as graceful as Joe Louis on tiptoe. It is supported on rows of sculptured and tapered *pilotis*, two stories high and as grandiose as the columns of Karnak. The slab itself (unlike most American slab buildings of the postwar years) is faced with an *irregular* egg crate, the irregularity being the result, in part, of the fact that the rows of two-story living rooms face alternately east and west (the two-story apartments interlock back and forth in the cross section of the building). While the rough concrete of the structure has a natural, pinkish-gray tint, the wall panels that separate adjoining balconies were painted in bright pastel colors—red, blue, yellow, and near-black.

These are part of Corbu's beautiful palette—"what I call the 'great gamut,' the earth colors and ochers, ultramarine, white and black," he once said. And he added: "We used to say: 'If you wish to paint black, take your tube of white; if you wish to paint white, take your tube of black.'" These plastic colors, not applied flat to the façade, but seen only through a sort of veil that represents the imaginary façade of the building, give the slab an added sense of three-dimensionality.

But it was really the roof garden, more than any other part of this building, that set the Marseilles structure apart from anything that Corbu, or anyone else, had done before. This roof garden is a huge plaza, bordered by a high parapet, and filled with intensely sculptural elements—great tapered funnels through which the air is exhausted from the building; vaulted structures that house a gymnasium; a concrete mountain range full of tunnels and caves, designed for children to play in; a nursery school, a pool, a restaurant, a row of curved concrete benches for mothers to sit on while watching their babies; a bold, free-standing vertical concrete slab on which to project movies at night; and a cantilevered balcony (the only element that punctures the high parapet) designed for lovers who might like to sit there in privacy and watch the sunset. This giant sculpture garden has been compared to all sorts of things: to the fantasies of the French eighteenth-century architect Claude-Nicholas Ledoux, whose marvellous geometric forms seem today a preview of the Machine Art era; and to the equally fantastic creations of the nineteenth-century architect Antonio Gaudi, whose Parc Güell may, quite possibly, have influenced Corbu when he saw it during one of his frequent visits to Barcelona.

But the greatness of the roof garden on the Marseilles building has little to do with traceable influences. The whole thing is an original, creative work of sculpture. The Marseilles building is located in a rather unattractive suburb; yet the roof garden, being surrounded by a high parapet, appears to be a strangely dreamlike piazza, located in space, suspended somewhere between the silhouettes of the Alpes Maritimes and the distant views of the Mediterranean and the Château d'If. It is, in a way, a modern sort of Acropolis. Corbu, when first visiting the Acropolis during one of his early trips through south-east Europe, had

Part of the roof garden above Marseilles apartments. The foothills of the Alps are just visible above the high roof parapets. (Photo: Richard Miller)

been overwhelmed by the grandeur of that sculptural abstraction raised up against the sky. He recalls saying to himself: "Remember the clear, clean, intense, economical, violent Parthenon—that cry hurled into a landscape made of grace and terror. That monument to strength and purity." And at Marseilles, some forty years later, he succeeded in matching that "monument to strength and purity" in his own way.

Corbu is a mixture of many things. He is an artist of incredible strength; a fighter of great passions; a pamphleteer of tremendous eloquence. He needed all these qualities to accomplish Marseilles: he must have written half a dozen books and pamphlets about this building, fought many more battles for it (at one time during the construction of the Marseilles project some delightfully archaic Society for the Preservation of the Beauties of France tried to have him forcibly restrained from despoiling his nation). Yet, to him, one of the happiest achievements at

Marseilles was a 1,000-foot-long cinder track that he was able to incorporate in the design of his roof garden. Corbu is a very wiry and *sportif* type, and he enjoyed this track almost as much as he enjoyed everything else about the building, posing proudly for photographers while trotting around his great "piazza on the roof," attired only in shorts, a sweatshirt, and a very professional-looking pair of track shoes. Obviously Corbu has always been very serious about becoming a "complete man."

There was a great celebration on the Marseilles roof when the building "officially" opened, at a CIAM party on a summer evening in 1953. Architects from every part of the world attended, including Corbu's old associate from the days in Behrens's office, Walter Gropius, who had by this time become the principal apostle of Machine Art architecture in the United States. Yet Gropius recognized at once that Corbu had created an entirely new architectural vocabulary. "Any architect who does not find this building beautiful," Gropius said on that evening, "had better lay down his pencil."

X V I I I

CORBU BECAME BEST KNOWN to people in the U.S. in the years after the end of World War II, when he served as the representative of France on the United Nations Headquarters Commission. (He had become a French citizen in 1930.) The job of this Commission was to select the site for the proposed UN Headquarters; and by the end of 1946 it agreed to accept an offer by John D. Rockefeller, Jr., of a seventeen-acre site located along the East River in Manhattan. Corbu published a little book on the job of selecting the site (as he was apt to do on just about every other job that came along), and that made it official, at least in his mind.

Following his work on the Commission, Le Corbusier became one of the ten architects selected from all over the world who were to plan the actual Headquarters buildings. Throughout the spring and the summer of 1947 Corbu was in New York, working feverishly to realize one of his greatest and oldest ambitions—to build a seat for a potential world government. It seemed to him that he was about to be compensated for the severe and unjust blow he had received at the time of the League of Nations competition; and it further seemed to him that the job of designing the UN Headquarters should very properly be his. For, after all, the very fact that here the authorities had turned to a group of *modern* rather than traditional architects represented final proof that the new architecture had won its battles. And no one had done more than Corbu to help win those battles—or so he felt.

To Corbu, the moral issue was quite clear: the UN had to be his; he deserved every bit of it! To partisans of Frank Lloyd Wright, of course, the moral issue was equally clear: Wright, rather than Corbu, had won the battle for modern architecture, so he was the obvious choice for the design of the UN Headquarters.

As things worked out, neither Corbu nor Wright was awarded the job. Once a site in the heart of Manhattan had been chosen, Wright was never seriously considered. His hostility toward the city was only too well known; and he had made no secret of his views of the proposed East River site. "Grass the ground where the proposed UN skyscraper would stand," Wright announced, characteristically. "Buy a befitting tract of land, say a thousand acres or more, not too easy to reach. . . . Sequester the UN. Why does it not itself ask for good ground where nature speaks and the beauty of organic order shows more clearly the true pattern of all peace whatsoever?" But the UN authorities were not willing to grass the ground and move out into the prairie; they *wanted* to be in New York, they *liked* the metropolis, they had no intention of sequestering themselves.

The basic decision about the character of the UN Headquarters was made almost without debate: the Headquarters was going to be urban, which meant that it would have to be designed by architects basically in sympathy with the city. So long as everyone was agreed that the architecture should be modern, this meant, almost inevitably, that it should be of the International Style.

Next, there were the obvious political problems: should the UN job go to a single architect? If there had been some degree of decisiveness and courage in places of authority, the answer might conceivably have been in the affirmative—in which case Corbu would, in all likelihood, have been chosen by general acclamation (including his own). But those in high places at the UN felt that an international Board of Design should be selected, to consist of ten architects from ten major countries: Corbu was chosen to represent France, Oscar Niemeyer to represent Brazil, Sven Markelius to represent his native Sweden, and several less well-known architects represented the USSR, Belgium, Canada, China, Great Britain, Australia, and Uruguay. The next logical step was to select a chairman; and here again a politically sound choice was made in the selection of the American architect Wallace K. Harrison. There were several reasons for the choice of Harrison: first, everyone realized that the Headquarters would certainly involve some very large structures, and Harrison's experience in the design of Rockefeller Center was bound to be very useful. Second, it was felt that an American should be the chairman, as no one outside the U.S. had had very much experience with the purely technical problems involved in constructing very tall buildings. And, third, it was recognized that the chairmanship of such a Board of Design would call for a man with the wisdom of Solomon; and while Harrison may not have measured up to that standard in every respect, no one in authority could think of another American architect who came closer to filling those specifications than he.

The result of all this careful diplomacy was exactly what might have been expected. From the very beginning Corbu's dynamic, indeed crackling personality dominated the situation. There were virtually no projects developed by any of the participants which did not, basically, reflect Corbu's concepts. The only disagreements in principle seem to have concerned matters of relative detail. All members of the Board of Design agreed that: (a) the Secretariat would have to be a tall, slablike building; (b) the General Assembly structure would be a relatively low and free form, derived largely from the pie-shaped assembly halls contained within it; and (c) the Meeting Halls would be contained within another low structure that somehow joined the Secretariat to the General Assembly. All were agreed, also, that there would be some sort of plaza and that the Delegations building then planned (but not immediately built) would be another slab (or, possibly, two slabs) that would help form that plaza in conjunction with the Secretariat.

This general layout is an almost exact duplicate of Le Corbusier's first 1936 project for the Rio Ministry of Education. No one could possibly deny this, and no one did. Yet Corbu wanted to be recognized as the sole designer of the UN Headquarters, not only in theory, but also in practice. The situation became increasingly tense as Corbu tried to run the show, and for a while it was partly Niemeyer's quiet tact that kept things on a more or less even keel.

When Corbu had appeared in Rio some ten years earlier, Lucio Costa decided that it was the better part of valor to withdraw discreetly from the Ministry of Education design team. Perhaps it would have been the better part of valor for Harrison to leave the field of operations to Corbu; yet this was hardly possible, for everyone at the UN seemed to be agreed that an architect with American building know-how was required to see the job through. So, Harrison stayed on; and after the Board of Design had arrived at its basic scheme, Harrison, as Director of Planning, was appointed to set up his own UN Headquarters Planning Office and to carry out the scheme developed by the Board of Design.

At this point the tension that had been building up around Corbu finally erupted into open hostility and verbal violence. Corbu announced to all the world that the design approved by the Board was actually his own proposal, which he had submitted to the Board on March 15, 1947. Corbu's proposal, identified by the number "23 A," was indeed almost identical with the project finally adopted, although that proposal also owed something to a series of sketches prepared by Niemeyer. Corbu has claimed that Scheme "23 A" formed the basis for all discussions by the Board of Design over a period of three months after he first submitted it, and this claim seems to be generally accurate. Corbu kept a sketchbook throughout the deliberations of the Board of Design, and his daily entries support the argument that it was his contribution, primarily, that shaped the UN.

As a matter of fact, there is no one who would care to argue this point, least of all, one imagines, Wallace Harrison. The point at issue in selecting the architect to *execute* the design was not whether he had made the principal contribution to its conception, but, rather, whether he had shown the organizational and diplomatic ability to carry out this complex and politically difficult assignment. Regardless of how much respect one may have for Corbu's creativity, it is hard to believe that Corbu would have been a more competent over-all administrator of the job than Harrison. The fact is that few people in the past had been able to work with Corbu on any terms other than submissive adulation (which may, indeed, have been his due); and, rightly or wrongly, the UN authorities felt that they had a better chance of getting the job done competently, smoothly, and well with someone like Harrison in charge than with an "eccentric" like Corbu running the show.

Corbu's own actions after the decision had been made hardly served to impress his critics or his admirers with his tact. He denounced Harrison, more or less publicly, as a "gangster" who had stolen Corbu's design and made it his own. Corbu hinted darkly that Harrison's relationship by marriage to the Rockefeller family had got him the job; and he hinted, even more darkly, that the famous sketchbook he had kept during the deliberations of the Board of Design had mysteriously disappeared in 1948, when the construction drawings for the UN were being prepared under Harrison's supervision, only to reappear just as mysteriously in 1950. In short, he showed himself to be that most regrettable of social beings, a Bad Loser.

Corbu's attacks on Harrison were both intemperate and unfair. Harrison is one of the most modest, gentle, and scrupulously honest professionals to be found in the U.S. or anywhere else. Although many critics disagree with Harrison's design preferences, few would be willing to deny that his ability as an organizer made him a natural choice for the top position on the UN project—Rockefeller or no Rockefeller. And, finally, the idea that "someone" might have stolen Corbu's sketchbooks in order to copy his ideas in developing the UN drawings is patently ludicrous. All of Corbu's suggestions were plainly on record at the UN, and there was no need for cloak-and-dagger methods to unveil his innermost thoughts: Corbu has never left such thoughts unpublicized.

Yet, after all has been said about Corbu's unfortunate actions in connection with the award to Harrison of the execution of the UN buildings, there still remains the unhappy fact that a UN Headquarters carried out by Corbu would have been a finer work of art than that standing on the East River today. For in almost every detail the UN buildings are too slick and, at the same time, too heavy-handed. The glass curtain wall, with its clumsy grilles along floors devoted to mechanical equipment, looks like a tinny caricature of Corbu's majestic façades. The lobby of the Secretariat, with its black-and-white marble square and great lighting boxes, looks like a giant bathroom. The stairs and ramps—those sculptural counterpoints Corbu has always turned into such lovely flights of poetry—are hardly more sensitive in design than those leading into Gimbel's basement. And the office spaces in the Secretariat are so undistinguished that their best feature, in all likelihood, is that nobody seems to have designed them at all—a blessing when one considers some of the "creative design" that has been employed to "jazz up" several of the more public spaces in the Headquarters.

The General Assembly building turned out to be a particular offender, and for a rather amusing reason. The scheme finally accepted by the Board of Design had two pie-shaped auditorium spaces in the General Assembly structure, placed back to back so that the over-all shape of the plan resembled a sort of hourglass, with the entrance at the narrow waist, and the two assembly halls spreading out from the central entrance lobby. As the working drawings were further developed, the UN decided to cut out one of the two assembly halls for reasons of economy. This would, normally, have forced a major change in the over-all shape of the General Assembly building, and thus involved a recall of the Board of Design (including Corbu) to reconsider that aspect of the plan. By this time Harrison was thoroughly fed up with Corbu's histrionics; the thought of having to cope with him again was too much to bear. So, he went to work, with the help of several bright, young designers, to try to retain the exterior hourglass shape of the plan, but fill it with only one assembly hall instead of two. This project proved to be about as easy as trying to fit a mermaid into a pair of pants, and about as successful. When the building was finally completed in 1952, the *Architectural Forum* hailed it as a departure from form-follows-function and "some loosening of surrounding dogma." That was perhaps the understatement of the year in architectural circles. Dogma was not the only thing that had to be loosened to get a single auditorium to fit a double-auditorium shell. Paul Rudolph, the young architect who was later to head the School of Architecture at Yale, was considerably more penetrating in his brash comments. "The interiors of the UN Assembly Building," he informed the readers of the *Architectural Forum*, "bring the so-called International Style close to bankruptcy. Of course the building is not really a product of the International Style but rather a background for a Grade 'B' movie about 'One World' with Rita Hayworth dancing up the main ramp. . . . Le Corbusier's dia-gram unfortunately did not indicate the way for the interiors of the UN Assembly Building." And Serge Chermayeff, one of the most articulate of the early members of CIAM, summed it all up by saying that "the geometry and texture of Le Corbusier's sketch are there and make their point, but the 'executed' detail and the concept do not jell. . . ."

Still, to most people, the UN Headquarters probably represents an impressive statement of the power of which modern architecture is capable. If so, this effect is due primarily to the sketch proposal made by Corbu (and the years of work that preceded it) and, secondly, to the technically competent execution of the sketch by Harrison. For the building does show a neat competence that few European architects would be able to equal: nothing has leaked (except for the windows, which were put to an unexpected test one day when it started to rain *upward!* The reason was that the glass façades created a violent updraft of warm air just outside the building, and this updraft carried gusts of rain with it. The windows were subsequently fixed to cope with both down- and up-pours); the elevators and the air conditioning work beau-tifully (which is more than can be said about certain European buildings); and life and work, in general, are pleasant in the gleaming Headquarters. Only by comparison with Corbu's executed work of the postwar years does the UN seem a failure in many of its details.

While Corbu appeared increasingly bitter and cantankerous during these years—to the outside world, at least—he remained, in the private reality of a few close friendships, a charming and warm person. One of his friends in New York was the sculptor Tino Nivola. Born in Sardinia of a peasant family, Nivola has the sort of primitive and uncomplicated charm that Corbu always felt he could trust. While the UN battles were being fought uptown during the day, Corbu spent many evenings and weekends in Nivola's 8th Street studio, in Greenwich Village, painting his passionate, brightly colored canvases. In later years, when Corbu had come to the conclusion that almost everyone in America was a potential enemy, Nivola seemed to be one of the few exceptions: on his occasional visits to the U.S., Corbu liked to go out to Amagansett, at the end of Long Island, where Nivola has an old-fashioned frame-and-clapboard house; and there the great man, dressed only in shorts, a sports shirt, and the inevitable black-rimmed glasses, would make sand sculptures on the beach, using a poured plaster process developed by his friend, or play with Nivola's children in the garden behind the house. On one such weekend Corbu decided to repay his host for his generous and uncomplicated hospitality: he did it by painting two huge murals on adjoining plaster walls inside the little clapboard house. In this setting, among children, trees, the ocean, and simple and friendly people, Corbu relaxed and showed himself to be a warm and kindly human being. Oddly enough, it was the city, which he loved so much, that produced most of his real or imagined enemies. "I first really began to understand Corbu when I met his wife," Nivola said. "She was a wonderful and funny, primitive type, the only person who never really took Corbu very seriously as a Great Figure." Le Corbusier must have found some of the same qualities in Nivola and in other close friends. These were the people he felt he could trust—not the sophisticates who were attracted by Corbu's own enormous sophistication.

X I X

CORBU'S REPUTATION as an *enfant terrible*, incapable of collaboration with others on an equal basis, cost him at least one other important commission that might have been his. Shortly after the UN Headquarters was completed in New York, UNESCO decided that it must have a Headquarters of its own, separate from the parent organization in Manhattan. Paris was the natural seat for UNESCO; and it appeared obvious that in Paris, at least, there could be no argument against having Corbu design the buildings. Just as an administrative center on the skyscraper-studded island of Manhattan seemed to call for a man like Harrison, who knew skyscraper organization better than just about anyone else of his generation, so a cultural center in Paris called for the one architect who represented with the greatest distinction the traditions of modern French culture. Yet, as a large part of the money for the UNESCO Headquarters was provided by the United States, officials of the State Department had a major say in the selection of UNESCO's architect. They felt that diplomacy must be an essential quality in the architect to be selected, as the Paris authorities tended to be hostile to a modern structure—and, in particular, to any *tall* modern building. Corbu had not distinguished himself particularly in his political dealings with French authorities any more than he had in his dealings with some American officials; and while this was due as much to the stupidity and narrowness of officialdom in Paris as it was to Corbu's aggressiveness, it represented an existing, political fact of life and had to be considered.

To make sure that Corbu would not get the UNESCO job, the UNESCO people and the State Department men most directly concerned decided to set up a board whose job it would be to select the architects for UNESCO, and then made Corbu a member of that board. Everyone realized that this was a transparent device to take Corbu out of the running, as the board could hardly select one of its own members. As a matter of fact, the board did select three excellent men: Marcel Breuer, the Hungarian-born American architect who is probably the closest counterpart to Corbu in the U.S.; Pier Luigi Nervi, the brilliant Italian engineer whose speciality is precast, reinforced concrete and who could teach Corbu and others a thing or two about the technical problems involved in handling this material; and Bernard Zehrfuss, a young French architect of tact and good political connections. This team completed its job in 1958, when the UNESCO Headquarters on the Place de Fontenoy were opened to the general public. The achievement was considerable; and though it owed much to Corbu in its details, it reflected many original contributions that had been arrived at independently of Le Corbusier. Throughout the planning stage of UNESCO, Corbu tried, by all sorts of means, to get his hand in. It was tragic to see how bitterly hurt he was to have been denied this third (and possibly final) opportunity to realize his League of Nations Palace.

There is really nothing reprehensible in Corbu's inability to work harmoniously with others. Art-by-committee is a ridiculous notion; even Walter Gropius, who greatly favors collaboration among technicians to solve today's architectural and planning problems, does not really believe that a great work of art can emerge from such collaboration unless a great architect dominates the collaborative effort. (The UNESCO job was largely dominated by Breuer.) Yet the world of Organization Men is constantly on the lookout for other, safe Organization Men to whom it can entrust its problems; and the result—most clearly visible in the postwar buildings in Manhattan—is a mess of mediocrity. The criticism so often leveled against Corbu that he is "unreasonable" is no criticism at all; if Corbu had been "reasonable," he would never have succeeded in doing what he did. "When we began our symphony," Corbu once said, "our continual role was to appear as tough guys, with dirty, muddy boots stamping into an elegant and tranquil society in order to assert our ways of thinking. And so it happened that our attitude was insolent, despite ourselves. . . ." The tragedy of Corbu's life has been not that he has grown bitter, but that he knew, almost from the start, that the price he had to pay for achieving his objectives was to live a life of bitterness. And the greatness of Corbu's life is his indestructible optimism in spite of that bitterness.

When he completed the Marseilles block in 1952, Corbu demonstrated several obvious things: first, he showed (at long last) what he meant by his vertical city of gardens and piazzas in the sky. Second, he showed that he was capable, at an age that would lead most architects to thoughts of retirement, to start out on an entirely new and brilliant career as a plastic artist—a career so dazzling as to leave his many younger followers once again far behind. But he showed something else, far less obvious: he showed that he knew that the role of an artist cannot be to try to gain popular acceptance, but that artists must be willing to challenge popularly accepted men and ideas with creative, individual statements of a strength that no one could ignore.

In a sense, Marseilles liberated Corbu from his fruitless struggles of three or four decades to try to become an accepted, "well-integrated" member of society. From now on, Corbu seems to have felt, he was not

going to deal with political situations; now his work would be a statement of what he thought, not as a frequently rejected member of polite
society, but as a creative artist, standing alone.

The buildings constructed by Corbu from 1950 on have a plastic
inventiveness and grandeur comparable to some of the most powerful
monuments produced by man since the beginnings of recorded history.
Each of the great structures completed by him during those years
seemed to be another brilliant sculptural achievement. From the massively formed chapel at Ronchamp in the Vosges Mountains, all the
way to the High Court building at Chandigarh, the new capital of the
Punjab, Corbu—once the man of the cube and the cylinder—brought
back into architecture a magic world of plastic form and virile texture
which had been notably missing in the work of all modernists except,
perhaps, in that of Frank Lloyd Wright. Yet, where Wright's plasticity

*The interior of the chapel at Ronchamp. The deep slots
in the wall are filled with brightly colored glass. (Photo:
Lucien Hervé)*

Ronchamp. (Photo: Lucien Hervé)

was often indistinguishable from the nature forms of the Art Nouveau (and, hence, dated), Corbu's new world of form seems to be timeless, conceivably the product of any and all ages, modern in every respect and ancient in every respect also. The great curved masses of Ronchamp might be the result of some acoustic determination, as Corbu declared; but they formed, together with the deep, irregularly spaced slot windows in the walls, a mysterious aura that was as reminiscent of the catacombs or the massive stone monasteries of the Middle Ages as it was of some dimly understood spatial concepts of today and tomorrow. "An implacable mathematics and physics reign over the forms presented to the eye," Corbu said. "Their agreement, their repetition, their interdependence, and the spirit of unity or of family which binds them together to form an architectural expression, is a phenomenon which is as supple, subtle, exact and implacable as that of acoustics." It is characteristic of Le Corbusier that even in as individual a sculptural statement as Ron-

Relief in concrete by Le Corbusier, based upon his Modulor figure. These figures can be found at the base of every apartment building by Le Corbusier. This one is from the apartments at Berlin, completed in 1958. (Photo: Peter Blake)

champ he tried to express and experiment with certain mathematical rules that would have broader application to the world at large. To Corbu, the idea of an art without a body of laws is totally irresponsible. Once, in Long Island, when he saw the late Jackson Pollock's "automatic" paintings, he said that he thought that painting, to be valid, must admit to certain fundamental rules. So, even this sprayed-concrete sculpture on a hill above the river Saône was an attempt to dramatize the rule of law in all life and in all art. To a Frenchman, there is nothing stultifying about a rule of law, as there was to an American radical like Wright. The rule of law is a poetic vision; and Corbu actually wrote and published a "Poem to the Right Angle" in the years when Ronchamp was being designed!

Throughout his life Corbu has searched for a rule of law in art. The idea that this made him a functionalist appalled and repelled him. "This frightful word was born under other skies than those I have always loved—those where the sun reigns supreme," he said, with a characteristic slap at the U.S., whose Horatio Greenough is generally credited with inventing the term "functionalism." Corbu's concept of a rule of law is intimately tied to a rule of life; and his Modulor system is a beautiful expression of what he means.

The Modulor is not a system of repetitive, identical dimensions of the dreary sort familiar to quantity surveyors and such, but, rather, a system of related proportions based upon the ancient "Golden Section" and the human figure that reflects that Section. In general, the Modulor starts with the division of the height of a man into two proportions, at the waistline. These two proportions, according to Corbu, govern all other dimensions of the human body: for example, a man with his arm naturally upraised creates another Modulor proportion, the distance between his head and his waist being in the proper relation to the distance between the head and his fingertips. Starting with this interlocking system of proportions—fingertips to head to waistline to soles of feet— Corbu developed a gradually diminishing scale of proportionate dimensions. In Corbu's atelier at 35 rue de Sèvres each draftsman and designer has a list of related Modulor dimensions pinned up on the wall next to his or her drawing board. The list consists of only two columns of ten numbers each. According to Le Corbusier this proportionate scale (applicable to the design of anything from a piazza to a bookshelf) has one further advantage: it is apparently the only numerical scale that relates the foot-and-inch system to the metric system, and vice versa.

It is characteristic of Corbu that a good deal of mysticism and poetic passion have surrounded the Modulor system. For while this is a real attempt to introduce a rule of law, related to both nature and art, into an industrial architecture, the project in Corbu's mind has nothing to do with the adding machine. It represents to him a system of ultimate truths; and, like all ultimate truths, the Modulor figures did not mean

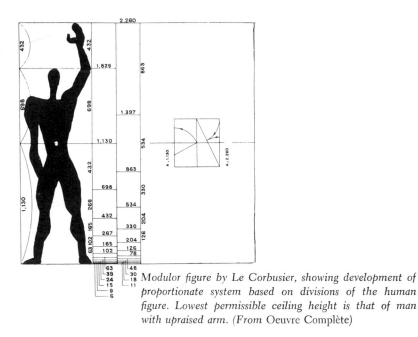

Modulor figure by Le Corbusier, showing development of proportionate system based on divisions of the human figure. Lowest permissible ceiling height is that of man with upraised arm. (From Oeuvre Complète)

much until he was able to reduce them to an extremely precise code. To anyone but a Frenchman this sort of thing might seem pedantic in the extreme; indeed, anyone but a Frenchman would probably be incapable of achieving a Modulor system. Not long ago Corbu became convinced that some "American gangsters" were trying to steal his Modulor by setting up a company called something like Modular Structures. Not only was he being silly, but he missed the most important point about his own invention: every modular system developed in the U.S. and elsewhere is a system based upon a single dimension, repeated and multiplied ad infinitum. (The most commonly used dimensions in the U.S. range from four inches to four feet, with multiples of four inches occasionally employed for certain prefabricated units.) But such systems are, of course, simple-minded by comparison with Corbu's Modulor, which does not use a single dimensional module, but only an infinite series of *related dimensions*. When Corbu showed the Modulor to the late Albert Einstein, in Princeton, Einstein told him that this was "a range of dimensions which makes the bad difficult and the good easy." This moral and poetic basis of the Modulor inspired Corbu to make the system, in a sense, the culmination of a life's work devoted to bringing a rule of law into art. Many critics, who admire Corbu's individual buildings, have scoffed at his various odes to the Modulor, not realizing that to this intensely moral man it was essential to develop a system that would "make the bad difficult and the good easy," to hand on to generations to come. It is an essential part of Corbu's greatness that he has *never* produced a single work that did not, in some way, contribute to the solution of a broader problem in architecture and city planning. The critics might admire the masses and spaces of the Marseilles block—and rightly so; but, to Corbu, one of the most important aspects of the Marseilles building was the fact that it is dimensioned completely according to the Modulor system of proportions. At the entrance to the building, cast in a slab of concrete, there stands Corbu's Modulor figure of a man with upraised arm; nearby, there is a concrete block on which the Modulor proportions used in this building are precisely incised. "It is in such moments as these," Corbu said, "that architecture soars, leaving the brutal and the material and attaining to spirituality." The rule of law by which civilized men live is the single, most moving political and moral achievement of the West. The rule of law which Corbu has tried to bring into architecture may, someday, be considered the single, most moving contribution he has made to our culture.

Although Ronchamp was almost pure sculpture, this chapel, too—according to Le Corbusier—was developed according to this moral code. But the use of the Modulor is much more evident in Corbu's several other apartment blocks built after Marseilles—the block at Nantes, the similar block in West Berlin (sadly defaced by Corbu's insensitive German clients), the new Brazilian Pavilion in the University City in Paris, the beautiful Secretariat Building at Chandigarh (which, incidentally, shows what a Corbu-designed UN Secretariat might have been like), and in several other structures done both in Asia and in Europe during the late 1950's. Each of these is a more extraordinary revelation of Corbu's mastery of brute forms than the one preceding it, each a more

Detail of the Brazilian Pavilion, University City, Paris, 1957-9. This building by Le Corbusier and Lucio Costa shows a highly refined use of "brute concrete" contrasted with handsomely precast surfaces. (Photo: Peter Blake)

Concrete pyramids set into a circular splash-basin at the foot of the Palace of Justice, Chandigarh. (Photo: Vernon Gibberd)

convincing proof of the importance of Corbu's "reincarnation" after World War II.

In these monumental and virile structures Le Corbusier has come to physical grips with the material he loves, the material he recognizes to be the most exciting structural development in our time: reinforced concrete, now become "reconstructed stone." Lewis Mumford, who once called Corbu's brutal use of concrete "sloppy," entirely missed the point: for Corbu is not only trying to leave the imprint of man on an architecture of the machine age—the imprint of man's hands in the rough formwork, and the imprint of man's scale through the Modulor; he is also saying that the people of the earth must face the fact that the sort of architectural slickness practiced nowadays in the U.S. becomes more and more unrealistic as our natural and industrial resources fail to keep up with the incredible growth in the earth's population. *Béton brut* is not only an aesthetic choice; it is the rational choice of a three to four billion population of the globe. It is the universal material, infinitely flexible, almost indefinitely available, and capable of receiving the imprint of man's hand.

Detail of the south-east façade of the Secretariat at Chandigarh. Although the pattern of balconies and sun-control louvers seems quite arbitrary, it was designed to adhere strictly to the proportionate scale of the Modulor. (Photo: Lucien Hervé)

SHORTLY AFTER Le Corbusier turned seventy, in the fall of 1957, his wife died. Few people knew how severe a blow this was to him. A few days earlier he had been in Berlin to open an exhibition of his work, and he seemed tired and not in the best of health. Things were not going as well as they might: in Berlin the builders of his Marseilles-type apartment block had ignored his drawings and changed the carefully designed fenestration into deadly bands of ribbon windows. Corbu's blasts at this and other examples of barbarism were, as usual, on the front pages of all local newspapers. But he did not seem to relish the battle as much as he once had. There were flashes of his old dynamism, though, when—during the opening of his exhibit—crowds of young

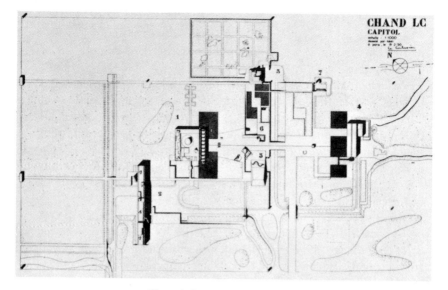

Plan of the capitol at Chandigarh, 1950-7. (1) is the Parliament Building or Assembly Hall; (2) is the Secretariat; (3) is the Governor's Palace; (4) is the Palace of Justice; and (7) is the "Monument of the Open Hand." (From Oeuvre Complète)

men and women jostled to get his signature on copies of his books, tried to shake his hand, applauded whenever he appeared. Even in the alleged capital of youthful nihilism, Corbu could stir young people almost as if he were a famous jazz or movie star. . . . He obviously enjoyed himself in those moments: and the crooked, slightly sarcastic smile on his thin face made him look very much younger than his seventy years.

Though his wife was dead, and he had broken with his collaborator of the postwar years, the young Yugoslav, Wogensky, Corbu was fortunate in at least one respect: Like Mies van der Rohe and others of their generation, Corbu was busier than ever before. Most of his work was at Chandigarh, the new capital of the Punjab, the city Corbu had been able to plan from scratch and whose center was being designed entirely by him. Chandigarh, until a few years ago merely a windswept plain at the foot of the Himalayas, was rising as the first city born entirely out of Corbu's genius.

Much of the work at Chandigarh had to be housing, of course; and for that part of the job Corbu brought in two English members of CIAM, Maxwell Fry and his wife, Jane Drew; and he also asked his cousin, Pierre Jeanneret, with whom he had been in partnership until the German invasion of France broke up their office, to come and help design the housing units. But the core of Chandigarh, the heart of this city, Corbu reserved for himself. This, he seemed to feel, was going to be the culmination of everything that went before.

And so it is. Words are not quite adequate to describe the power of Chandigarh. Its center is in the tradition of Corbu's project for Saint-Dié, though the elements that make up the great plaza are all governmental: a square Assembly building, the parliament; an 800-foot-long Secretariat, some eight stories high; a small, square Governor's Palace (fully designed but, as yet, unbuilt); the Palace of Justice; and several related elements of landscaping on different levels. Finally, there is the "Monument of the Open Hand," off to one side of the great plaza.

The first building to be completed was the Palace of Justice, a fantastic, vaulted structure topped by a huge, concrete roof umbrella that shelters a four-story, wall-less entrance lobby lined with concrete ramps and topped by arches. To both sides of this great lobby are court-rooms on several levels protected by an irregular concrete grille of sun breakers. Corbu's bright pastel colors—vermilion, pastel blue, lemon yellow, white—are used as accents behind the concrete grille and contrast brilliantly with the *béton brut* of the structure. Here the concrete, in all its unfinished roughness, has emerged looking as crude as a rock formation molded by thousands of years of wind and rain. Here, better even than at Marseilles, Corbu achieved the timelessness that will make his architecture a permanent treasure of man's history.

In the great courtrooms the necessary sound-absorptive surfaces are provided by huge tapestries designed by Corbu himself. Below the parasol roof, there are terraces and penthouses that overlook the plaza below and the city beyond—all the way to the foothills of the Hima-layas. Wherever you look, this building offers new and unexpected

Interior of the Palace of Justice, Chandigarh, 1953. Flying ramps connect the various levels of the building. (Photo: Lucien Hervé)

North-west facade of the Palace of Justice, seen from the Assembly Building one quarter of a mile away. A huge parasol of concrete catches the rainwater and cools and shades the building proper. The concrete vaults are irregularly spaced, but the spacing fits into Le Corbusier's Modulor scale. (Photo: Peter Blake)

spatial experiences—streaks of sunlight cutting through an opening in the structure, unexpectedly lighting up an interior concrete wall; ramps, balconies, arches, columns, a patch of the sky. Curiously enough, most of Corbu's achievements up to that time had been in the general area of form and exterior space. Here, in the Palace of Justice, Corbu showed himself a master of interior space as well.

The lovely scale models of Chandigarh, made for Corbu by turbaned and heavily bearded Sikh model makers, were carved out of solid blocks of walnut (or its Indian equivalent). In a sense, this abstraction of architectural forms through the use of a *natural* material (instead of plastic, say) is very revealing of Corbu's *rapprochement* to nature. It would have been inconceivable for him to make the models of the great "pure prisms" of the 1920's of anything but cardboard or metal, painted white, or plastics and glass.

The Secretariat was completed next. It is a building rather similar in character to the Marseilles block, though much more assured in its finish. Here, too, Corbu was able to show his fellow architects a few things they might study with profit: for example, while many U.S. architects think little of covering an 800-foot-long façade with a repetitive pattern of *identical* "curtain wall" units, it was quite obvious to Corbu that such treatment could lead only to endless monotony. The 800-foot-long façades of the Secretariat are broken in half a dozen places with projections, recesses, stair towers, changes in pattern, and the like. All these contrasting elements—like everything else at Chandigarh—are related to one another through the proportionate scale of the Modulor, so that all things have a family resemblance and general harmony. But apart from this over-all harmony, contrast is everpresent—contrast again as an expression of the selective, human act.

The third completed building at Chandigarh is the Assembly Hall—a roughly square structure in plan, with an open but roofed-over court at its center. The court is surrounded by several floors of delegates' offices; and in its space rise two majestic forms: a hyperbolic paraboloid, which contains the Assembly Chamber; and a pyramid containing the Council Chamber. Ramps and bridges join the main floor of the court

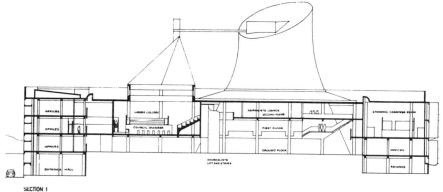

SECTION 1

Section through the Assembly Hall building, Chandigarh, 1956. The pyramidal structure at left is the Council Chamber; the hyperbolic paraboloid at right contains the Assembly Chamber.

Southeast façade of the Assembly Hall building, showing the forms of the two chambers rising above the roof. The Secretariat is at left. (Photo: Peter Blake)

to various levels within these two chambers. A huge parasol of concrete, shaped (in cross-section) rather like a sacred cow's horn, forms the monumental entrance portico that faces south-east. Like the parasol roof above the Palace of Justice, this concrete portico catches the rainwater—and scuppers at each end permit the overflow to spill into the huge pool along this side of the building.

The Assembly Hall's programmatic requirements were similar to those for the UN General Assembly Building in Manhattan—though much smaller, of course. Still, the magic play of spaces, forms and light which Corbu achieved here in Chandigarh suggests what opportunities were, in fact, missed when the UN decided to build itself a home designed by a committee.

The fourth major building in Chandigarh's government center was fully designed and detailed by Le Corbusier, but has not been constructed as of this writing (1976)—and may, unhappily, never be built. It was intended, initially, to be the Governor's Palace; when the Governor balked, it was redesigned by Corbu to be a "Museum of Knowledge"; finally, it was left unbuilt. Le Corbusier's many Indian collaborators—he spawned a veritable resurgence in Indian architecture during his years at Chandigarh and Ahmedabad—possess the original drawings, as well as the skill, to complete this building—the counterpoint so essential to Corbu's grand design. Alas, the political situation in the Punjab has significantly altered the status of the city of Chandigarh—and thus downgraded the importance of its monuments.

There are two aspects to the great center at Chandigarh that are not always understood by those who have not seen the space (except in photographs)—and sometimes not even understood by those who have. The first is the fact that all automobile (and other vehicular) circulation is entirely out of sight, located in a system of "canals" cut into the great plain. The pedestrian is king—and only where you cross one of the vehicular canals on a pedestrian *level*-crossing (not via an awkward pedestrian overpass) are you aware of the surprisingly heavy vehicular traffic that criss-crosses the center, and serves it.

The second aspect that is not apparent in the standard documents is the dramatic use of water as a form-giving element in the great center. Louis Kahn, the American architect most profoundly influenced by Le Corbusier (he once wrote "I dreamed I lived in a City called Le Corbusier"), suggested that the most valid symbols in an Indian townscape had to be monuments to water. At Chandigarh, those monuments are everywhere: not only the great pools outside the major buildings (including an elaborate system of pools projected for the approach to the unbuilt Governor's Palace or Museum); but also the flat slab-bridges that traverse these pools, and the great "catchments"—the concrete parasols—that shade the Palace of Justice and the Assembly's portico, and gather up the rainwater, and spill its overflow, through sculptured scuppers, onto splash basins and, finally, into the large reflecting pools themselves. To Le Corbusier, the realities of Indian life had become clear—not merely in the tourist attractions at Fatehpur Sikri and the Taj Mahal, but in the villages as well. At Chandigarh, he translated those realities into architectural form.

Another monument remains unbuilt in Chandigarh—"The Monument of the Open Hand." This monument is a marvelous fantasy, reminiscent of Corbu's proposed memorial to Vaillant-Couturier, done right after the end of World War II. It is a fifty-foot-high structure of wood, covered with hammered iron in a process that is in common use in the Punjab, and set on a huge ball bearing so that the great upraised hand might turn in the wind like a weathervane "to indicate, symbolically, the state of affairs. . . ." Regardless of the validity (or presence) of any symbolism of government, this is really Corbu's personal symbol of man vis-à-vis nature—the white, upraised cube, held against the sky; the upraised Acropolis, silhouetted against the sky; the upraised hand of the Modulor figure—a kind of Atlas figure supporting man's noblest creation, architecture, and offering it up to the sun.

Chandigarh was only a part of Corbu's work in the late 1950's. At Ahmedabad, the center of India's cotton-spinning area, he had completed his first museum, much along the lines proposed by him twenty years earlier. At Ahmedabad, also, he had built several beautiful houses of *béton brut*, as strong as some medieval monastic structures; and a building for the mill owners' association, with an assembly hall of sweeping, curved forms. There was more work in Asia, the Middle East, and Europe—another museum, this one in Japan; the landscaping for a dam in India; houses; exhibitions (including the extraordinary sculptural pavilion at the Brussels World's Fair for the Phillips Industries— a structure of precast concrete units forming a series of interlocking hyperbolic paraboloids). And then, at long last, there was a commission in the United States as well—to build a new Visual Arts Center for Harvard University.

José Luis Sert, one of Corbu's oldest and closest associates, was the Dean of the Graduate School of Design at Harvard, and determined to have at least one building designed by Le Corbusier in the United States before it was too late. Sert persuaded the University to set aside a site next to the Fogg Museum, between Quincy and Prescott Streets; and the University found a donor to finance the project. The only problem seemed to be that there was really no specific program for any sort of building on that site and at that time. The only specification, more or less, was that the new building should be a center for the visual arts.

Le Corbusier's solution was therefore rather fanciful. Since no specific function was spelled out, Corbu had to invent a function as well as a form—a process which, to most modern architects, tends to a disaster. What Corbu did was to invent a series of interior functions— studios, classrooms, quarters for artists-in-residence, and so on—and then to invent a major urbanistic function for the building: he proposed to make it a gateway from the old Harvard Yard to the then residential areas to its East. These areas, in Le Corbusier's eyes, offered a potential for the future expansion of the Yard and of Harvard's educational facilities. (He did not know very much about the growing power of community groups in the United States, and their increasing determination to block bulldozer expansion, whether initiated by government, by business, or by a university.)

So the Carpenter Center (as it was to be known) became a theoretical exercise both in its internal organization and in its urbanistic intentions. The latter were dramatized by the Center's most visible

Carpenter Center, Harvard University, 1964. View from Quincy Street. The ramp that swings up to and through the building is visible at right. (Photo: Harvard University News Office)

element: an elongated S-shaped pedestrian ramp that rises from the level of Harvard Yard to the third floor of the Carpenter Center, then penetrates the building at that level, and thereupon descends eastward until it rejoins the ground. It is a great tour-de-force—the form of the ramp (which was somewhat altered to fit the constraints of the site) was determined, in Corbu's mind, by the diagonal patterns of walkways in Harvard Yard; and the movement generated by the ramp was intended to dramatize the almost unlimited possibilities of restructuring pedestrian circulation on several levels within existing (or newly created) urban systems.

The drama is there, all right, though it is a mini-drama at best: ascending the ramp from Harvard Yard, one feels as Hannibal may have felt as he was crossing the Alps; alas, it is not the Po Valley, but only Prescott Street that meets the eye at the Alpine Pass—i.e. the third floor level of the Carpenter Center, at which elevation one is meant to enter the building.

Still, like so many of Corbu's earlier structures, this one is a powerful manifesto, in miniature as it were, of an idea with much more grandiose implications. Like so many of his last buildings and complexes, the Carpenter Center was concerned with movement systems—with people moving up and down, and changing direction in space, of entering structures and emerging from them in entirely novel and unconventional ways. As in the Palace of Justice at Chandigarh, and at the Millowners' Building at Ahmedabad, the ascending and descending ramps, leading to entrances at various levels, suggest a new freedom of pedestrian movement not previously available to mankind, except on isolated and rare occasions.

The Carpenter Center is full of Corbu's more familiar gestures as well: the *brises-soleil* are there, as are the roof terraces, the *pilotis*, the plastic concrete forms, and the Modulor-divisions in the fenestration. The building was executed by Sert's architectural firm in Cambridge, and finished rather more smoothly than most of Le Corbusier's other work, especially that in India. Some of the detailing of window and door frames seems not entirely in character with the stark contrasts preferred by Corbu in his European and Asian work—e.g. glass set directly in brute concrete. Still, it is a remarkable piece of work, matched in strength by very few of the University's buildings before or since.

It is a curious and slightly disturbing fact that the Carpenter Center seems to function rather better in its interior spaces than many of Corbu's strictly "functional" buildings—although it was not really designed for any specific functions at all! What this does to the cornerstone of modern dogma—i.e. that form must follow function, or else—is a question that will interest revisionist historians in years to come.

X X I

DURING THE LAST half dozen years of his life, Le Corbusier designed and built a surprisingly large number of structures, both in Europe and in Asia. He also developed a number of projects that may some
day, or may never, see the light of day.

The number of buildings and of projects was surprising because, to
most of his contemporaries, it seemed as if he were withdrawing more
and more from the architectural scene. He seemed to spend an increasing amount of time in his tiny vacation house at Cap Martin, in the
South of France, and devoting most of his time to painting large canvases that, in the eyes of most European and American critics, seemed
rather less interesting than his early, Purist works. Moreover, Corbu's
office in Paris appeared to be fairly dormant—only a very few of his

earlier associates remained, others having detached themselves and opened their own architectural offices.

In fact, however, Corbu was doing an extraordinary amount of work. There were more than half a dozen new buildings in Chandigarh, outside the Government Center, and some of these were not completed until well after his death. There were several major structures in France—especially the Youth Center and the *Unité d'Habitation* in Firminy-Vert, about forty miles south-west of Lyons, in France; and there were projects and buildings in Switzerland, Italy, and Brazil.

Two completed buildings and one project during these last half dozen years seem, in retrospect, of very special significance. The first of these is the Dominican monastery, *Sainte-Marie-de-la-Tourette*, constructed at Eveux, near Lyons, and dedicated late in 1960; the second

Sainte-Marie-de-la-Tourette Monastery, Eveux, 1960. View from the north. The "funnels" at left are two of the three skylights that illuminate the chapel on the lowest floor. (Photo: Lucien Hervé)

is the *Maison de l'Homme,* a prefabricated steel structure designed in 1963 for the Swiss art gallery owner, Heidi Weber, and completed by her in Zurich two years after Corbu's death; and the third, late work of special significance is the project (as yet unbuilt) for a hospital complex in Venice. If Le Corbusier had built and planned nothing else, these three projects would have assured him a prominent place in the history of the Modern Movement: *La Tourette,* as a classic work of art, a beautiful play of light, texture, color and form, and a profound influence upon modern architects everywhere; the *Maison de l'Homme,* as a virtuoso effort in prefabrication and industrialization of buildings (and in a few other things as well); and the Venice hospital, designed by Corbu in 1964 (and somewhat redesigned just before his death in 1965), as an extraordinary departure, a fundamental re-orientation of modern architecture, away from some of Corbu's own pioneering work, and toward new insights that are only just beginning to be understood, ten years after his death.

La Tourette is a curiously medieval structure—a kind of fortress, rectangular in plan, with a central court, very much in the tradition of early Dominican monasteries. It is from three to five stories in height, and its walls are poured-in-place or precast concrete, of different degrees of roughness. The fenestration is extremely varied: some of it divided irregularly, according to the Modulor scale, by vertical mullions; elsewhere, divided into abstract panels of glass alternating with white-washed concrete. The building's plan is quite rigid, but its walls and its attached forms—bell towers, chimneys, stairs, scuppers, skylights and other appendages—are free in form. It is a remarkable piece of sculpture, rich enough in ideas to nourish an entire new generation of architects.

The most successful space at *La Tourette* is the large chapel along the north side of the building. It is a rectangular room without real windows, and arranged on several levels. Off to one side is a small chapel, with the Stations of the Cross; and this free-form space is also the principal source of natural light: three truncated, cone-shaped skylights reach out from it toward the sun, and capture and bounce it off the walls within. These walls (and some of the ceiling surfaces)—board-formed concrete, like much of *La Tourette,* and painted in brilliant primary colors—create an ambiance of spirituality hardly matched by any architect in this century, most certainly not by one so non-religious. To Corbu, this building, with its poverty-level budget—indeed, because of it—became a supreme challenge: its materials, sunlight and shadows, cost nothing; in his hands, these cheapest of all building materials produced an act of faith.

La Tourette has been copied and bastardized the world over. In Boston, a vast City Hall, the size, roughly, of a beached aircraft carrier, has been built in the image of *La Tourette;* and there have even been

Detail of the side chapel, La Tourette. The board-formed concrete wall at right is painted a bright red; the ceiling is sky blue. The floor reflects the slope in the ground. (Photo: Lucien Hervé)

Detail of concrete penthouse housing stair to the roof of La Tourette. The glass is set directly into the board-formed wall. (Photo: Lucien Hervé)

laundromats and banks that borrowed from this modest and proud monument to poverty. It is a building that does not travel well—but that will inspire generations of architects who take the trouble to travel to it.

The *Maison de l'Homme*, in Zurich, designed for Heidi Weber, is a very different kind of structure—though it contains certain elements that can be found at *La Tourette* as well. Unlike the monastery, this little pavilion is insistently twentieth-century: prefabricated, industrialized, hard-edged and as modern as a space shuttle. Some of its forms—the *inverted* and "outverted" and connected roof parasols—had intrigued Corbu for several decades, but had not been previously realized, except at Chandigarh, in brute concrete; the colors, the connecting details, the articulation of mechanical systems, the roof garden, the ascending ramp, the irregular fenestration arranged according to the *Modulor*—all these existed in earlier structures, but rarely with such precision. The building was originally designed to be an actual house (complete with an air raid shelter, to comply with local law); but both in intention,

*Exhibition Pavilion "Maison de l'Homme," Zurich, 1965.
The roof parasols are of steel and the brightly painted
wall panels are of aluminum, porcelain-enamel, and glass.
(Photo: John Messina)*

and in detail, it is clearly an exhibition pavilion, easily superior to the
finest ones then being constructed at various world's fairs.

It is a particularly interesting structure, because Corbu had previously built very little in steel; most of his work had been of reinforced
concrete. Yet this structure, with its cross-shaped horizontal and vertical
struts (filled in with glass or porcelain-enamel panels) is entirely self-
assured in its technology—somewhat influenced, for sure, by the work
of Le Corbusier's friend Jean Prouvé, who pioneered much prefabrication in France in the 1930's and after that.

The pavilion was built in typically bravado fashion: first the tri-
angulated steel parasols, on their supporting columns; then, after these
were in place, the Modulor grid of cross-shaped struts was assembled
under it, protected against the weather. The spatial arrangements, unlike the structural grid, are reminiscent of earlier Corbu houses: open
spaces, connected by ramps and free-standing stairs, and topped off by

a sheltered roof garden. The building today houses some of Corbu's finest murals, drawings, sculptures and pieces of furniture.

The third project of major significance developed by Le Corbusier before his death in 1965 was the hospital for the city of Venice. It is still, as of this writing, unbuilt; it may never be started or finished. Yet it will certainly count as a most significant part of Le Corbusier's legacy to future generations of architects.

Its significance lies in the fact that, unlike all of Corbu's earlier work, the Venice hospital is not a building, but a system; it is, in fact, a non-building.

The program was, initially, for a 1,200-bed facility, with all the attendant operating rooms, nurses' residences, administration offices, kitchens, and so on. Yet, as in all hospital programs, the future was unpredictable: the building would surely have to expand, and the nature of some or all of its services would have to change.

Project for a hospital, Venice, 1965. The plan is a system of multi-level streets, with hospital wards "plugged into" the system. The patients' rooms are skylit. (Photo: Oeuvre Complète)

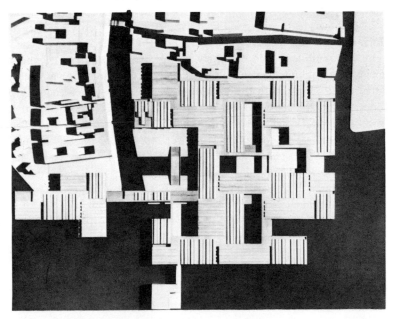

The site was on the northern edge of the city, behind the railroad station, and roughly in the direction of Mestre. Part of the site was on land, but most of it extended out over the water. In fact, the hospital would largely stand on stilts in a lagoon.

Many years earlier, Le Corbusier had pointed out that Venice was one of the most "modern" cities in the world—an urban system in which different modes of transportation had been sorted out from one another, and connected at points of intersection: high-speed transport (on the great canals); neighborhood transport (on local waterways); pedestrian avenues and plazas (and the points at which they connected with the waterways); and local streets and alleys (and at the bridges that crossed canals and also, invariably, connected with *vaporetti* stops). All these, together with peripheral railroad station, highway, and airport, made Venice an urban organism as astonishingly "modern," in Corbu's view, as the most advanced "megastructure."

His scheme for the Venice hospital was clearly influenced by such earlier thoughts; it was also, even more clearly, influenced by the work of his close American friend, and one-time apprentice, the late Shadrach Woods, who had won a competition for a new campus for the Free University of West Berlin in 1962, with a scheme very similar to the 1964 project for the Venice hospital. (Corbu, in a generous mood, told Woods how greatly the grid-like "system" of the Free University influenced him in the Venice design.) For the Venice plan was, quite simply, a multi-level grid, infinitely flexible (in its infill spaces, and in theory), and infinitely extensible in almost all directions. It was a structure on four levels, with the bottom three levels an "infrastructure" of services, and the top level the domain of patients, with each bed lit from a grid of skylights.

How radical a departure this project represented for Le Corbusier can be understood only when it is compared with the plan for the center of Saint-Dié, proposed by him in 1945. That plan was an asymmetrical (but still quite rigidly composed) piece of urban design—much admired and much copied since, and perhaps rightly so.

But the Venice hospital project was a radical, irreversible departure from Saint-Dié: an urbanistic prototype that rejected rigid composition, and welcomed unpredictable change—and, thus, formless growth.

In both philosophical and practical terms, this is a fundamental change in direction—and one that has been recognized by Corbu's more perceptive followers, though not by his latter-day sycophants. Corbu's final collaborator, the Chilean architect Jullian de la Fuente, has attempted to carry the Venice project forward; and because the basic concept is infinitely flexible, Jullian has been able to adjust the form to changing functions. The building may never see the light of day—indeed, its multi-level grid may have found its initial expression in Shadrach Woods' Free University, in West Berlin. It probably won't be its last.

Although Le Corbusier was approached by more and more clients in the early 1960's, he seemed increasingly to withdraw from the scene. Buildings were being built in his imprint in Asia and in Europe; and projects were being drawn by his hand. But, more and more, he seemed to withdraw from the world that had treated him so shabbily. He spent more and more time in his little cubicle-studio at Cap Martin, painting and writing. On August 27th, 1965, he went for his usual swim. His Swiss chronicler reports that he died at 11 a.m., in the water, of a heart attack at the age of (almost) seventy-eight. The chronicler forgot to mention that Corbu's death marked the end of a heroic era.

It was a staggering shock to those who were committed to a new era and to a new architecture. When Frank Lloyd died, one felt that he had lived and fulfilled his time; but when Le Corbusier died, in the waters off Cap Martin, one felt that his incredible intelligence had only just begun to jolt our time.

This, it seems, was the way Corbu was, posthumously, viewed in France. In a ceremony held in the Cour Carrée du Louvre, on September 1st, 1965, André Malraux, Minister of Cultural Affairs of the French Republic, said some admirable things about this man, whom the French Republic had managed to reject and ignore quite soundly before Malraux resurrected him.

Perhaps there is another sort of tribute to Corbu, to be found in the hearts and minds of a young generation that sensed his passion. Many years ago, in *Vers une architecture*, the young Le Corbusier had written this about two men—Michelangelo and Phidias: "Intelligence and passion; there is no art without emotion, no emotion without passion. Stones are dead things sleeping in the quarries, but the apses of St. Peter's are a drama. The drama of architecture is that of the man who lives by and through the universe. As the man, so the drama, so the architecture. We must not assert . . . that the masses give rise to their man. A *man* is an exceptional phenomenon, occurring at long intervals, perhaps by chance. . . .

"Michael Angelo is the man of the last thousand years, just as Phidias was the man of the thousand years before. The work of Michael Angelo is a *creation*, not a Renaissance . . . A passion, an intelligence beyond normal—this was the Everlasting Yea.

"Phidias, the great sculptor who made the Parthenon. There has been nothing like it anywhere or at any period . . . For two thousand years, those who have seen the Parthenon have felt that here was a decisive moment in architecture.

"We are now at such a decisive moment."

Phidias, Michelangelo, Le Corbusier. Intelligence and Passion; the Everlasting Yea; the Decisive Moment.

MIES VAN DER ROHE

and the Mastery of Structure

Mies van der Rohe in Chicago (Photo: Morley Baer)

I

ON ALMOST ANY DAY of the week, around lunchtime, a massive man will climb up the delicate white steel and travertine staircase of the Chicago Arts Club. Although he now walks with a limp (due to recurring attacks of arthritis) and, generally, has to lean on a cane, Ludwig Mies van der Rohe seems remarkably nimble for his weight and age. His clothes are extremely elegant; most of his suits were tailored by Knize and make him look slim and agile. He is, indeed, something of a dandy in a subdued way: there is generally a very soft, very expensive handkerchief trailing out of his breast pocket, and he obviously likes fine quality in all his personal belongings.

Yet there is nothing dandified about his features: his head looks as if it had been chiseled out of a block of granite; his face, infinitely lined, has the massively aristocratic look of a wealthy Dutch burgher by Rembrandt. As he walks across the generous space of the Arts Club, which he designed in 1951, Mies—as everyone has learned to call him —may notice an acquaintance or greet a friend. When he does, his shy face suddenly lights up in a charming, rather toothy grin, and he may even say a word or two in a deep, hesitant voice. Later, after a couple of Martinis and lunch, Mies will pull out one of his huge cigars, relax, and even talk. It will then be about 2 P.M. Chicago time, and Mies will be ready to start on a new day in earnest.

No one seeing this large and impressive figure would suspect that Ludwig Mies (he added his mother's family name, van der Rohe, to his own when he started to work as an architect) was born the son of a rather humble mason and stone cutter. Nor would anyone suspect that this conservative gentleman, whose appearance is that of a Chairman of the Board of U.S. Steel or of some comparable Captain of Industry, has been considered a dangerous radical throughout a large part of his life. Indeed, as late as 1953, when Mies was already beginning to look a little bit like his own monument in rock, the editor of a woman's magazine hysterically attacked him as a "threat to America" and hinted, darkly, that Mies was in league with Communists, Fascists, and other nihilists. All of this came as a surprise not only to Mies himself, who is without question the gentlest radical ever to have renounced a barricade, but also to his friends, who have tried for years to protect him from the day-to-day tensions and conflicts of a neurotic era. The relative isolation in which he has lived has enabled him to concentrate, in peace and quiet, upon the search for simple truths which has been the central mission of his life as an architect.

Mies has not always been able to live so dedicated a life. He was born on March 27, 1886, in Aachen in the German Rhineland. His family's circumstances did not permit him to obtain any but the most rudimentary schooling. But the fact that his father was a master mason gave Mies a knowledge of building materials which many, more formally trained architects have never been able to acquire. "My father had many wonderful blocks of marble and other stones in his shop," Mies recalls, indicating with his hands a block of marble about a cubic foot in size. "I learned about stone from him." While attending elementary and trade schools, Mies earned a few pennies by working as a runner on construction projects, together with other boys of his age. "We had to go out and get boiling hot water for the carpenters framing in the roof," Mies recalls. "They used the water to make coffee. And if we didn't get the water fast enough, they would throw one of their sharp axes after us to make us hurry up." Mies is rather pleased with himself for having gone through this rough and tumble schooling, for having learned building not from the drafting board, but from the dirt and noise of the building site. When he is at ease—generally late in the evening, with a group of friends—he likes to talk about the days when he learned to put brick on brick. "Now, a brick, that's really *some*thing," he will say, with his infectious smile. "That's really *building*. Not paper architecture." There is some doubt as to how many bricks Mies ever really laid one on top of the other, for his father was a *stone* mason; but there is no doubt that he learned much of what there was to be known about building, in the traditional way, long before he drew a single line on paper. More than fifty years after he was born in the one-time seat of the Holy Roman Emperors, Mies made one of his rare, brief and—to him—painful speeches at his inauguration as Director of Architecture at the Illinois Institute of Technology. On that day, in 1938, he said: "All education must begin with the practical side of life . . . [along] the road of discipline from materials, through function, to creative work . . . How sensible is the small, handy shape (of a brick), so useful for every purpose! What logic in its bonding, pattern and texture! What richness in the simplest wall surface! But what discipline this material imposes! · . . ."

"Discipline"—this has been the watchword of Mies's life and work. Discipline, order, clarity, truth. Aachen, the city of his birth, is located near the border between the Catholic Rhineland and the Low Countries, and Mies was born a Roman Catholic. Although he was never a practicing member of his faith, the code to which he subscribed from his youth to this day—the code to which he added his own beliefs—is the moral code of St. Augustine and of St. Thomas Aquinas. He told that audience at Illinois Tech, in 1938: "Nothing can express the aim and meaning of our work better than the profound words of St. Augustine —'Beauty is the splendor of Truth.'" To Mies, there has never been any doubt about the rightness, the truth—and hence the beauty—of what he was trying to do. Every step along his way has been a clear step —sure, steady, uncomplicated, uncompromising. The first step is the brick, the simple fact of the material. The second step is to understand the meaning of one material, and the meaning of all materials. The third step is to understand the materials characteristic of our time— steel, concrete, and glass. The fourth step is to understand the needs of our epoch: the need to provide vast amounts of shelter (the mass need); and the need to make each man free (the individual, human need). And the inevitable result of this clear and uncompromising progression is to insure "the splendor of truth." How could it be otherwise? "Our practical aims measure only our material ,progress," Mies said. "The values we profess reveal the level of our culture. . . . We must make clear, step by step, what things are possible, necessary and significant." Mies's critics have sometimes tried to provoke him into arguments, to get him to defend his point of view. Mies considers such debates a waste of time; to him, logic—uncompromising logic—leads to truth, and truth leads to beauty. There is really nothing to discuss.

After leaving elementary school, Mies entered a local trade school, always concentrating on the practical aspects of building, always working, part time, on various buildings his father or his father's friends were putting up. When he was only fifteen years old, Mies left the trade school and apprenticed himself to several architects around Aachen. One of his major assignments of that period—a job he recalls with considerable amusement and some pride—was to make full-size drawings for neoclassical ornaments to be rendered in stucco on the façades of various buildings. "We had to draw those things on huge sheets of paper pinned on a wall," Mies recalled not long ago. "No drawing boards for us: we had to stand up, and draw this stuff swinging our arms in a big arc, covering the entire sheet with volutes and other decorative nonsense. That was real training in draftsmanship!" It was also about as tough a job, physically, as splitting rocks on a chain gang, and Mies was delighted when, after two years of this particular kind of torture, he was offered a job by a Berlin architect. He left Aachen for the German capital in 1905. He was quite "uneducated" in the conventional sense of the term. But, at an age when most young, would-be architects were just starting out at some academy, Mies knew much of what there was to be known about building, much of what there was to be known about drawing, and much of what there was to be known about self-discipline. At only nineteen he had acquired more valid knowledge than many architects acquire after years of academic training and apprenticeship.

I I

MIES DID NOT STAY on his first Berlin job for very long. Upon discovering that his new employer worked primarily in wood, and upon realizing, furthermore, that he himself knew very little about that material, Mies went to Bruno Paul, the leading furniture designer of the period (who, like everyone else, was strongly influenced by Art Nouveau), and asked to become Paul's apprentice. After two years of apprenticeship, Mies had filled this particular gap in his working knowledge of building, and he left Paul's office. That year, 1907, Mies obtained his first commission, a house for a Professor Riehl in Neubabelsberg, a suburb of Berlin. Although the finished building was quite traditional in concept and detail, its perfect execution seemed almost incredible in a first work by a twenty-one-year-old apprentice.

There was one man working in Germany during the first decade of the twentieth century who appeared to have gone beyond the concept of the architect as an apostle of Arts and Crafts and a defender of man against the onslaught of the machine. That architect was Peter Behrens —the same Behrens to whom Le Corbusier was drawn in 1910, and who had employed the young Walter Gropius as one of his chief designers. When Mies finished his house for Professor Riehl, Behrens offered him a job in his office, and Mies accepted with delight; for three years Mies remained with Behrens and there, in effect, completed his architectural education.

Oddly enough, Behrens was important to Mies in two seemingly opposed ways: first, Mies learned from Behrens something of that potential interplay of architecture and industry which impressed Gropius and Corbu so much during their periods in Behrens's office. But this was only a part of Behrens's work, however important; for, in addition to his industrial structures for the A.E.G. (the German electrical industry), and in addition to his "product designs" for that same company, Behrens was occupied with another sort of practice, which, to some of his admirers, seemed at violent odds with the "advanced" work done for A.E.G. This other side of Behrens was his monumental, neoclassical work, generally for government agencies. And that work affected Mies almost as much as the "new spirit" of industrialized building that was exemplified by Behrens's factories and exhibition structures.

This is not to suggest that Mies was really taken in by neoclassicism —or, for that matter, that Behrens was taken in. Around 1900 Behrens had been a leading apostle of Art Nouveau; he had designed some extraordinary plant-shaped glassware; he had done woodcuts almost indistinguishable, to a layman, from those being imported from Japan; and he had painted some delightfully sentimental canvases entitled *Mourning, The Kiss, Butterflies*, etc., that would have done credit to the most lachrymose pre-Raphaelite. By 1905, or thereabouts, the basic fallacy of Art Nouveau became shockingly apparent to Behrens, and he was looking for the cleansing influence of a clear and logical discipline—a classical discipline, to be precise—to help him pull out of the sentimental morass of Art Nouveau. He found that discipline in the neoclassicism of the great German architect of the early nineteenth century, Karl Friedrich Schinkel.

To Behrens, and to his young draftsman, Mies, the most interesting aspects of Schinkel's neoclassicism were three: first, they felt that Schinkel had a way of placing his structures on wide pedestals or platforms that gave the buildings a considerable nobility; second, they saw that Schinkel had a feeling for rhythm, proportion, and scale which was applicable to buildings of *any* period; and, third, Behrens and Mies saw in Schinkel's buildings a purity of form which held even greater meaning for a time whose architectural forms and spaces were bound to become increasingly bold and simple.

In 1930, when Behrens published a brief review of his work, he omitted all illustrations of the neoclassical buildings of the years before World War I. Yet it is very likely that Mies was influenced at least as strongly by the revelation of Schinkel's concepts of form as he was by Behrens's excursions into industry. The fundamental principle of classicism—the development of universal solutions, universally applicable to a wide variety of problems—was to interest Mies more and more in years to come.

Behrens's office was an extremely busy place while Mies and Gropius worked there as designers. But if one were to single out two buildings of that period which inspired Mies more than any others, these would have to be the famous Turbine factory for the A.E.G., done in 1909, and the German embassy in St. Petersburg, the construction of which was to be supervised by the young Mies. These two buildings showed Behrens at his best and in his two extremes: the first was, probably, the most important steel-and-glass building prior to Gropius's Fagus factory of 1911; and the second was, probably, the most accomplished piece of neoclassicism to come out of Behrens's office.

The Turbine factory was a huge hall framed in steel arches spanning some eighty feet and about one hundred feet high at their crowns. These arches were placed about twenty-five feet apart, and the space between, up to the roof line, was filled with a "skin" of glass. This great room was planned to be more than 600 feet long, but only a first stage of 400 feet was actually constructed. The corners of the hall were closed off with massive-looking "piers" of concrete, scored horizontally to contrast with the march of the vertical steel arches along the 400-foot façade. Actually, these concrete corners were quite thin, also, and carried no loads. This is a rather significant aspect of the building, for it shows that Behrens—unlike Auguste Perret, for example—was perfectly willing to deviate from structural purism and create an effect by means other than purely functional. Those massive concrete corners of the A.E.G. Turbine factory are a poetic image of strength and power, not a true representation of structural framing. Whether Behrens was justified in using images of this sort in a building whose actual bone structure might have been used to convey the notions of strength and power more convincingly is open to question. Nowadays the sort of imagery practiced here by Behrens is often abused by industrial designers to create a suggestion of speed, or power, or uplift which does not correspond to the reality of structure at all. But these are, of course, decisions dictated largely by taste. In the Behrens building the notion of "power" was conveyed so convincingly by the great fortresslike concrete corners that no one could possibly have mistaken this structure for anything but what it was. When Mies, many years later, was faced with the problem of how to express a quality of structure despite building-code requirements that forced him to conceal the very structure he was trying to express, he may have thought of Behrens's images of power as a way of conveying the meaning and the content of his buildings.

The German embassy in St. Petersburg belonged to the neoclassical category of Behrens's work, and, in retrospect, it does not seem particularly inventive to us today. Its proportions were impressive and noble; its interior finishes were of the finest quality; its sculptural decoration, including an equestrian group over the main-entrance portals, was restrained by comparison with some of the other work of the period. Still, none of this was really very exceptional in a time that saw much more advanced work being done by Wright in America, by the Perrets and Garnier in France, by Gropius and Bruno Taut in Germany.

Yet the St. Petersburg embassy contained several spaces of quite extraordinary elegance. If we were able to look at the monumental ground-floor lobby today (unfortunately the building was badly damaged during World War II), we would find a space formed almost entirely by regularly spaced columns whose bays were filled with floor-to-ceiling panels of glass. The glass areas (some of them French doors) opened the lobby space out toward a very formal court to the rear of the main building. Elsewhere the columns would become pilasters, holding between them floor-to-ceiling panels of wall area or of doorways—all treated as a modular unit fitted neatly and tightly between the expressed structural system. Even the grand staircase leading up from the lobby floor was fitted into a column bay and hence treated as an integral part of the structure and the plan of the building. This pattern of verticality imposed upon the building by its expressed column structure was not new to classical architecture; but to Mies it seems to have suggested a way of creating formality and monumentality to which he resorted in several buildings in later years.

While Mies was in Behrens's office he took on several small commissions to carry out on his own. One, a house for Hugo Perls, was in the straight tradition of "cleaned-up Schinkelism" which Behrens and other German architects of the period employed, generally with good taste, if occasionally with too heavy a hand. The house was two stories high, quite symmetrical, stuccoed, endowed with a very simple but pronounced cornice line, and a fairly low-pitched tile roof with a low parapet (rather than roof overhangs). Few people passing by the house would give it a second look today; yet anyone willing to take a closer look would find in this house a refinement of proportions, of details, and of simple forms that suggest that its designer was more than a mere follower of Schinkel or of Behrens.

But perhaps the first suggestion of Mies's independent creativeness came in a project done in 1912, a year after the Perls house was completed. For some time Behrens had been working on the design for a truly palatial home to be built for Mme H. E. L. J. Kröller, near The Hague in Holland. Behrens's design was very Schinkelesque—a two-story block with a recessed portico topped by a balcony, a pronounced roof cornice suggesting a flat roof, and a partly walled patio to one side. Mme Kröller, the owner of the famous Kröller-Müller collection of modern paintings, went so far as to have Behrens build a full-scale wood-

Kröller house project for The Hague, Holland, 1912.
(Courtesy, Museum of Modern Art)

and-canvas model of the house on its intended site. The photographs of this mock-up that still survive show a rather massive and ungainly pile of building blocks, distinguished primarily by the orderliness of its vertical fenestration.

Mies, who had been working on the Kröller job in Behrens's office, went to The Hague in connection with the construction of the mock-up. For various reasons Mme Kröller decided not to go ahead with the Behrens proposal; instead she asked Mies to stay at The Hague and to design his own version of a house for the same site. Mies stayed at The Hague for a year (he considers time one of the cheapest commodities an architect can spend in the design of a building), and came up with his own version, which was reproduced, full scale in wood and canvas, just as the original Behrens design had been.

The comparison between the two projects is striking. Where Behrens's proposal was a compact, somewhat heavy-looking structure two stories high throughout, Mies had developed a rather low-slung, extended complex of one-story wings and colonnades grouped around a central, two-story-high block facing on various interior patios. The details were still quite neoclassical, but the massing of the building, with its great, horizontal sweeps of colonnades, was quite different from the tight verticality of a Schinkel building. Unfortunately, this villa never went beyond the mock-up stage, either; but its design gave Mies a chance to go beyond Behrens for the first time.

By 1913 Mies returned to Berlin to open his own office. During the eighteen months or so of peace that remained before the outbreak of

World War I, he designed several villas much in the manner of his Perls house three or four years earlier. All were done more or less in the Schinkelesque manner, though the greater use of glass (French doors in particular), the simplification of detail, and the emphasis on fine proportions set his designs apart from similar work done by other architects of those years. Although Mies was still a classicist in terms of form, it was apparent that structure, as an overriding discipline, had begun to interest him more and more. During his year at The Hague he had seen some of the work of H. P. Berlage, the Dutch architect whose unaffected work in brick seemed to Mies to express the honest, structural possibilities of that material to perfection.

The notion of "honesty" in structure and structural expression was something that Berlage had acquired from men like Ruskin, who had used the concept initially to attack the pretentions of neoclassicism and eclecticism. Their opposition to those latter evils had, in turn, taken them back to the alleged structural honesty of early medieval architecture. Under the influence of this sort of rationalization Mies became increasingly critical of the surface trappings of Schinkelism. It seemed to him that Behrens and others like him were primarily interested in form for form's sake, while he was learning, from Berlage, to accept structure as the great, underlying discipline. Some years later Mies put it very clearly when he said: "We refuse to recognize problems of form, but only problems of building. Form is not the aim of our work, but only the result. Form, by itself, does not exist. Form as an aim is formalism; and that we reject." Those were brave words—and good words, as far as they went. Just as Behrens had felt the need to cleanse himself of Art Nouveau sentimentality by turning to Schinkel's classicism, so Mies now felt the need to cleanse himself of formalism by finding a moral rationalization of architecture which would, incidentally, determine form, but not be dominated by it. It was a necessary step in Mies's development; and the fact that he was destined one day to swallow some of those words and become one of the first modern architects to return to the creation of eloquent forms does nothing to subtract from the validity of his beliefs in those early days.

I I I

I N 1918 MIES returned to Berlin from military service in the German army. He had been an enlisted man in the engineers, building bridges and roads in the Balkans. (Not being a university graduate, he found it impossible to become an officer in the old German army.) Upon his return from the Balkans, Mies found himself in the midst of several revolutions, all taking place simultaneously. First, there was the political revolution—the transfer of power from the Kaiser's defeated empire to the new, Weimar Republic. Next, there were political upheavals within republican ranks—all the way from the extreme left, which managed, briefly, to establish Soviet-style dictatorships in several German states, to the near-monarchist right, which was hoping against hope to prepare for the eventual return of the Hohenzollern family to the German throne. But, in the midst of these wild political upheavals, a whole series of upheavals took place in the world of art: there were the German *im*pressionists, holdovers from the prewar years, fighting for a comeback; there were the new *ex*pressionists, very much in vogue though soon to be eclipsed; and there was a sudden influx of ideas from France, Holland, and Russia, all dealing with different aspects of the new Cubist movement. Germany had been completely cut off from these latter developments throughout the war years and, to some extent, even before. Now that the war and the Kaiser were over and done with, now that *any*thing that represented a new point of view could receive a hearing in Germany, the young artists of Mies's generation (he was just over thirty years old) were irresistibly drawn to everything that seemed to represent a new world.

In this exhilarating atmosphere Mies found it possible to make the final, absolute break with the past. He designed one more house in the vaguely classical manner he had developed before 1914; but that house was never built, and it was Mies's last attempt to reconcile neoclassicism with the needs of our time. In the same year in which this last, conservative house was designed, Mies produced so radical and daring a sketch for a skyscraper that modern architecture, quite literally, has not been the same since.

The sketches Mies developed in 1919 were for an all-glass tower, twenty stories in height, with a central core of services from which extended three wings of office spaces, sheathed from street level to the roof line with an uninterrupted skin of glass. This sheer cliff of crystal was a staggering piece of imagination and daring in itself; coming from a young man who, only a few months earlier, had been content to design a rather "safe" and conservative villa in a neoclassical vein, these drawings were almost incomprehensible. For here, with a single stroke of the pen, as it were, Mies laid the foundation for all the great glass-and-metal skyscrapers we see about us today.

Mies would be the first to admit that this sketch in 1919 was merely the foundation, the beginning, of a vast amount of work on his part and on the part of others. Yet what a beginning, what a step for-

Glass office-building project for Berlin, 1919. (Courtesy, Museum of Modern Art)

ward! The plan for this building was still oddly fanciful in outline, angular and jagged in shape, rather like an expressionist pattern. The reason for its odd shape, according to Mies, was not any preoccupation with expressionist forms, but, rather, an attempt to study the reflections of light in the many-faceted glass façades of the building. "I placed the glass walls at slight angles to each other to avoid the monotony of over-large glass surfaces," Mies wrote. "I discovered by working with actual glass models that the important thing is the play of reflections and not the effect of light and shadow, as in ordinary buildings." A year later

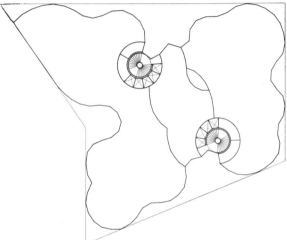

Glass skyscraper project, 1920-1. (Courtesy, Museum of Modern Art)

Plan of glass skyscraper. (Courtesy, Museum of Modern Art)

Mies produced a second set of sketches for another all-glass skyscraper, this one to be thirty stories high. It was even more extraordinary than the first one: in plan it consisted of a complex of free forms; each floor was enclosed by a continuous curtain or skin of glass, arranged to follow the compound curves of the outline of the plan. Yet this curved glass skin was made up of dozens of identical flat window units that changed direction on every mullion line, like the sides of a polygon. As a result, the same play of reflections Mies had tried to achieve in the first scheme was carried still farther on the multi-faceted skin of this building. The model of the structure prepared by Mies showed, behind the skin of glass, a stack of reinforced concrete floor slabs cantilevered out from interior column supports and expressed in a knife-edged metal strip on the glass façade.

Why do these two projects for glass skyscrapers seem so important in retrospect? The answer is in three parts: first, while there had been glassy buildings designed and even constructed before 1919, no proposal had ever been so radically all-glass, so completely uncompromising a statement of what the new technology could produce. Second, the glass skyscrapers were amazingly "right" for their time—right in terms of their cantilever structure, in terms of their simple, aesthetic expression, in terms of their decisive clarity. And, third, these two projects seem important now because they suddenly pushed Mies into the forefront of the modern movement and assured him a place he has never relinquished since.

For these projects revealed a quality in Mies which has been his most impressive characteristic throughout his career. That quality is the ability to produce architectural statements of such overwhelming precision, simplicity, and single-mindedness that their impact is that of a major revelation. Bold and singlehanded statements have been used for centuries as devices to attract attention to a new dogma or a new personality. But in Mies's case the single-mindedness and precision of his architectural statements has never been meant to attract publicity to his ideas or to himself. (Indeed, Mies is so self-effacing and withdrawn a person that, in the 1940's, his students at the Illinois Institute of Technology once petitioned to have an annual Christmas party at which they might have a chance to meet him!) The startling simplicity of his revelations is, instead, the result of an endless process of purification and crystallization of an idea—until that idea becomes so disarmingly simple, so overwhelmingly "obvious" that it must, according to Mies's beliefs, represent the ultimate truth. His famous saying—"less is more"—is not only typical of Mies as a man of few and well-chosen words; it is also descriptive of the method by which he works, a method of distilling ideas to the point of ultimate purity.

As a matter of fact, the logic of Mies's glass towers appears now, in retrospect, almost predictable. Once Mies became disenchanted with formalism and began, through Berlage's work, to think in terms of structural clarity and honesty, it could only be a matter of time for him to investigate the logical consequences of steel, reinforced concrete, and glass, and to arrive at a statement of "honesty" as he saw it when applied to those new materials. To him the answer was perfectly clear: steel and concrete represented strength; these would be the "bones" of his buildings. Glass was a shimmering veil that could be draped over the skeleton to form the "skin." Gropius and Behrens had, of course, done steel-and-glass buildings; but their structures showed the "bones" clearly on the exterior, with glass used as a fill-in panel set into the spaces between the structural skeleton. In Mies's skyscraper projects the bones and skin became completely separated—the skeleton inside, the skin of glass outside—so that there was no possible visual confusion between what supported the floor and roof loads and what kept out the weather. "Skin and bone construction" is what Mies called it, and the description has stuck.

Despite his relative isolation, Mies was undoubtedly influenced by certain movements in painting and sculpture which swept across Europe in the years immediately after World War I; and the qualities found in his glass-tower projects were present in some of these movements as well. For example, the Russian Suprematist painter, Kasimir Malevich, in his famous *White on White* (now in the permanent collection of the Museum of Modern Art) had made the same sort of uncompromising statement about painting which Mies was to make about architecture with his glass towers a couple of years later. For just as Malevich's painting was, in effect, a clean slate offered to the world, to receive an entirely new set of images, so Mies's glassy façades were giant mirrors held up to the world to reflect an entirely new set of forms. And Mies had seen, too, how the Russian Constructivists like Lissitzky and Tatlin, in their mechanistic sculpture of the same period, always articulated different parts of a structure, both by separating the parts and by making them of different materials. Mies, like everyone else of his generation, was conscious of these movements abroad: exhibitions were held in Berlin of Suprematist and Constructivist painting and sculpture, and Mies became a member of the Novembergruppe—an organization of artists in many fields interested in finding a channel through which to bring their work to the attention of the public. (The Novembergruppe was generally Left Wing in its politics, having been named after the month in 1918 which saw the revolution that created the Weimar Republic.) Mies, as head of the architectural section of the Novembergruppe, helped arrange several exhibitions of advanced architectural projects, and his own two skyscraper proposals were first shown within that context.

In a sense, the idea that Mies should associate himself with a movement motivated—in part, at least—by political objectives seems odd. His own political inclinations are practically nonexistent; on at least one occasion, during the years after World War II, when told by a friend that another German architect of some prominence—who, unlike Mies, had remained in Germany during the Hitler period—had received an important post despite his past Nazi connections, Mies flared up angrily, saying, in effect, that he didn't give a damn about the man's politics, but *was* concerned with the fact that the man was a rotten architect! Mies's own personal tastes—his preferences for quiet, expensive clothes, for restrained but near-precious building materials—seem to have led him in later years into associations with wealthy conservatives rather than Bohemian radicals. Still, in the years following the end of the Kaiser's Reich it was simply not possible to be an *avant-garde* artist without becoming associated with Left Wing republicans. Mies, of course, didn't care, just so long as his fellow artists were good—as artists. . . .

Mies's next project—an office building of reinforced concrete and glass—was also exhibited by the Novembergruppe. It was a design startlingly different from the rather exuberantly free forms of the two glass towers; for here Mies took the most rational plan form, the pure rectangle, and framed it with a regularly spaced grid of reinforced concrete columns. These, in turn, carried concrete floor slabs that were cantilevered out beyond the face of the outside columns and turned up to form continuous, concrete parapets at each floor level. Above each parapet and reaching up to the floor slab above, Mies placed ribbon windows that ran, uninterrupted, around the perimeter of the building.

Today this starkly horizontal structure seems very familiar; in debased form it has been built in most large American cities. But, in the

Concrete office-building project, 1922. The entrance portico is seen at left. (Courtesy, Museum of Modern Art)

year 1922, when Mies designed this austere and uncompromising structure, its form was anything but familiar. Eric Mendelsohn, who was perhaps more directly influenced by this project than any other architect of the period, did not build his famous ribbon-window department store for Schocken, in Chemnitz, until six years later; and Peter Behrens did not take up the theme until 1935, in his tobacco factory at Linz, Austria. Since then, of course, the ribbon-window building with cantilevered floor slabs around the periphery has become the single, most commonly used office structure in the world.

Unfortunately, most of Mies's imitators never really investigated his 1922 project as closely as they might have done. For Mies incorporated in it several ideas that are worth exploring further. For example, there was more than one good reason for making this building a strong horizontal structure: first, of course, there was Mies's feeling that reinforced concrete lent itself uncommonly well to this sort of cantilevered structure, and that cantilevers, being the projection of horizontal elements beyond the vertical column frame, tended to create horizontal rather than vertical patterns. Still, in his two glass towers Mies had used cantilevered floor slabs also; yet the exterior expression of the glass skin had been a series of closely spaced, vertical mullions dividing the glass and running the full height of the building, from sidewalk to roof line. Theoretically, Mies might have done the same thing in his 1922 project; yet he chose, instead, to make this building an uncompromisingly horizontal composition.

The reason is really quite simple: while the glass towers were to be twenty and thirty stories in height, respectively, the 1922 building was going to be only eight stories high. Its proportions were going to be largely horizontal in any event; therefore Mies felt that it was necessary to underline the horizontal nature of the building rather than fight it with a vertically patterned skin of glass. Many of the ribbon-window buildings we see nowadays in New York or Chicago are twenty or thirty stories high, with the result that the horizontal emphasis of the ribbon pattern is at disturbing odds with the vertical "soar" of the building mass. It was perfectly obvious to Mies that no building could be a clear statement unless its proportions and details were related, from the smallest unit to the over-all form.

Out of his decision to make this a horizontal building, Mies developed a second set of details which have been largely ignored by his imitators. In a vertical building, Mies felt, it was possible to let the verticals rise straight up into the sky, without cutting them off in any formal fashion. (Louis Sullivan's "cap," terminating the vertical ascent of his expressed columns, always seemed a little incongruous, especially as Sullivan knew that the only way to stop his soaring verticals was to make the cap a heavy "lid" to hold down the building. . . .) But a horizontal building, Mies saw, needed a definite horizontal line to terminate the sweep of ribbons, and it had to be decidedly different from the ribbons below it. Mies's slim-edged roof slab on top of the 1922 building was a simple and convincing answer.

Finally, there was the problem of how to get into a horizontal building. (It is a matter of constant bafflement to the average layman that architects find it so hard to design entrances; yet this is just about the most difficult aesthetic problem in the development of any building.) In Mies's horizontal structure, there was no way of inserting a meaningful entrance without interrupting the pattern of the horizontal ribbons in some manner. Most architects would have cut into the horizontal pattern with a heavily framed entrance rectangle, hoping that no one would pay too much attention to the violation of formal and structural principle involved. Mies, as usual, cut the Gordian knot by simply interrupting his second-floor ribbon for the width of the entrance lobby. The width of the entrance was not framed in any way; instead, the gap between the horizontal ribbons was filled with a rather monumental (and classical) flight of steps revealing for the first time the great concrete columns recessed behind the façade of the building. No better and more direct way of entering a horizontal ribbon building has been discovered since.

Here, as in the glass towers, there emerges something of Mies which has set him apart from most of his contemporaries. The fundamental concept of the building is, as usual, astonishing in its simplicity. Yet, beyond the seemingly "obvious" simplicity of the concept, there appear a host of carefully developed details as unobtrusive as the fine stitching on a well-tailored suit, but just as important. "God," Mies likes to say, "is in the details." He says it only half jokingly.

I V

SHORTLY AFTER MIES completed his design for the ribbon-window building, he produced two other projects of far-reaching importance. Like the glass towers and the office building, these two projects—a brick villa and a concrete villa—were never built. They, too, were first exhibited by the Novembergruppe; and, like the earlier projects, these two designs can be traced in part to outside influences in the related arts.

As a matter of fact, Mies has always denied that he was influenced directly by painting or sculpture. "One day, when Henry-Russell Hitchcock (the well-known critic and historian) came to see me," Mies once said, "he was surprised to see my collection of Klee paintings. He was sure that I would have some Mondrians on my walls!" However that may be, the painters, sculptors, and architects of Mondrian's persuasion —all members of the Dutch De Stijl group—*did* exhibit in Berlin in the early 1920's, and the leader of the De Stijl movement, Theo van Doesburg, had visited Berlin regularly from 1922 on. So, it is at least possible that Mies's extraordinarily linear and asymmetrically composed plans for the two villas were influenced by the interlocking lines, squares, and rectangles of De Stijl painting. Indeed, the brick villa, with its interlocking rectangular glass and brick volumes looks very much like a De Stijl sculpture by Vantongerloo; and the plan is clearly reminiscent of Mondrian's early paintings. All of this work was well known to Mies. In 1923 he and the De Stijl abstractionist, Hans Richter (who worked primarily with films), had begun to produce the magazine G—a publication devoted to all the arts. (G stood for the German word *Gestaltung*, or, creative action.) And Mies, being primarily involved in exhibition design, saw all the exhibits of De Stijl and Russian Constructivism that reached Germany.

Yet Mies was also bitterly opposed to formalism. "We reject all esthetic speculation, all doctrine, all formalism," he wrote in the first issue of G. "Architecture is the will of an epoch translated into space; living, changing, new . . . To create form out of the nature of our tasks with the methods of our time—*this is our task*." In other words, he not only rejected the De Stijl formalism as an influence (just as he rejected the then rampant expressionism as an influence), he actively opposed both; and his published writings of the period prove that this is no wishful afterthought on Mies's part today. Still, the graphic means employed by Mies to present his projects, especially in the plan drawings, are strongly reminiscent of the graphic means developed by De Stijl artists.

Much more fundamental was the influence of architects like Berlage and Frank Lloyd Wright. Mies had seen the great Wright exhibition that came to Berlin in 1910. "The dynamic impulse emanating from Wright's work invigorated a whole generation," he wrote later. The brick villa, especially, shows how strongly Mies felt that "dynamic impulse." The building is planned exactly like a typical Wrightian

Concrete villa project, 1924. Different elements of the plan are clearly articulated. (Courtesy, Museum of Modern Art)

country house: a core of rooms, screened from one another, but also partly open to one another to permit the easy flow of space between them; and an extension of this core of rooms far out into the landscape by means of long walls that reach out from the interior all the way into the surrounding gardens. This general principle had been followed by Wright in many of his early houses during the first decade of the century. Although the principle was sometimes obscured—because Wright tended to be fussy and ornate in his details—it was nonetheless visible to a trained eye. What Mies did with this principle is almost as astonishing as what he had done with Behrens's neoclassicism a few years earlier: with a single stroke of the pen he brought Wright up to date and made him modern! The plan of the brick villa, done in 1923, is in fact a preview of the sort of simple and strong statement which Wright himself was to make with his Usonian houses of the 1930's.

In its plastic composition, however, the brick villa owed very little to Wright. Its brick nature seemed to suggest to Mies the sort of blocky, squared-off composition which Berlage had handled to perfection. In a way the villa is an extension of brick-building—masses and volumes formed by bricks and interlocking much in the way in which bricks interlock. Although the brick villa was a radical statement for its time (especially as no *avant-gardist* worth his salt would have seriously thought of building with as old-fashioned a material as brick!), it now seems somewhat dated in everything but its dynamic, entirely modern plan.

The concrete villa Mies designed in the following year has none of this dated look. In plan composition it owes something to Wright, although the courts and formal pedestals (with formal flights of steps) show that Mies never forgot the valuable lessons he learned from Schinkel. But, in structure and form this villa is a typically Miesian statement, clear and precise, and unmistakably of reinforced concrete. There are great, sweeping cantilevers, long ribbons of glass, corner windows, and deep roof overhangs. There is a dynamic quality in this building which not only spells "reinforced concrete" to perfection, but also seems to suggest some sort of "American" style. Where the brick villa, despite its expanding, pinwheel-shaped plan, seemed rather tight and confined in its volumes, the concrete villa is an expanding organism that somehow suggests a spacious continent. Its wings, arranged in a modified S-shaped pattern, separated areas of different function much as the "articulated" house plans of today try to do. Although it was never built, the concrete villa had an influence upon some of Mies's contemporaries comparable to the influence of his ribbon-window building. It looks so familiar and modern to us today because it is so similar to the kind of house made popular in California by men like Richard Neutra.

By the end of 1924 Mies had not built a single important modern building. The very precarious economic and political situation in Germany, with its wild inflationary cycles and its severe unemployment, had greatly curtailed building activities throughout the country. Mies and others of his generation built very little during those early years after World War I; indeed, most of their work consisted of projects that were published, exhibited, widely discussed, and discarded. To "practical men," Mies's projects seemed of questionable value; but, among *avant-gardists*, Mies's concepts, with their enormous precision and clarity of statement, were greatly admired. Still, the acid test was yet to come: would Mies be able to build what he preached? A contemporary writer on architecture spoke condescendingly of Mies as having made some "valuable suggestions," and hoped that his "beautiful, idealistic projects" would withstand the "fire of practicality." He need not have worried; the only obstacle Mies has ever had to face is the obstacle of an outdated, outdistanced technology.

V

B Y 1925 MIES's astonishing and well-publicized projects made him sufficiently known so that private and public clients began to come to him more and more often. He built several brick- and-glass villas for wealthy businessmen in the fashionable suburbs of Berlin and in the Rhineland, while at the same time constructing a monument to the German Communist leaders, Karl Liebknecht and Rosa Luxemburg, and designing a low-cost housing project for the City of Berlin. Although none of these structures had the daring of his glass towers, they all revealed Mies to be, in all likelihood, the best *builder* among the modernists of his generation. The brickwork used in his elegant villas can be compared only to some sort of inlaid mosaic of precious stones.

(Mies often went down to the kilns to make a painstaking selection of the bricks he wanted before they were shipped to any of his jobs.) Indeed, the villas were designed with infinite care so that all their dimensions would be multiples of the standard brick dimension, with the result that no "fudging" of edges or openings occurred anywhere.

Although some modernists in Europe had begun to use brick by 1925, most of Mies's contemporaries insisted upon using smooth surfaces of stucco in the hopes of achieving the sort of "Machine Art" effects that were such a favorite with Le Corbusier and Gropius. Actually, these surfaces were little more than a pretense, for behind the skin of stucco most architects concealed a traditional wall of concrete block. Still, everyone was hoping to see the great day when industry would produce large, smoothly finished sheets of building materials in modular dimensions, so that architects could assemble their structures using big building components rather than the small-scale stones and bricks of the past. The hope became father to the completed building, and the typically modern house or store of 1925 was a smoothly surfaced affair that looked as if it had rolled off the assembly line—although, in reality, it had been put together by the same old-fashioned building methods used by every architect for a hundred years and more. The only difference was that as the surfaces were smooth, rather than decorated, every streak and other blemish began to show almost immediately!

In his purist attitude toward structure, Mies rebelled against this sort of sham. He was convinced that only an architecture honestly arrived at by the explicit use of available building materials could be justified in moral terms. Because brick and brick masons were available, he built brick houses. But, because he, better than most of those who paid lip service to industrialized building, knew what this could mean to architecture, he insisted in his brick-bonding upon a degree of precision that tended to impose even upon the *craft* of brick-building all the discipline of industrialized construction. For Mies saw it very clearly indeed. "I consider the industrialization of building methods the key problem of the day," Mies said in 1924. "Once we succeed in this, our social, economic, technical and even artistic problems will be easy to solve. How can industrialization be carried out? . . . The problem before us is [to effect] a revolution in the whole nature of the building industry. The nature of the building process will not change as long as we employ essentially the same [traditional] building materials, for they require manual labor. . . . Our first consideration, therefore, must be to find a new building material. . . . It must be a light material which not only permits but requires industrial production. All the [building] parts will be made in a factory and the work at the site will consist only of assemblage, requiring extremely few man-hours. . . . I am convinced that traditional methods of construction will disappear. In case anyone regrets that the house of the future can no longer be made by hand workers, he should remember that the automobile is no longer manufactured by carriage-makers." All very familiar to us today, some thirty-five years later. But, in 1924 Mies's clear perception of the central issues facing the building industry—and, hence, architecture—was remarkable, to say the least. For Mies was really drawing up, in those few words, a precise prescription for exactly the sort of building panel that modern industry is now, at long last, beginning to mass produce: a plastic or light-weight metal panel designed to be bolted together on the job so rapidly that in 1955 a twenty-five-story office building in Manhattan could be completely enclosed with such panels in a matter of twelve hours—or, to use Mies's prescription of 1924 again: "the work at the site will consist only of assemblage, requiring extremely few man-hours."

Meanwhile, until such building materials were available, Mies felt that the traditional ones would have to do the job. "The old brick masonry has many advantages," he said. And indeed it has; one of the most important is that it weathers well if handled properly. Few *avant-garde* houses built in Europe in the early 1920's have stood the test of time as well as those built by Mies. His traditional training, his experience both in his father's shop and on building sites in the Rhineland, had served him extremely well; for he was one of the few modernists who was not a *theoretical* architect, but a master builder with experience firmly rooted in the past.

It is not his traditional building experience alone that has served Mies well throughout his career. It is also his early training, in Behrens's office and before, in the classical tradition. It was fashionable in the

1920's (as it is today) to scoff at the academies and to deny the validity of their teaching. Yet the traditionalists knew (and the few surviving ones still know) a good deal about architecture which the modernists could study with considerable profit. They knew not only how to get their buildings to weather well, to stand the test of time; they also knew how to relate their buildings to one another and to the landscape around them. Many Americans, having heard Louis Sullivan's and Frank Lloyd Wright's laments about the 1893 Chicago exposition, in which the disciples of the Paris Beaux Arts Academy stifled the exuberant sprouts of a new and originally American architecture, now equate the Beaux Arts with the devil. Yet the Chicago exposition, for all its fakery, had unity; all its component buildings related to one another; their cornices all lined up; the progression from space to space, from level to level, indoors and, just as importantly, outdoors, was carefully studied. Compared to the hideous shambles of the Brussels World's Fair of 1958, Chicago was a dream of planning and of unity.

The most impressive quality possessed by Mies's early modern villas —apart from their precision of detail, their large and simple areas of glass, their daring concrete roof cantilevers, and their openness in interior planning—is their classical serenity of setting. The first radical houses built by Le Corbusier, Gropius, Breuer, and others often seemed to be almost dropped out of the sky to settle where they might in the landscape. Mies's houses, on the other hand, are always sited on terraces, surrounded by retaining walls, reached by means of short, easy, almost monumental flights of steps. They look as though they belonged in their setting from the day they were completed. Wright, who was the past master of siting a building in the country, used other than classical means to achieve that same sense of belonging. Mies, a classicist in spirit though not in practice, adapted the devices of Schinkel and of those who inspired Schinkel to achieve a similar effect.

Knowledge of how to build and of how to place the building, and a calm, self-assured, instinctive knowledge of what was truly "modern" and what was a passing fad—these qualities have made Mies's houses of the 1920's almost timeless. Where much of Corbu's work of the same years has the charm, in retrospect, of a brilliant period piece, Mies's

Monument to Karl Liebknecht and Rosa Luxemburg, Berlin, 1926. The massing of horizontal forms foreshadows some of Wright's later houses. The monument is, actually, a thick wall treated as a massive relief. (Courtesy, Museum of Modern Art)

houses of those days might well be built in the 1950's by anyone sufficiently well-to-do to afford such perfect workmanship.

The monument to the martyred German Communist leaders, Karl Liebknecht and Rosa Luxemburg, was built of brick also. It was a composition of superimposed and cantilevered masses of masonry, somewhat like Vantongerloo's De Stijl sculpture, but, unlike it, very structural in feeling. (In Vantongerloo's compositions the rectangular masses always interlocked to create a play of forms almost equally valid regardless of which side was "up." Whereas Mies's monument was an assembly of massive, rectangular "slabs," one always resting upon the one below, each cantilevered out from a clearly defined base, or recessed above a similarly defined projecting plane.)

In some respects Mies's monument is much closer to Wright's Larkin building in Buffalo, done in 1904, or to certain details in Wright's Robie house in Chicago, built in 1908, though here again, as in his brick-villa project, Mies seemed to "modernize" Wright by stripping his dynamic forms of all their superfluous, Art Nouveau trimmings.

Indeed, there almost seems to have been an unconscious give-and-take between Wright and Mies during the 1920's and 1930's: for the Lieb-knecht-Luxemburg monument of 1926, while based in part upon Wright's earliest work, also appears like a preview of Wright's most famous house, "Falling Water," at Bear Run, Pennsylvania, the stunning composition of planes and cantilevers jutting out over a waterfall.

As recently as 1957 the U.S. Department was deeply disturbed that Mies's "dossier" contained evidence of his having built a monument to two German Communists. Mies, with characteristic honesty, never tried to explain away this excursion into political architecture. To him, people are admirable when they hold deep convictions and act according to them. Needless to say, Mies has never tried to ignore the quality of such convictions: his dealings with the Nazi charlatans are clear evidence of his deep-seated moral sense. But, what was the quality of Lieb-knecht's and Luxemburg's convictions when judged, not in retrospect or in the light of today's experience with Soviet imperialism, but in the light of the German revolution against the Kaiser and against the Kaiser's war? To Mies and to many of his contemporaries, Karl Lieb-knecht and Rosa Luxemburg stood for social justice, for economic as well as political democracy, for planning, for peace—in short, for all the things the Kaiser's Germany had more or less denied its citizens. Mies felt then (and feels today) that these two Communist leaders held honest convictions and lived according to them. He was not particularly interested in their party allegiances; he was interested only in their moral caliber. When they were assassinated by extremists of the Right, Mies felt honored to be chosen to build their monument. No one can tell where Liebknecht and Luxemburg would have stood after the great Soviet purges of the 1930's, after the Hitler-Stalin pact, after the rape of Hungary. To judge Mies or anyone else by political criteria established in retrospect is obviously preposterous, and it is to the credit of the State Department that it has apparently reversed itself and awarded Mies the commission of building the new U.S. Consulate at São Paulo, Brazil, thus certifying him as politically pure.

Although Mies was to return to brick masonry frequently in later years, the completion of the brick villas and the brick monument were a distinct milestone in his career. He was now sufficiently well known to be appointed, in 1926, First Vice-President of the Deutsche Werk-bund—the organization that, in 1914, had given Gropius his chance to build the glass- and-steel exhibition structure in Cologne. The Werk-bund had been founded by a group of architects, artists, and indus-trialists to attempt to achieve an integration of art and industry in order to raise the level of German product design. Mies's elevation to the effective leadership of the Werkbund at that time was to prove of tre-mendous importance to the future of modern architecture; for the or-ganization was about to hold its second, major exhibition at Stuttgart, and Mies was appointed Director of that effort. What he did with the Stuttgart exhibition advanced the popular cause of architecture more decisively than any other single event of the 1920's.

V I

THE SIGNIFICANCE of the Werkbund exhibition in Stuttgart was twofold: first, it represented a kind of summary of the total achievement of modern European architecture and furniture design up to that moment, and suggested some of the future potentialities of the movement. And, second, it told something about the qualities of its Director—Ludwig Mies van der Rohe—who, as first Vice-President of the Werkbund, had been put in charge of this extraordinary undertaking.

If Le Corbusier or Frank Lloyd Wright had been placed in a similar position, the chances are that the Weissenhof development would have been a one-man exhibition—admittedly exciting, but, still, a vehicle for the propagation of a single point of view. Mies, self-effacing as he is, did the almost inconceivable: he laid down the general ground rules for the exhibit, and then threw the whole exhibition open to every modern European architect of any note! And even the ground rules laid down by Mies were liberal in the extreme. "I have refrained from laying down a rigid program," he explained, "in order to leave each individual as free as possible to carry out his ideas. In drawing up the general plan I felt it important to avoid regulations that might interfere with free expression." Mies's first "general plan" was quite prophetic of today's most advanced city-planning concepts: he proposed to have all circulation *within* the Weissenhof limited to pedestrians, and to provide parking facilities for automobiles along the perimeter of the development. This, however, implied some sort of central ownership and control of the whole area, and the City of Stuttgart found it necessary to have the Weissenhof exhibit designed in such a way that each building could, eventually, be sold to an individual owner. To facilitate this, Mies adjusted his site plan to provide through streets and individual parking areas for each residential unit.

There were thirty-three of these residential units in all; some of them were single-family houses, others were apartment blocks containing as many as twenty-four flats. In drawing up the list of participants, Mies showed a high degree of discrimination: almost every modern European architect of importance was included, although several of them had not achieved their present recognition when Mies made his choice. In addition to Le Corbusier and his cousin, Pierre Jeanneret, Mies invited Gropius; J. J. P. Oud, the leading Dutch architect of the De Stijl group; Victor Bourgeois, the Belgian modernist who had produced some rather fantastic city-planning projects during the first decades of the century; Bruno Taut; Hans Poelzig; and Peter Behrens—all of them German pioneer architects whose work is still in high regard today; Hans Scharoun, whose strikingly individualistic style has dominated German architecture throughout the years since the end of World War II; and several others. Eric Mendelsohn was invited, but was unable to participate. Mies himself designed a long apartment block.

The scope of the Weissenhof development was remarkable. Here was a full-scale exhibit concerned with the most advanced theories of construction and design, and financed by a relatively small, provincial city and an association of artists and industrialists—all operating in a defeated and impoverished nation! Nothing comparable has been done since in any other country; several attempts to duplicate the Weissenhof experiment in the U.S. failed because no one in the U.S. building industry has had sufficient vision or guts to put up the required funds— even temporarily! More than thirty years after it was built, the Weissenhof exhibit is still unique—a remarkable testimony to the vision and courage of a nation and its industry.

Mies had a very clear idea of what the Weissenhof experiment ought to achieve. "In spite of its technical and economic aspects, the problem of the modern dwelling is primarily one of building-art," he said. "It is a complex problem of planning and can therefore be solved only by creative minds, not by calculation or organization. Therefore, I felt it imperative, in spite of current talk about 'rationalization' and 'standardization,' to keep the project from being one-sided or doctrinaire. I have therefore invited leading representatives of the modern movement to make their contribution. . . ." The different contributions varied both in quality and in emphasis: Corbu's two buildings have been described earlier; they were perhaps the most imaginative structures at the Weissenhof. Gropius built two houses made entirely of prefabricated wall and roof panels, equipped with prefabricated storage walls and furnished with Marcel Breuer's airy tubular steel chairs. These two houses remain the most rational statement of prefabrication to have been achieved to date, and no prefabricated house built since the Weissenhof opened in 1927 has gone very far beyond Gropius's remarkable demonstration. When Gropius turned seventy, in 1953, a party was given for him in Chicago at which Mies, who is usually the most taciturn guest at any such occasion, rose to make what must have been the longest speech of his career. "I am glad I had once the possibility in Stuttgart to give Gropius a hand so that he could demonstrate his ideas on industrialization and prefabrication," Mies said, among other things. "He built two houses there which were the most interesting ones in the exhibition." As usual, Mies was being excessively modest, for his own block of apartments was a beautiful and clear-cut achieve-

Apartment house at the Weissenhof exhibition, 1927. Garden side of block, showing sheltered roof terraces above. (Courtesy, Museum of Modern Art)

ment as well: steel-framed, finished in stucco, topped with sheltered roof gardens and endowed with long bands of glass and prefabricated partitions and storage walls, this block would be remarkable in any development of garden apartments put up in the 1950's. By no means other than perfectionist detail and perfect proportion, Mies succeeded in creating one of the best housing units put up in Europe in the 1920's. Indeed, the only comparable structure of its type at the Weissenhof was the strip of five row houses designed by Oud—a neat demonstration of small-scale housing which continues to influence planners to this day.

The Weissenhof exhibit was an important event in the history of modern furniture design as well. Probably the most famous and most widely used chair designed since World War I is the so-called tubular steel "cantilever chair"—a chair whose profile is, roughly, S-shaped, and whose frame consists of a continuous steel tube. It is today a familiar staple in every restaurant from Bangkok to New York.

The history of this particular chair is full of twists and turns, and full of bitter conflicts—all of which, somehow, culminated at the Weissenhof exhibit. The first man to use tubular steel for the frames of chairs and tables was the young Hungarian-born architect Marcel Breuer, who had been put in charge of the furniture workshop at Gropius's famous design school—the Bauhaus—in 1924 when he was only 22 years old. Sometime in 1925 Breuer, who used to ride around on a bicycle in those days, realized that the tubing that formed the handlebars of his bicycle could be bent into more complex shapes to form the supports for pieces of furniture. He approached the manufacturers of this sort of tubing to obtain their assistance in the development of a few experimental chairs. Like many practical men faced with a new idea, the manufacturers thought that Breuer was mad, but finally consented; and Breuer began to produce a whole series of chairs and tables of elegantly curved steel tubing, with seats and backs formed of stretched canvas or caning, and table tops formed of polished plywood slabs screwed to the tubular frame.

The best and simplest of Breuer's tubular-steel inventions was undoubtedly a little stool whose continuous frame, in profile, looked like an upside-down letter U, and whose top was either of stretched canvas or of wood—depending upon whether the piece was to be used for sitting on, or as an occasional table. This stool was mass produced for the new Bauhaus buildings designed and built by Gropius in Dessau in 1926. When these buildings were nearing completion, the Dutch architect, Mart Stam (who was also to be represented at the Weissenhof in 1927), came to visit the Bauhaus, and Breuer showed him around. When they came to the U-shaped stools, Breuer picked up one of them, set it down on its side, so that it seemed to "kneel" on one side of the U, and said: "That's going to be my next chair!" Mart Stam, who was doing some tubular steel furniture of his own at the time, may or may not have remembered the incident. In any event, shortly after Stam returned to Rotterdam from Dessau, he produced an S-shaped cantilever chair remarkably similar to the "kneeling" version of Breuer's U-shaped stool. It was a rather crude affair, consisting of straight lengths of plumber's pipe with elbow connections at all corners, rather than continuous tubing. To the "kneeling" U shape was added an extra length of pipe to form the back.

Original "cantilever chair," designed in 1926. (Courtesy, Museum of Modern Art)

While all this was going on, Mies had been working quietly and independently on a cantilever chair of his own—a similarly curved frame based on much the same principle both Breuer and Stam seemed to be exploring. However, Mies's chair was the first of the three to be completed, and a patent was issued to Mies which assured him of royalties on the basic design for years to come. As a matter of fact, it is highly unlikely that Mies had been influenced by Breuer's chairs and tables, except insofar as Breuer had been the first to use chromium-plated, tubular steel for furniture. Mies's chairs were quite different in profile from the almost angular S shapes arrived at by Stam and Breuer; *his* had the slow, graceful curve of a Brancusi sculpture and the ample width of Mies himself. Moreover, unlike the Stam and Breuer models, Mies's chairs, though exceedingly beautiful, had a disconcerting tendency to tip forward and propel the sitter across the room as he or she tried to get out of the chair. A later adjustment helped to fix that.

At the Weissenhof, Stam exhibited his own, rather clumsy S chairs; Mies exhibited his very suave and elegant S chairs; and Breuer (who furnished Gropius's houses) could only show some of his many early, revolutionary tubular steel chairs and tables, but not his own version of the S chair, which, in fact, was not to appear on the market until the following year. It was a tragic thing for Breuer, who had done all the pioneering in this field: not only was his best design to be developed by others first, but—to make matters even worse—*his* version of the S chair turned out to be the one that is still mass produced the world over, and at no profit to himself. Only Mies ever obtained a mechanical patent on the basic idea of a cantilever chair, and Mies's S chairs, because of their fairly high cost and somewhat impractical (though beautiful) performance, were never really mass produced at all!

Despite this little storm in a teacup, the Weissenhof development in the hills above Stuttgart was a huge success. A handsome book on the development was published by the Werkbund, and each architect explained his contribution in detail. Mies, the man of few words, had built the largest structure in the exhibition and, characteristically, contributed the briefest statement in the book—twelve lines of tight-lipped prose, entitled "About My Block," as opposed to some 200 lines of descriptive matter written by Gropius to explain his small, prefabricated units. Each word in Mies's statement reads as if it had been put down under extreme duress, and the whole statement could hardly have been drier or more reserved. His contention that "less is more" has always provided Mies with a perfect excuse for cutting short his own public statements.

Perhaps the finest compliment paid to the Weissenhof was unconsciously contributed by the Nazis, who singled out the development as a prime example of Kulturbolschewismus and Degenerate Architecture. One of the first "cultural" acts performed by the Nazis after they came to power in 1933 was to print photo-montage picture postcards of the Weissenhof showing its streets populated by Arabs and their camels. The montage and its caption—"Arab Village, Stuttgart"—was meant to convey the depths of depravity to which the Weimar Republic's architects had descended. Next, the guardians of German culture put pitched roofs on top of the flat-roofed Weissenhof structures, thus infusing them with a shot of Blood and Soil. Still, the development was almost recognizable until Allied air raids did serious damage to some of the structures (and, especially, the glass walls) during World War II. After that, the window openings were bricked or boarded up, or narrowed down in size to preserve precious heat during the winter. By 1945 the Weissenhof was but a hollow and deformed shell of its former self. In the late 1950's, however, efforts were under way to restore the Werkbund's spectacular achievement to its former glory. The Bonn Republic's first President, Theodor Heuss, had once headed the Werkbund and now saw to it that the Werkbund's finest achievement was salvaged for posterity.

V I I

T
HE SUCCESS of the Weissenhof exhibit gave Mies considerable
standing among modern architects in Germany, so that when the time
came for the German government to select an architect to design its
Pavilion for the 1929 International exposition in Barcelona, Mies was
chosen to do the job.

The first thing that needs to be said about the Barcelona Pavilion is
that it is considered by many—to this day—the most beautiful modern
building to have been constructed anywhere. This is so for several reasons: first, Mies decided that the German exhibit was going to be the
Pavilion itself, not something displayed inside it. (After all, who could
remember what had been exhibited inside Paxton's Crystal Palace, or

Main approach to Barcelona Pavilion. Walls at right are of green Tinian marble. (Courtesy, Mies van der Rohe)

inside Sullivan's Transportation building at the Chicago Fair in 1893?) As a result, there were practically no functional requirements worth mentioning, so that the Pavilion could, in fact, be a pure exercise in spatial composition. Second, there was the fact that money seems to have been no object: somehow, Mies was able to specify Roman travertine, Tinian marble, gray transparent glass, onyx, chromium-plated steel columns—in short, the most precious materials available to any architect. And, finally, there was Mies's phenomenal display of genius. No doubt the Barcelona Pavilion showed the usual "influences"—some stronger than others. But it showed, above all, the hand of an artist of such elegance and perfection that no modern building put up since—except, perhaps, one or two of Mies's later works—has been able to escape invidious comparisons with the detailing of this lovely structure!

Here, at last, was the fulfillment of the promise of Mies's glass-tower projects. Here was the tangible evidence of the genius that had lain dormant during the years of the well-proportioned, well-built (but rather dry) brick villas and stucco apartments. Here, at last, was the emergence of a master equal in every way to Wright and to Le Corbusier—a master with so sure a hand that no one would ever again be able to question his prowess.

The Barcelona Pavilion was a small, one-story jewel of a building placed upon a wide pedestal of travertine, part of which held a pool lined in black glass. The building itself consisted of a sweeping, horizontal roof plane supported on eight chromium-plated steel columns, cross-shaped in section (rather than H-shaped like most standard steel columns.) Below this roof, there was a rectangular composition of glass and marble walls that formed a series of beautiful spaces, all open to one another and open to various outdoor areas beyond the glass. The only objects shown inside these spaces were several elegant chairs and tables especially designed by Mies. The glass walls were divided by slim, vertical bars of chromium-plated steel; some of the glass was a transparent gray (a shade in increasing use in American buildings since 1945 to reduce sky glare); other walls were of etched glass, two sheets back to back, with light sources between the glass sheets to make the wall a brilliantly luminous panel.

In their asymmetrical, rectilinear composition, the walls of the Barcelona Pavilion looked in plan very much like a De Stijl painting. In the third dimension, the building had some of the sweep of Wright's Robie house. And the pedestal seemed reminiscent of Schinkel's neoclassicism. Yet, even if these influences were present (and they probably were), Mies improved upon each of them: Van Doesburg never painted as beautiful a composition as the Barcelona plan; Schinkel never designed a pedestal more elegant than the travertine base that supported Mies's Pavilion; and Wright never composed a more modern, more striking sweep of horizontals than those that gave the Barcelona Pavilion its magnificent verve.

At one end of the Pavilion the green Tinian marble walls that enclosed the interior seemed to slide out, under, and beyond the roof plane to form an enclosed sculpture court whose floor was largely taken up

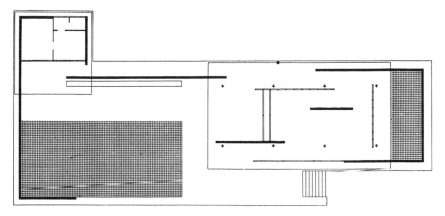

Plan of Barcelona Pavilion, 1929. Shaded areas are pools lined with black glass. (Courtesy, Mies van der Rohe)

Pool and principal exhibition area of Barcelona Pavilion. (Courtesy, Museum of Modern Art)

by another reflecting pool, also lined with black glass. On a small base in this pool Mies placed a statue by Georg Kolbe, and the resulting composition has become a favorite example of those who advocate collaboration between architects on the one hand, and sculptors and painters on the other. The Kolbe did, indeed, look beautiful in this setting; but, while Mies always intended to put a figure into this little court, the idea that he collaborated with Kolbe in the design of this setting is, unfortunately, a myth. The truth is that Mies was very anxious to borrow a Lehmbruck figure for this spot; and when this proved to be impossible to arrange, he grabbed a taxi on one of his last days in Berlin before leaving for Barcelona, drove out to Kolbe's studio, and borrowed the best substitute he could find. . . . Although the success of the Kolbe in this classic court does not prove that collaboration between artists and architects is unnecessary, it does suggest that there may be other and better ways toward integration of the arts.

In addition to the Kolbe statue, there were only about a dozen objects exhibited in the Barcelona Pavilion—and all were exquisite. Specifically, the exhibit consisted of a couple of Mies's so-called Barcelona chairs, half a dozen Barcelona stools of related design, and two or three glass-topped tables also generally related to the chairs in concept. That concept was to take two modified X shapes of flat, chromium-plated steel bars, join them with crossbars in two or three places, apply to them a web of broad leather straps, and rest leather-covered pillows on the webbing to form the actual seating surfaces. In the case of the tables, the modified X frame was topped by inch-thick slabs of glass.

The delicate curvature of the X-shaped legs, the perfect finish of the plated steel and the leather upholstery, and the magnificent, almost monumental proportions of the pieces—all these factors have made Mies's Barcelona furniture "timeless," rather than easily dated. Like everything else Mies did at Barcelona, these pieces were expensive to make; but they were made to last through the ages, both in terms of solidity and in terms of design.

Unfortunately, the Barcelona Pavilion was dismantled at the close of the exhibition and shipped back to Germany in pieces. Where it ended up, Mies was never able to discover. Yet its influence upon mod-

Sculpture court of Barcelona Pavilion with statue by Georg Kolbe. (Courtesy, Mies van der Rohe)

Interior of Barcelona Pavilion with Barcelona chairs and stools. (Courtesy, Mies van de Rohe)

Barcelona chair, 1929. (Courtesy, Museum of Modern Art)

ern architects the world over has been tremendous. Some of Wright's best Usonian houses of the late 1930's were quite clearly influenced by the grandiose simplicity of the Barcelona Pavilion—just as Mies had been influenced by the sweep of Wright's Robie house of 1908. But quite apart from Wright (who, needless to say, never acknowledged any such influences), there were and are numerous others—especially among the younger generation of modern architects—who are unable to this day to escape the powerful impact of this jewellike structure. Most of Paul Rudolph's early houses in Florida, in the late 1940's and early 1950's, were variations on the Barcelona theme; I. M. Pei's penthouse office for William Zeckendorf, on a roof top above Madison Avenue, is in part almost a replica of the 1929 Pavilion—as are some of the beautiful details of the plaza at the base of Pei's Mile High Center in Denver, Colorado. In Los Angeles, of course, a highly successful firm of architects built a near-copy of the Barcelona Pavilion out of stucco and sheet aluminum and turned it into the firm's offices. From Tokyo to Stockholm the Barcelona Pavilion has been copied in large or small part, in cheap or precious materials, again and again. And the monumental Mies-sized chairs and tables designed for Barcelona remain to this day the only standard modern pieces the leading architects of the U.S. and Europe find suitable for the furnishing of important spaces in public buildings. Indeed, the reception room in the offices of Skidmore, Owings & Merrill, in New York—a firm that has designed and built more "Miesian" buildings than Mies himself—is furnished entirely with Mies's Barcelona chairs, and lined with the same glass walls set in chromium which Mies developed for Barcelona!

Mies's critics have pointed out, with some justification, that he is at his best when there are no serious functional problems to solve and when there are no budget limitations worth mentioning. They have said that Mies is really an architectural sculptor—admittedly a master at the manipulation of spaces and forms, materials and finishes—but that architecture is a mixture in equal parts of function and aesthetics. Mies's answer to this is that buildings have a long life; that most of them outlive their original function and must adapt themselves to different uses; and that the only permanent ingredient a building can be expected to possess is beauty. History, of course, is on Mies's side; nobody remembers whether the Parthenon ever worked really well, but everyone remembers what Phidias did there for the eternal splendor and glory of architecture. By the same token, no one will long remember that the German Pavilion at Barcelona contained no exhibits—and could not have contained any exhibits—in the conventional sense; but history will record that in 1929, on a hill above Barcelona, Mies van der Rohe built the most beautiful structure of an era.

V I I I

THE BARCELONA PAVILION was no isolated flash in the pan. During the two or three years after the Pavilion was dismantled, Mies produced half a dozen houses, exhibits, and stores of similar simplicity, precision, and clarity. The best of these were two residences: the Tugendhat house in Brno, Czechoslovakia, built in 1930; and the exhibition house for the Berlin Building exposition of 1931.

What the Villa Savoye is in Corbu's career, what the Robie house is in Wright's work, the Tugendhat house is in Mies's development. In fact, it would be possible to tell the broad story of modern architecture in terms of these three houses—Savoye, Robie, and Tugendhat. It is difficult to imagine that many of today's modern houses would look the way they do without the prior creation of these three.

Living area in Tugendhat house, Brno, Czechoslovakia, 1930. Study is at left. (Courtesy, Mies van der Rohe)

Although the Tugendhat house was, actually, a very practical affair full of closed-off bedrooms, dressing rooms, kitchens, pantries, and all the other "functional" areas that are supposed to give Mies so much trouble, it will be remembered best for its magnificent living space—a huge, open area, walled on three sides with glass extending from floor to ceiling, and subdivided into four or five different and smaller spaces by the merest suggestion of a screen or a free-standing cabinet (today's "space-divider"). To all intents and purposes, the Tugendhat house was the first "glass house"—the first of a whole series of spacious and airy constructions that allowed the trees and lawns to form the visual boundaries of the interior. In many ways the Tugendhat house was very similar to the Barcelona Pavilion in its extraordinarily open plan and its

2 1 7

completely free flow of space—much freer than anything ever attempted by Wright up to that time.

Like the Barcelona Pavilion, the Tugendhat house had cross- rather than H-shaped chromium-plated steel columns spaced far apart to support the roof slab; like the Pavilion, it had free-standing walls of the most precious materials available to the architect—gold and white onyx for some walls, striped black and brown Macassar ebony for a truly majestic semicircular screen around the dining area, black and beige shantung for the curtains. The floors of the Tugendhat house were of white linoleum.

Into this most elegant setting, Mies carefully placed several of his Barcelona chairs and stools, together with a series of new chairs and tables just as beautiful as those he had designed for Barcelona. The finest piece—another classic still in common use today—was a glass-topped coffee table supported on a cross of flat, chromium-plated steel bars. As in every one of his designs, from skyscrapers to dining chairs, Mies reduced each object to its essential elements, and then refined each detail to a point of almost breathtaking beauty and eloquence. There was nothing in this house which did not reflect this process of distillation to the point of utter perfection—not a window mullion, not a heating pipe, not a lighting fixture, not an ash tray. The Barcelona chairs and the special Tugendhat chairs designed by Mies—an upholstered version of the cantilever-chair principle patented by him—were covered with natural pigskin or white vellum; a square rug of natural wool formed an "island" in the open space, defining the main living area; and a Lehmbruck bust on a square pedestal formed the focal point of that space.

No wonder Gropius is supposed to have said, when seeing this villa, that it was a "Sunday house." It is difficult to imagine the place overrun by hordes of happy, mud-caked children. Yet this is almost what happened after World War II, when the local Czech authorities turned the empty and somewhat damaged Tugendhat house into a gymnasium —with parallel bars along the walls—and painted the white linoleum a bright red. A visiting American student was able to take a snapshot of

Living room at night, Tugendhat house. The chairs were specially designed for this house. (Courtesy, Mies van der Rohe)

the house, which she showed to Mies. "And you know," Mies said later, with a grin, "it didn't look bad at all!"

In its prime the Tugendhat house made several points about architecture in a masterly way. Its site was difficult, as the land sloped abruptly and the entrance had to be on the uphill side. Mies treated the top or entrance floor somewhat like a Corbu roof garden, with curved and rectangular forms making a free and open composition. However, one of the most difficult aspects of siting a building on a steep slope is not the question of entrance levels, but the question of how to treat the *sides* of the building. Most architects simply let the natural slope of the land continue past the short sides of their structure, hoping that no one will catch a side view of what looks like a building taking a toboggan ride downhill. Mies, who never leaves a detail to chance (for "God is in the details"), cut back into the slope and framed the Tugendhat house between two level courts carved out of the hillside. As a result, the house looks solidly anchored in the hill, surrounded by terraces that dramatize the natural slope and make the hill "architectural." (This sort of thing would, of course, be frowned upon by Wright's followers, but Mies felt —with Corbu—that if you are an architect, you might as well treat your site architecturally, rather than let the site swallow you up in its own untrammeled contours.)

The Tugendhat house showed Mies intensely sensitive to color. Actually, there were no real *colors* in the house at all—only the muted, natural tones of marble, wood, silk, and leather. Mies's palette is just about confined to whites and off-whites, and blacks and off-blacks. There are never any bright color accents as there are in Corbu's work. One reason for this is that in the glass houses Mies developed since Tugendhat, the ever changing colors in nature are a major part of the spatial experience indoors. "When you have a white house with glass walls," Mies said some years later about his Farnsworth house near Chicago, "you see the trees and bushes and the sky framed in white— and the white emphasizes all the beautiful colors in the landscape." So, in the Tugendhat house, Mies made the landscape his "wallpaper"; indeed, one of the glass walls was really a glass case, filled with planting that lent touches of color to the interior in every season.

Those who denounce Mies as "cold" and call for a more "romantic" approach have completely failed to see how he has used the resources of nature—of the trees and the sun—to make his architecture vibrant with life and color. From the outside, his glass walls reflect the changing seasons, the drifting clouds, the colors of sky and leaves. In the glass skyscrapers, Mies had taken a leaf from Wright's book: he had made each glass wall a many-faceted diamond whose every face would reflect a different sort of scene. The result was a mosaic of refractions and reflections, for each sheet of glass was set into its frame at an angle slightly different from that of the adjoining sheets, so that each sheet tended to reflect a slightly different image. In a house, Mies felt, such a system would produce too many window divisions, and these would obstruct the view from the inside out. The view *out* of a glass *house* is just as important as its exterior appearance; for the landscape suddenly becomes the space within which you live, and the building itself dissolves in its natural setting. The view *out* of a glass *office building*, on the other hand, is less important, and here Mies felt that closely spaced window divisions could be justified. On an urban or suburban site, a house with unshielded glass walls obviously makes no sense, and Mies designed a whole series of beautiful court or patio houses, with walled-in gardens, to cope with the problem of privacy combined with the need for spaciousness presented by just such sites. These court houses are, in reality, a single space; part of it is roofed over and faced with glass where it looks out over the rest of the court; the balance is a walled garden, and each interior space partakes of that garden. Between 1931 and 1938 Mies designed and built several such court houses, and projected others in his airy and brilliant sketches. These projects remain a prime source of inspiration to many architects building in crowded suburban areas.

Despite the colorful and ever changing reflections and views of nature made possible by Mies's glass buildings, it is obvious that he always shied away from bright colors and brilliant contrasts of light and dark. He was, and is, after all, the man of eternal understatement, and bright colors and bright sunshine have no appeal to Mies's reserve. "I remember the first time I ever went to Italy," Mies recalled recently. "The sun and the blue skies were so bright, I though I'd go crazy! I couldn't wait to go back to the north, where everything was gray and subtle." To somebody as preoccupied as Mies is with the extraction of the finest nuances from the simplest object, the brightness of the Mediterranean was nothing but sheer bombast. Even in commissioning photography of his American buildings, Mies has tried hard to get the same sort of gray, slightly grim, and very contrastless pictures of his buildings which he used to be able to get in Germany in the 1920's. . . .

The year after Tugendhat was completed, Mies built another sort of house—a full-sized dwelling unit shown in the great hall of the Berlin Building exhibition. This house was all on one level; its plan presup-

Living room in house for the Berlin Building exposition, 1931. Pipe columns were chromium-plated. (Courtesy, Museum of Modern Art)

posed a relatively small site, so that most of the glass walls faced a court or patio surrounded by garden walls. This was a very practical house, by Mies's standards, zoned for different kinds of activity, yet extremely open in plan. Like the Tugendhat house and the Barcelona Pavilion (which it resembled in plan), its rooms were modulated and defined only by free-standing walls that overlapped and produced compositions of planes and volumes which, in turn, allowed all interior spaces to merge with the surrounding gardens. The roof was again supported on a few columns—in this case, pipe columns that had been chromium-plated like those in the earlier structures. (The chromium-plating, incidentally, turned the column surfaces into reflecting mirrors that tended to make the columns seem much more slender than they actually were.) All furniture was, as usual, by Mies, and it included some beautifully de- tailed storage walls and the by then standard assortment of cantilever and Barcelona chairs and tables. Although the finishes employed here were not as precious as those used at Barcelona and Tugendhat, the white-walled exhibition house had a tremendously elegant and costly look. At the same exhibit, Mies also showed a "bachelor's apartment" consisting of a single space divided, by various means, into sleeping, living, and dining areas. Here, as in the exhibition house, Mies incorporated some of the finest contemporary paintings and sculpture in the architectural setting. And here, as in all his work since Barcelona, Mies showed a calm mastery ·of detail and of total composition which made his work the most self-assured modern architecture then being created in Europe.

N 1930 MIES was appointed Director of the Bauhaus in Dessau. The Bauhaus had been Gropius's great experiment; he had taken over the school at the end of World War I, when it was located in Weimar. An arts-and-crafts school originally, the Bauhaus had been founded in 1902 and had been directed prior to the war by the great Belgian architect Henry van de Velde. Gropius turned it into the first serious laboratory for the development of an *industrial* art. "Art and *technology*—the new unity" had become the Bauhaus slogan; and the work done at the Bauhaus, under Gropius, completely transformed product design in Europe in less than a decade. Some of the finest architects, designers, and painters had been brought together by him to run the school: men like the architect Marcel Breuer, the designers Herbert Bayer, Joseph Albers, and L. Moholy-Nagy, and the painters Paul Klee, Wassily Kandinsky, and Lyonel Feininger had helped him make the Bauhaus the outstanding center of modern architecture and modern design of its time in the world.

By 1926 the Bauhaus had grown to the point where new quarters were required, and Gropius moved the school from Weimar to Dessau. There he built one of the most extraordinary complexes of buildings to be erected anywhere in the 1920's. The principal element of this dynamic complex was a structure sheathed entirely in glass. It was a logical extension of the two glass-and-steel structures Gropius built before World War I, and quite similar in concept to Mies's proposal for a glass "curtain wall" to be draped over the "bones" of his two skyscrapers.

The Bauhaus was beset by problems from the start. This was, of course, unavoidable in any effort based on as radical a concept as that proposed by Gropius. Some of the difficulties arose from philosophical conflicts: the early days of the Bauhaus were strongly influenced by German Expressionists and their arts-and-crafts romanticism. Other difficulties were political: although Gropius was determined to stick to the central issues he himself had outlined for the school, there were political pressures from the extreme Left inside the Bauhaus, and the extreme Right outside the Bauhaus. Still, all went reasonably well until February 1928, when Gropius decided that it was best for him and the Bauhaus if he resigned his post as Director. There followed a more or less chaotic period during which, at one time, a group of Communists dominated the direction of the school; until finally the Dessau authorities (the Bauhaus was a public institution) decided to make a clean sweep of it and put the Bauhaus back in order. They asked Gropius for his recommendations of a man to serve as Director, and Gropius suggested Mies.

One of the first things that happened to Mies when he took over at Dessau was that he was faced with a minor scandal. A woman instructor was involved, and there was to be an investigation. Mies, who had not the slightest idea of what was going on, called up Kandinsky and asked him if he would come along to the hearing to help out. "Kandinsky, who was trained as a lawyer, said he'd be delighted," Mies recalls. "He thought it might be fun!" Next, Mies telephoned Paul Klee with the same request. "Klee said that he'd rather go to see a dentist than listen to this sort of mess," Mies continued. "That's when I really began to like Klee."

The next thing that happened to the new Director was that a student delegation appeared to inform him that there would be a student strike unless certain demands were met immediately. Mies looked at the delegates coldly, and said: "You are here to work and learn. Anyone not present at his classes in the morning will be expelled." Within a remarkably short time the Bauhaus had stopped being a circus for Bohemian radicals and had gone back to being a workshop.

Still, political developments in Germany and, more particularly, in the Province of Anhalt (in which Dessau was located) began to endanger the Bauhaus. By 1932 Anhalt was dominated by a Nazi governor and a Nazi legislature, and the Bauhaus was forced to move to Berlin. Mies rented an empty factory and set up the school inside it. "We just painted it all white inside," he recalls. "It looked fine." But the situation was getting to be increasingly difficult in Berlin as well. In January 1933 Hitler came to power, and the Bauhaus was again under attack. The Nazis not only objected to the Bauhaus because it had once been briefly identified with Communist influences; they objected to its sort of design and to its sort of architecture, which they considered "Bolshevist" and "degenerate," as well as "un-German."

Mies and a few collaborators tried to hold the fort, but by the fall of 1933 the situation had become virtually hopeless. Mies arranged an interview with one of the Nazis' "cultural experts," Alfred Rosenberg, and they met late one night in Rosenberg's office. "We talked for an hour or more," Mies has said. "It was quite a peaceful discussion. Rosenberg told me: 'If only you would drop the name, Bauhaus, then we might be able to work things out.' I said: 'But that is a wonderful name —Bauhaus (House of Building)—in fact, it's almost the best thing about the school!' Finally, Rosenberg agreed to let us continue." Mies left the Nazi leader's office and went across the street to a restaurant where some of his close associates had been waiting anxiously, afraid that he might be arrested for having had the nerve to stand up and talk back to a Nazi boss. Lilly Reich, the brilliant furniture designer who had collaborated with Mies on some of the exhibitions in the 1920's, was among those waiting for him. Mies reported on his interview with Rosenberg, and everyone was elated. There were drinks all around. Then Mies said, quietly: "I have something to tell you. Now that they have agreed to let us continue, *we* are going to close the Bauhaus! I have written out a statement saying that the Bauhaus cannot continue to exist in this atmosphere." There was shock and deep consternation, but Mies prevailed. The Bauhaus, in its original form, was closed forever. . . .

Mies stayed on in Germany for another three or four years. He was able to build a few smaller houses (though to do a modern house was becoming increasingly difficult in the face of Nazi pressures to force all architecture into neoclassicism or romanticism), and he had time to develop several beautiful projects for court and row houses. Many of these projects never went beyond the stage of eloquent sketches, but even these sketches have served to inspire a whole new generation of young architects in the U.S. and elsewhere. There were also two projects for office buildings: the first, was an entry in a competition for the headquarters of the Reichsbank in Berlin; it was rejected in favor of other designs more in conformity with the Nazi party line in architecture. The second, an administrative center for the German silk industry, was—like the Reichsbank building—symmetrical, monumental in scale, but entirely rational in expression. Neither one of these two office structures was ever built.

In the spring of 1937 the American architect Philip C. Johnson, who had long been an ardent admirer of Mies, suggested to Mr. and Mrs. Stanley Resor (of the J. Walter Thompson Advertising Agency) that they should engage Mies to design for them a country house on a spectacular site in Jackson Hole, Wyoming. Johnson had had several earlier contacts with Mies: he had visited Germany on a number of occasions and met Mies when the latter was Director of the Bauhaus. Together with the critic and historian Henry-Russell Hitchcock, Johnson had, in 1932, arranged the Museum of Modern Art's exhibition of "International Architecture" and published the famous accompanying catalogue—a book in which the term International Style made its first public appearance. Mies's work was, of course, included in the Modern Museum exhibition, as were photographs and models of buildings by

*Resor house project for Jackson Hole, Wyo., 1938. Because
the landscape is all-important in a glass house, architectural
elements were underplayed to emphasize the view. (Courtesy, Mies van der Rohe)*

Frank Lloyd Wright, Le Corbusier, Gropius, and others. In short, Mies
was quite well known to the American *avant-garde* by the time the in-
vitation came from the Resors to visit America.

Mies arrived here in the summer of 1937, and went out to Wyoming to study the site. (Though the Resor house was never built, Mies's
studies for it are as clear a demonstration as he ever made of the importance of the landscape in glass architecture.) On one of his trips
through Chicago he met the architect John Holabird, who was then
looking for a man to head the School of Architecture at Chicago's
Armour Institute (later to be known as the Illinois Institute of Technology.) Holabird thought that Mies was exactly the man for the job,
and asked him what his terms were. "A completely free hand, and
$10,000 a year," Mies answered. Holabird telephoned President Heald,
of Armour, then turned to Mies and said: "You can have a free hand,
but they can't quite afford the salary." Mies accepted nonetheless and,
in 1938, moved to Chicago for good to become the Director of Architecture at Heald's Institute. Twenty years later, when the age limits of
the Illinois Institute of Technology (I.I.T.) finally forced Mies to retire,
he had set up one of the most impressive—and unusual—Schools of
Architecture in the world, and trained some of the best men now heading the staffs of American architectural offices. I.I.T., for its part, had
given Mies the chance to design its entire campus (and build a large
part of it), and to construct, also, some of the faculty and student housing along the perimeter of the campus. I.I.T. also had, by the time Mies
retired, managed to raise his salary to the amount he had originally requested.

X

LADIES AND GENTLEMEN," Frank Lloyd Wright said, his arm across
Mies's shoulders, "I give you Mies van der Rohe. But for me, there
would have been no Mies. . . . I admire him as an architect and respect and love him as a man. Armour Institute, *I* give you *my* Mies van
der Rohe. You treat him well and love him as I do." With that, Wright
stepped down off the platform and walked out.

The occasion was a dinner in the ballroom of Chicago's Palmer
House, given to present the new Director of Architecture to the faculty
and trustees of Armour. Mies had asked Wright to introduce him, and
Wright did it in his own, inimitable style. Mies's English, in those days,
was practically nonexistent (it later became quite fluent, if a little
rough), and he replied in German with a speech that must have taken

him a year or more to write—or, to be exact, a lifetime. But before he started out on his prepared speech, Mies paid an eloquent and extemporaneous tribute to Wright. Although no record remains of that tribute, Mies did, a couple of years later, write an appreciation for the Museum of Modern Art's catalog to its 1940 Wright exhibition. The catalog was never published because disagreements arose between Wright and the Museum regarding some of its contents, but Mies's tribute to Wright is on record. "In his undiminishing power," Mies wrote, "Wright resembles a giant tree in a wide landscape which, year after year, attains a more noble crown." Mies is so painfully modest about certain aspects of his own work that he never seriously objected to Wright's bombastic assumptions of fatherhood for the entire modern movement. In later years, after World War II, Mies was hurt by Wright's intemperate attacks upon him and the International Style in general, but never ceased to admire Wright's own work.

What Mies had to say in his inaugural address at Armour was, in a sense, completely autobiographical. It is worth quoting almost in full, for, in these aphorisms, Mies told not only the story of his own life and work, but laid down the law to Armour Institute's students of architecture and established a code of discipline and of morality which will live long after Mies is gone.

"True education is concerned not only with practical goals but also with values," Mies began. "Our aims assure us of our material life; our values make possible our spiritual life. In its simplest form, architecture is rooted in entirely functional considerations, but it can reach up through all degrees of value to the highest sphere of spiritual existence, into the realm of pure art.

"In organizing a system for architectural education we must recognize this situation if we are to succeed. . . . We must fit the system to this reality. Any teaching of architecture must explain these relations and interrelations. *We must make clear, step by step, what things are possible, necessary and significant.*

"If teaching has any purpose, it is to implant true insight and responsibility. Education must lead us from irresponsible opinion to true, responsible judgment. It must lead us from chance and arbitrariness to rational clarity and intellectual order. Therefore let us guide our students over the road of discipline from materials, through function, to creative work.

"Let us lead them into the healthy world of primitive building methods, where there was meaning in every stroke of an axe, expression in every bite of a chisel. Where can we find greater structural clarity than in the wooden buildings of old? Where else can we find such unity of material, construction and form? Here the wisdom of whole generations is stored.

"What feelings for material and what power of expression there is in these buildings! What warmth and beauty they have! They seem to be echoes of old songs."

Mies went on to describe, with unexpected passion, the quality of stone and brick, its texture, pattern, bonding, the richness of its color. Several years later, when Nikolaus Pevsner, the historian and an editor of the British *Architectural Review*, wrote to architectural schools throughout the world to discover what methods they used in teaching design, Mies answered for I.I.T. by saying that he first taught his students how to build with wood, then with stone, then with brick, and, finally, with concrete and with steel. By that time, Mies continued, the students were just about ready to graduate from I.I.T.; and after a few years of additional, practical experience, some of them might be expected to become designers! Pevsner, who thought that Mies had misunderstood the question, wrote again, but Mies simply explained the system in additional detail. If such an educational program seems only reasonable to the layman (who assumes that one must learn to walk before he learns to run), it should be explained that most modern architectural schools take a very different view: they believe that it is quite proper for students to be designing skyscrapers long before they have been taught anything about the steel or concrete structure or the elevator systems without which skyscrapers cannot work. Only at Mies's I.I.T. and at Wright's Taliesin did students first learn the fundamentals of building before they were permitted even to think about problems of design.

Mies made this point clear in his inaugural address when he came to speak of modern materials. "Each material has its specific character-istics which we must understand if we want to use it," Mies said. In other words, no design is possible until the materials with which you design are completely understood. "This is no less true of steel and concrete [than of wood, brick, and stone]. We must remember that everything depends on how we use a material, not on the material it-self. . . . New Materials are not necessarily superior. *Each material is only what we make it.*

"We must be as familiar with the functions of our buildings as with our materials," Mies continued. "We must learn what a building can be, what it should be, *and also what it must not be.* . . . And just as we acquaint ourselves with materials, just as we must understand functions, so we must become familiar with the psychological and spiritual factors of our day. No cultural activity is possible otherwise; for we are de-pendent on the spirit of our time." What did Mies mean by the "spirit of our time"? He explained by saying that "at this point, the problem of technology arises. . . . Technology not only promises greatness and power, but also involves dangers; good and evil apply to it as they do to all human actions; it is our task to make the right decision." And then, in a precise and characteristic sentence, Mies said: *"Every decision leads to a special kind of order."*

The decisions Mies referred to have to do with emphasis. Is archi-tecture to be based primarily upon the material and functional require-ments of the day? No, Mies said. "Means must be subsidiary to ends and to our desire for dignity and value." What about some idealistic principle of order as a basis for our architecture? Again Mies said no; such ideal systems of order overemphasize form and have nothing to do with simple reality or our sense of what is practical. What, then, is the alternative? "We shall emphasize the *organic principle of order* as a means of achieving the successful relationship of the parts to each other and to the whole. . . . The long path from material through function to creative work has only one goal: to create order out of the desperate confusion of our time. We must have order, allocating to each thing its proper place and giving to each thing its due according to its nature. And here," Mies concluded, "we shall take our stand."

Material, function, creative work—here "we shall take our stand!" This rational progression, as stern a discipline as was ever developed by a religious order, has not only been the foundation of Mies's own work, but the foundation of Mies's school at I.I.T. as well. The students who soon came under his influence had to reconcile themselves to living a serious life of simple dedication: each had to measure up to the precise standards of draftsmanship and of structural knowledge which Mies had once trained himself to meet; or else they had to go on to a less single-minded school. Under the circumstances, it is not surprising that a kind of hero worship of Mies soon sprung up at I.I.T.—a development that Mies, unconsciously, helped to cultivate by his extreme reticence and shyness in public. Mies brought with him a number of old associates, including the architect and city planner Ludwig Hilberseimer, who had built one of the Weissenhof structures in Stuttgart ten years earlier. Some of his associates have tended to surround Mies with the aura due to an éminence grise and overly to protect him from the outside world. When strangers are finally brought into Mies's presence, they are often surprised to find a simple, friendly, unpretentious man who loves to reminisce over a few drinks after dinner, and whose pleasures—in addition to living and breathing architecture, reading the works of German philosophers, and looking at his beautiful collection of Klee paintings—are largely confined to puffing away at huge cigars.

Mies's own mode of living in Chicago contributed quite a bit to the aura of mystery which has surrounded him ever since his arrival in the U.S. He inhabits a spacious apartment in an old building a block away from Lake Michigan. He generally lives there alone, though one of his three daughters, an art historian, used to share the apartment with him. (Another daughter, now back in Germany, is a successful actress in Munich. Mies's marriage to their mother ended in divorce in the early 1930's.)

On the surface, Mies lives much like any other quiet, sometimes lonely, elderly gentleman. Yet his apartment is anything but typical, for it has remained, for all intents and purposes, quite unfurnished ever since Mies moved into it. Except for the living room, which contains several well-proportioned, black-upholstered settees and easy chairs of square silhouette, the apartment has almost no furniture at all. Its only décor is Mies's magnificent collection of Klees, carefully hung on white and otherwise empty walls, and just as carefully lit. An occasional marble shelf completes the "decorative scheme."

Mies lives in this monastic setting according to a rather peculiar schedule established by himself and respected by his friends and associates. As he rarely talks until after dinner (when, in the right sort of atmosphere, he may become very voluble and cheerful), he does not go to bed until the early hours of the morning, and does not rise until fairly late the next day. No one who values Mies's friendship would telephone him before 11 a.m., at which time he may, under extreme duress, produce a few pleasant and thoughtful grunts. By the time lunch is over, he may feel inclined to become a little more articulate; in his office he is likely to sit and examine a scale model of one of his latest buildings, asking an assistant to shift walls around very slightly—or back again just as slightly. (This process may consume several weeks or months; the "simpler" the building looks, the longer it is likely to take.) During these sessions with scale models of buildings and full-size mock-ups of building parts (all the walls in Mies's buildings are studied in precise, full-size mock-ups prepared in a model workshop that is as well equipped as any jeweler's), Mies may communicate with others by an occasional smile between puffs at his ever present cigar. There are not likely to be very many spoken words, and the atmosphere tends to be that of an operating room while a great surgeon is preparing to perform a revolutionary operation for the first time.

Mies was able to establish his own private architectural practice in Chicago shortly after taking over the position at Armour Institute; for the President of Armour, Dr. Henry Heald (later to become President of the Ford Foundation), decided to entrust the planning and design of the entire new I.I.T. campus to him. Mies's designs for the campus covering eight city blocks were so radically different from anything he had attempted before—and so convincing in terms of American building technology—that the I.I.T. buildings are now among the most influential works of architecture ever produced in the U.S.

This is doubly astonishing, for when Mies attempted I.I.T., he was

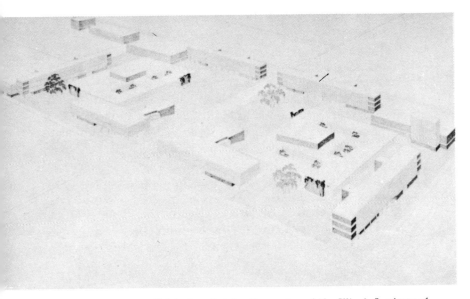

Original project for the campus of the Illinois Institute of Technology, Chicago, 1939. (Courtesy, Mies van der Rohe)

more than fifty years old and could easily have been expected to concentrate on a further development of his European work; conversely, he could hardly have been expected to see the nature of modern American building technology with as much clarity as he did—for, after all, he was only a newcomer. Yet the I.I.T. buildings are so simple, so obvious, so entirely reasonable in structure and structural expression, that it remains a major mystery why no one else had built these buildings long before Mies arrived in Chicago!

Gordon Bunshaft, Mies's admirer and the designer of Lever House, has said that "America is largely a steel-building country." Mies saw this clearly as soon as he arrived in Chicago, and proceeded to draw the logical conclusions: a skeleton of steel becomes a simple cage, with columns and beams set at regular intervals. Such a cage may be filled with many different materials: brick, glass, concrete, or what have you. Once Mies understood the nature of the steel cage, it seemed to him that brick and glass were the obvious, economical, and natural complements of steel. Brick is small in scale, easily handled, easily fitted around the flanges of steel columns and beams, easily recognized for its familiar size—a fact that immediately gives any onlooker a true sense of the scale and the dimensions of the building before him. Glass, set into steel or aluminum frames, could be attached with similar ease to the flanges of a steel cage and could be given a proper scale by divisions into window-panes of different (or identical) sizes. And because glass is transparent, it clearly reveals the structural cage. The obvious solution for a modern, industrial enclosure, therefore, was a straightforward grid of steel filled in with brick and glass.

Material—function—creative work. Mies had found the right materials. What about the function? Here Mies developed a concept so radical within the modern movement that it is still being fought by many of his contemporaries. Louis Sullivan had said that "form follows function"—or, at least, Sullivan's partner, Dankmar Adler, had said it, and Sullivan had accepted the idea with a grain or two of salt. But Mies decided to find out whether this was really a valid maxim. Did not buildings tend to outlive their original functions? Did not functions change with increasing frequency in the modern world? Was it really possible to predict, in 1940, what functions the laboratories and machine shops and classroom structures at I.I.T. might be called upon to fulfill in 1950 or 1960 or in the year 2000? Obviously not, Mies decided. The only function one could be sure of in any building built to last was *the function of flexibility of use throughout its lifetime.* So, the only kind of building which would make sense, in terms of functionalism, would be a building not adjusted to any specific function at all!

This conception of the "universal building" probably came to Mies out of his knowledge of Schinkel and the classical tradition. For the greatest contribution the classicists had made to our civilization—from the Parthenon to the Greek Revival—was the idea of universality. They believed that mankind needed not *special* but *universal* solutions—solutions as applicable to a temple as they might be to a palace, as reasonable in a museum as in a customs house. What Mies did at I.I.T. was to take the classical notion of universality and translate it into steel, brick, and glass. I.I.T.—a campus dedicated to research into the wide world of ever changing sciences—became a collection of beautifully detailed standard units, based upon an identical module, and designed to be so flexible as to be capable of accomodating almost any kind of activity in the years to come.

How radical a notion this was for the U.S. in particular is not always clearly understood. An American businessman, to whom one of Mies's friends explained this notion of universality, was horror-struck! "Do you realize what this means?" he asked. "Don't you know that the entire economic system of the U.S. is based upon the rapid obsolescence of our buildings, cars, consumer goods? If buildings were designed with so much flexibility that they would never wear out—well, that would wreck our whole building industry!" This shortsighted point of view formed the real basis of many hysterical attacks upon Mies during the years immediately after World War II; only in the late 1950's, as it

Typical court on I.I.T. campus (Photo: Hedrich-Blessing)

became evident that even the U.S. would have trouble in providing the amount and variety of shelter needed by an exploding population, did Mies's earlier critics begin to understand how much sense his "universal space" concept would make on a globe populated by three billion people or more.

Material and function were solved at I.I.T. with Mies's characteristic clarity and simplicity. What about "creative work"? One Chicago architect, looking at the first I.I.T. buildings, said that they looked to him like little more than warehouses thrown up by some contractor. He was absolutely right, though not in the way he meant it. For the "little more"—the "little" difference—made *all* the difference. Marcel Breuer once listed all the ingredients that went into the design of his buildings, and ended up with "that intangible one per cent which is art." Mies might raise that to ten per cent or even thirty-three per cent, but he would agree that regardless of the percentage, the quality that is art is intangible and elusive. Yet it is much less so in Mies's work than it is in the work of Wright or Le Corbusier. "What makes Mies such a great influence," Philip Johnson once said, "is that he is so easy to copy." There are plenty of Miesian buildings that tend to disprove this dictum; but the fact is that Mies has always been able to reduce his ideas and methods to a precision unequaled in our time. At I.I.T. the intangible, unifying force "which is art" is the repeated use of a standard unit, a structural bay twenty-four feet wide, twenty-four feet deep, and twelve feet high. This structural bay appears on most façades as a steel-framed rectangle twenty-four feet long and twelve feet high, i.e., a double square, one of the oldest and most effective proportional systems in architecture. This double square may be filled with brick or glass (or a combination of the two); but its dimensions are constant. Behind this rectangular façade system, there may be a variety of spaces: open workshops, classrooms, research labs, or what have you. But the universal façade embraces them all.

The second, intangible quality that makes I.I.T. a "little more" than a collection of warehouses is the quality of the spaces between the various rectangular buildings (most of them two or three stories in

Boiler plant at I.I.T., 1950. (Photo: Hedrich-Blessing)

height). Mies conceived of the I.I.T. campus as a group of some twenty buildings forming a series of quadrangles; but, unlike the classical quadrangles of Oxford (or even of Harvard, with its gaps between buildings), Mies's quadrangles were a series of subtly interlocking spaces whose movement leads the visitor on from one court into the next, through a variety of spatial and formal experiences. This effect was achieved by making the planes and volumes of the individual buildings overlap in such a way that beyond each structure another one would become visible in the distance, "sliding out" from behind the buildings in front of it and suggesting an unseen continuity of space beyond. Mies had achieved the same effect in his overlapping wall planes in the Barcelona Pavilion and in the Tugendhat house; here he was doing it on a grand, urban scale for the first time.

Mies's first building at I.I.T. was completed in 1943. Thirteen years and a dozen buildings later, Mies completed his part of the I.I.T. campus. His great friend, Dr. Heald, had long before moved on to New York, and the new administration of the Institute decided, rather arbitrarily, that they wanted some other architects to try their hands at doing a building or two on the new campus. In 1958, therefore, I.I.T. approached Skidmore, Owings & Merrill, the big and highly skilled firm whose New York office was headed by Mies's friend, Bunshaft, and whose Chicago office was full of Mies's former students. Bunshaft, who was very disturbed by I.I.T.'s sudden rejection of Mies, suggested to him that he associate with the Chicago office and act as designer of the new building. Mies was rather touched and grateful, but told Bunshaft that he preferred not to "come in through the back door. Anyway," he added, "the whole campus is already designed. Why not just carry it out?" Still, the gratuitous insult was unmistakable, and the I.I.T. student paper ran a front-page protest. Mies decided that he was much too busy to bother with the small minds now in charge of I.I.T. and that it was a waste of time to fight. In any event, the Skidmore, Owings & Merrill office was likely to produce something reasonably close to a Mies building; and it was also likely to respect Mies's site-plan concept. In short, the over-all harmony of the campus was not likely to be seriously affected. Still, in an age that has plenty of individual buildings— individual statements—by self-important, individual architects, and depressingly few unified *groups* of buildings, the opportunity missed at I.I.T. is likely to hurt architecture more than the powers-that-be may have realized.

Chapel at I.I.T., 1952. (Photo: Hedrich-Blessing)

X I

THE HOUSE that Mies designed for the Resors in Wyoming—and that was his immediate reason for coming to the U.S.—was never built. But shortly after the end of World War II, Mies began work on another house, which has probably had as great an influence on recent domestic architecture in America as any single work of the postwar years.

The client for this house was Dr. Edith Farnsworth, a brilliant Chicago physician who had been a close friend of Mies for several years. In 1946 she bought a piece of land on the Fox River in Plano, Illinois, about an hour's ride from Chicago, and Mies began to design a house for her to be built on that site.

The Farnsworth house is, in all likelihood, the most complete statement of glass-and-steel, skin-and-bones architecture Mies or anyone else will ever be able to make. It is, also, the ultimate in universality, the ultimate in precision and polish, the ultimate in the crystallization of an idea. The house is a rectangular structure of eight steel columns, set in two parallel rows some twenty-eight feet apart. In the long direction of the plan the steel columns are spaced twenty-two feet apart. Between these eight columns there are held two slabs framed in steel—the floor and the roof. These slabs seem to float in the air (the floor slab is about four feet above the ground, and the ceiling plane is about nine feet above that), and they are held between the steel H columns as if by some magnetic force. At each end the floor and roof slabs cantilever out six feet beyond the last row of columns.

Between these two floating slabs there is a simple, glass-enclosed living space and porch. The living space is, to all intents and purposes, a single room, divided into sleeping, living, kitchen, and service areas. The floor throughout is of Italian travertine; the ceiling is white plaster; the few interior partitions are finished in natural primavera; the curtains inside the glass skin are of natural-colored, off-white shantung; and the steel frame itself is painted white.

As a matter of fact, the steel frame was carefully polished before the coats of white paint were applied: first, all the welding marks at the connections between columns and beams were ground down; next, Mies had the steel sand-blasted to get rid of the "rough" texture of the rolled, structural sections; then he had a coat of zinc sprayed over the sand-blasted surface to prevent rust; and, finally, the white paint was applied with such care that the finished surfaces look almost baked on.

One reason for the elevation of the floor plane above the grade is that the Fox River tends to rise and overflow its banks in the spring, so that the house looks like a pier or a boat during those days. Another reason is that Mies wanted a quality of airiness, of space-in-motion, which an earth-bound house would not have had to the same degree.

It took Mies six years to design and build this perfect jewel of a house. During this period his disciple, Philip Johnson, went ahead and built his own famous glass-and-steel house in New Canaan, Connecti-

Farnsworth house, Plano, Ill., 1950. View of entrance porches. Again the architecture is made to frame and reflect the surrounding landscape. (Photo: George H. Steuer)

cut. Johnson has always made a point of saying that his house was designed *after* Mies had first developed the Farnsworth concept and that it was, therefore, based upon the Farnsworth house, although the latter was not completed until two years after Johnson moved into his own home. Actually, Johnson is unnecessarily modest in crediting Mies with all the qualities of his own house, for the Johnson and the Farnsworth houses—apart from being all steel and glass—are completely different in character. Johnson's house is symmetrical in its elevations; the Farnsworth house has a porch and a lower deck at one end and is quite dynamically asymmetrical. Johnson's house sits on the ground like a delightful little classical temple; the Farnsworth house is virtually airborne. Johnson's house has dark gray steel columns at all corners, containing the volume within the glass shell; the Farnsworth house has open corners and cantilevered ends, so that the interior space is projected outward into the landscape as in any structure by Wright. Finally, the Johnson house has a strong post-and-beam look, a feeling of compression in the columns; whereas the Farnsworth house has a sense of tension, of steel being stretched out to its ultimate potentials. (The white steel columns of the Farnsworth house are so precisely welded to the horizontal steel fascias of floor and roof planes that the steel "sings" like a tuning fork when it is lightly tapped. . . .)

These differences between Johnson's and Mies's glass houses are more significant than they might seem. For what they add up to is this: Mies's house was a very "American" sort of statement—dynamic, cantilevered, almost in motion; whereas Johnson (who was born in Ohio) had built a tiny, classical *palazzo*—a static, columnar, serene temple of a house. Mies's responsiveness to America—a continent of motion—began long before he came to Chicago; indeed, this quality of motion is already quite apparent in the Barcelona Pavilion (although the Pavilion *did* sit on a pedestal), and it is the quality Mies undoubtedly derived from Wright's Prairie houses.

Although the Farnsworth house was exquisitely simple and beautiful as an abstract statement about structure, skin, and space, it was hardly a "house for family living." Needless to say, it had never been intended to be that: it was meant to be a pleasure pavilion for a lady living alone, and it was a perfect and expensive solution for that. Unfortunately, as the house neared completion, Mies's friendship with Dr. Farnsworth broke up, and there was an extremely unpleasant aftermath, involving lawsuits (which were decided in Mies's favor), recriminations in public and private on the part of Dr. Farnsworth, and denunciations of Mies as a menace to American architecture. This latter campaign, a rather ludicrous and silly bit of hysteria in retrospect (though it did hurt many of those involved), took the form of a concerted attack upon the International Style by the Hearst magazine *House Beautiful.*

In her April 1953 issue the editor of *House Beautiful* came forward with a ringing editorial denouncing the "Threat to the New America." The gist of the editorial was that a sinister group of International Stylists, led by Mies, Gropius, and Corbu, and supported by the Museum of Modern Art, was trying to force Americans to accept an architecture that was barren, grim, impoverished, impractical, unlivable, and destructive of individual possessions, as well as of individuals themselves. There was a hint or two that Communists were behind the whole thing. A list of International Style characteristics was published to warn readers of *House Beautiful* against the "threat"—much in the same way that the FBI warns the public against the "ten most wanted" criminals of the day.

But the lady's principal ire was reserved for Mies's dictum: "less is more." This was the threat in a nutshell. "We know that less is *not* more," she wrote. "It is simply less!" She was on pretty firm ground there, arithmetically speaking, though many of the great artists of all periods would have agreed with Mies on aesthetic grounds. For the purity of a miniature by Fra Angelico, say, is as much the result of a process of aesthetic distillation as is the Farnsworth house.

Although the attack was probably good for *House Beautiful's* advertising and circulation, it was, perhaps, a little less good for some of the people most directly involved. Mies was shocked and unhappy. To him, the concept of universality in architecture implied the highest possible degree of freedom. For, after all, a building reduced to "almost nothing" (Mies's phrase) represents the ultimate in noninterference on the part of an architect with the lives of his clients. To Mies, the architure of "nothingness" suggests a maximum opportunity for free expression on the part of those who use the building: they can furnish it in any way they like, use it for anything they like, change its interior spaces in any manner that seems most suitable. If this theory does not always work out in practical terms, it does at least suggest a degree of self-effacing modesty on the part of the architect who formulated it that is somewhat at variance with the image of a totalitarian monster. A few

Project for a museum for a small city, 1942. This collage shows Picasso's Guernica *among other works of art displayed. As the museum was designed to serve the paintings displayed within (rather than vice versa, as in Wright's Guggenheim Museum), there is an almost complete anonymity of architectural expression. (Courtesy, Mies van der Rohe)*

years earlier Mies had designed an ideal museum for a small city, and here again he had tried to make the architecture "almost nothing" and the paintings and sculpture (for which the museum would be built) everything. His beautiful drawings and collages for this project show a large, glass-enclosed space, lightly subdivided by free-standing walls and screens against which to hang paintings or place sculpture. Indeed, Mies's incredible modesty was never better expressed than in the collages he prepared for this project: for in these the only elements visible at first are the photographic reproductions of important paintings and pieces of sculpture; one must actually search with a magnifying glass for any evidence of the architecture that is supposed to enclose these works of art, for the only indication of any building whatsoever is a series of fine lines suggesting a few slender columns and the paving pattern of the floor. How different from Wright's Guggenheim Museum, whose powerful, plastic forms overwhelm all but the most self-assertive works of art!

Nor was the *House Beautiful* episode very edifying for Dr. Farnsworth. She let herself be persuaded to grant an interview to the magazine, and her quoted remarks were not in the best of taste. "Something should be said and done about such architecture as this," she told *House Beautiful*, "or there will be no future for architecture. . . . I thought you could animate a predetermined, classic form like this with your own presence. I wanted to do something 'meaningful,' and all I got was this glib, false sophistication." Her principal complaints were that the house cost far too much to build ($73,000), that it was terribly impractical in many ways, and that it was expensive to maintain. Many of her criticisms would have been entirely justified if her house had been meant to be a model for "family living." But obviously there was no such intention. The Farnsworth house was meant to be, and succeeded in being, a clear and somewhat abstract expression of an architectural ideal—the ultimate in skin-and-bones architecture, the ultimate in "less is more," the ultimate in objectivity and universality. And it was meant to show that even when architecture approaches nothingness, its spirit can be romantic and beautiful. The glass prism built by Mies for his friend was a mirror held up to a lovely landscape; it was not a very practical house for Levittown, say, and it was not intended to be. But it was a clear and precise statement that other, lesser architects have found very helpful indeed as a point of departure. Mies's insistence upon an all-glass skin was no arbitrary defiance of "practicality"; it was an attempt to arrive at an absolutely clear, visual separation of structure and nonstructure. All great houses by great architects tend to be somewhat impractical; many of Corbu's and Wright's house clients find that they are living in too expensive and too inefficient buildings. Yet many of these same clients would never exchange their houses for the most workable piece of mediocrity "designed" by means of a consumer survey.

And, finally, Frank Lloyd Wright was involved in the *House Beautiful* affair as well. "The 'International Style' . . . is totalitarianism," Wright announced. "These Bauhaus architects ran from political totalitarianism in Germany to what is now made by specious promotion

General view of Crown Hall. The roof is hung from deep steel girders overhead. (Photo: Hedrich-Blessing)

to seem their own totalitarianism in art here in America. . . . Why do I distrust and defy such 'internationalism' as I do communism? Because both must by their nature do this very leveling in the name of civilization. . . . [The promoters of the International Style] are not a wholesome people. . . ." Wright's fundamental disagreement with skin-and-bones architecture was nothing new, and, in many respects, was valid indeed. But his personal attack upon Mies and others was both new and unworthy of him.

Mies designed two other important "universal" structures during the year after the Farnsworth house was completed. In 1952 he completed the plans for the Architecture and Design Building at I.I.T., and in 1953 he submitted his proposal for a National Theater to be built at Mannheim, in Western Germany.

These two structures carry the concept of a universal, entirely open, and entirely flexible space to its logical conclusion. Both buildings are framed in steel, with deep steel girders or trusses spanning the distance between outside columns. As a result, there is no need for any interior supports at all, so that the enclosed space can serve any number of

*Detail of entrance to Crown Hall, I.I.T., designed in 1952.
This building houses the School of Architecture. (Photo:
Hedrich-Blessing)*

Stair at Crown Hall. (Photo: Hedrich-Blessing)

different and changing functions. In both buildings the deep girders are *above* the roof plane, so that the roof ceiling (which was hung from the overhead girders) becomes a flat slab uninterrupted by any dropped beams. All exterior walls between columns are of glass.

The Architecture and Design Building—"Crown Hall"—was completed in 1955, and it now houses both the School of Architecture and the Institute of Design (known as I.D.). The latter—an offspring of the Chicago version of the Bauhaus, originally started by Moholy-Nagy in the 1930's and long housed in a neo-Romanesque castle north of the Chicago Loop—was absorbed by I.I.T. in the early 1950's. Mies, who was somewhat critical of the Institute's "undisciplined" method of operation, put the I.D. spaces into a semi-basement space below the huge drafting rooms reserved for the architecture students on the main floor. While this may seem a cruel jest, the I.D. spaces are actually well lighted by high clerestory windows all around the perimeter of the building.

The Mannheim Theater remained a project. Together with a dozen other architects, Mies had been invited by the City of Mannheim to submit a proposal for its National Theater. His design consisted of a rectangular cage of gray-tinted glass, 530 feet long, 270 feet wide, and forty feet high, suspended between fourteen huge steel columns joined, in pairs, above the roof by seven deep steel trusses that spanned the entire 270-foot width of the building! The glass cage was held within this framework about fifteen feet above the ground level, and the entrance to the theater was from below. Within the huge glass cage, there was room for two separate theaters, complete with workshops, dressing rooms, and other services.

Although Mies's proposal attracted the greatest attention and was highly praised as an original contribution to architecture, the City of Mannheim chose another design, which has since been built. The completed theater owes a good deal to Mies, but it has none of the verve and daring of his own proposal.

In developing the Mannheim project, Mies again made the point that only a universal space, free of all interior columns and infinitely flexible in interior arrangement, could hope to satisfy all the functional needs that might arise in the course of the life of the building. This notion of universality has one serious drawback, demonstrated both in the Farnsworth house and in the I.I.T. building: because the large, universal space is so dramatic and exciting, Mies (and most other architects) are tempted to leave the space as undivided as possible, never carrying partitions within all the way up to the ceiling plane if this can be avoided. The result is that many of these universal spaces do not offer very satisfactory answers to problems of acoustics and controlled lighting. At Crown Hall, for example, where all partitions separating drafting rooms stop short of the ceiling plane, there are disturbing squeaks every time a student moves his drafting stool an inch this way or that, and the constant squeaks are "universally" audible. And in the Mannheim Theater project it might well have been necessary to enclose the universal space with heavy curtains to keep out disturbing natural light.

Mannheim Theater project, 1953. Huge steel trusses span the entire width of the building and hold the roof plane. Small human figure at left suggests scale of the building. (Photo: Hedrich-Blessing)

All these minor and major irritations could easily be avoided if Mies were a little less stubborn. Unfortunately, he became so annoyed with some of his critics, who believed that you could substitute "climate control" for architecture, that he adamantly refused for many years to try to do anything about these mundane problems of practical living. Still, some of his most recent work suggests that he has at last decided to face up to the more prosaic facts of life, and that he is perfectly capable of coping with them. He does not particularly like to admit this, saying, when asked about such things as air conditioning or garbage collection, that "this is not my *métier*"; but he and his associates have found that there is really no good reason why a beautiful building cannot work efficiently as well. In 1950 Mies made one of his rare speeches at I.I.T. and said, among other things, that "some people are convinced that architecture will be outmoded and replaced by technology." This was a sly "dig" at the Institute of Design. "Such a conviction is not based on clear thinking," Mies continued. "The opposite happens: wherever technology reaches its real fulfillment, it transcends into architecture. It is true that architecture depends on facts, but its real field of activity is in the realm of significance." Only thirty years earlier most *avant-gardists* of Mies's generation were convinced that anything that expressed function and technological advance was, *ipso facto,* beautiful. Mies, of course, had never believed such nonsense; but he had found it necessary to expose the fallacy that "functionalism must equal beauty" on more than one occasion. He may, perhaps, be forgiven if the fallacy of this equation finally persuaded him—for a short while, at least—that functionalism was, in fact, the *enemy* of beauty. . . .

X I I

S OMETIME IN 1946, while Mies was still Director of Architecture at I.I.T., he met a young man, a former philosophy student, called Herbert Greenwald, who had, by a series of accidents, become a real-estate investor and builder just before the outbreak of World War II. Greenwald was only twenty-nine years old when he met Mies, but the two got along well from the start. The chief reason was that Greenwald was not a builder primarily for profit, but, rather, an idealist interested in "leaving his stamp on the scene," as Mies put it, by means of creating the finest architecture possible within the framework of modern technology and modern economics. Another reason was that both liked to talk about philosophy.

Two years after Mies and Greenwald met, the first Mies-designed

Greenwald building, the Promontory Apartments, rose on Chicago's Lakeshore Drive. It was a concrete-framed structure, whose bays were filled in with brick and glass. The principal innovation—apart from the austere simplicity of the façades—was the way in which Mies handled the column expression: as columns obviously carry smaller loads at the top floors than they do at street level, Mies stepped back his columns at various levels on the principal façades to make the columns progressively smaller as they rose up to the roof line. The result was a subtle elongation of the façade similar to that achieved by stepped-back buttresses on medieval structures. Several years later, when Mies designed and built the faculty apartment blocks that today adjoin the I.I.T. campus, he used the same stepped-back concrete frame to give his buildings an exaggerated vertical perspective—a rather subtle variation on the plain, rectangular "slab" buildings then, and now, in vogue.

When the Promontory Apartments demonstrated the success of Mies's simplicity and logic combined with Greenwald's practical idealism, the two proceeded to bigger and more exciting things. In 1950, on another site on the shores of Lake Michigan, two steel-and-glass towers designed by Mies rose to demonstrate in full scale and for the first time what Mies tried to say in his glass-tower sketches of thirty years before. The apartments at 860 Lakeshore Drive—which soon became known, among architects all over the world, simply as "860"—were the strongest, purest, and most deceptively simple statement of his ideas which Mies had ever made.

The two towers at "860" are rectangular in plan and twenty-six stories high. They are spaced a short distance apart and set at right angles to one another, so that each apartment gets the best possible view of Lake Michigan. The buildings are all steel and glass; columns and beams are covered in black steel plate, and vertical I-beam sections of black steel spaced about five feet apart are welded to the exterior. These I-beam rails run the full height of the building, and floor-to-ceiling panels of glass framed in natural aluminum are set between the rails. There are four apartments to each floor in one building, eight in the other. At ground-floor level the two towers are connected by a black steel canopy.

Apartment houses at 860 Lake Shore Drive, Chicago, 1951. The sides of the towers receding from view seem opaque because of the overlap of deep vertical rails that rise to the full height of the façades. (Photo: Ezra Stoller)

The structural expression Mies chose for "860" is unusual and original in the extreme. While the buildings are steel-framed, the Chicago building code required the steel to be fireproofed with two inches of concrete all around. If Mies had just left his buildings as a "bare" fireproofed structure, he would have had two vertical cages of concrete filled in with glass. The result would have been an indeterminate building, neither vertical nor horizontal, for the column and beam pattern would have created a series of *horizontal* rectangles twenty-one feet wide and about nine feet high, while the complete façade itself would have been decidedly *vertical*.

To avoid this visual conflict, Mies finished all his concrete-covered columns and beams with black steel plate, and then welded on to this black steel plate a pattern of slim, vertical I-beam rails eight inches deep, which soar up from the second-floor line of the building in a pattern of closely spaced vertical strips all the way up to the roof line 250 feet above. These slim rails give the façades a fluted appearance that suggests the vertical fluting found in the late Gothic cathedrals. They make the "860" towers the most vertical-looking skyscrapers ever built.

Needless to say, the functionalists were horrified: here Mies was using steel (a structural material) as applied ornament! It was inexcusable! Mies, who takes great delight in making the functionalists squirm, explained his heresy with engaging frankness and wit. "Now, first I am going to tell you the *real* reason for those mullions," he told an interviewer, "and then I am going to tell you a good reason by itself." Where the I-beams formed window separations, he explained, they made perfectly good sense. You had to have a metal rail to separate the windows from one another, and you might as well make the mullions deep and narrow instead of wide and flat. But what about then taking those same deep and narrow I-beams and welding them onto the black steel that covered the concrete, which, in turn, covered the *real* column? Wasn't that a pretty far-fetched way to "express" a structural frame? "It was very important to preserve and extend the rhythm which the mullions set up on the rest of the building," Mies said, coming back to the *real* reason. "We looked at it on the model without the steel I-beams attached to the corner columns and *it did not look right*. That is the *real*

Connecting canopy between apartment towers at 860 Lake Shore Drive. (Photo: Hedrich-Blessing)

reason. Now, the other reason is that the steel I-beams were needed to stiffen the plates which cover the columns so these plates would not ripple, and also we needed the I-beams for strength when the sections were hoisted into place. Now, of course, that's a very *good* reason—but the other one is the *real* reason!"

The *real* reason turned out to be enormously persuasive. One of the results of having a pattern of deep, vertical I-beams running up and down on all four sides of the building is that it makes the rectangular towers infinitely more plastic than a flat façade. For when you see the towers head on, one façade on each tower appears to be all glass—a huge mirror reflecting the sky and the clouds, as well as one another. But the other façade that recedes from the onlooker appears completely opaque and solid. As one walks around the buildings, the façades that were formerly glassy become opaque, and the façades that were formerly opaque become open and glassy. This extraordinary play of transparency and opacity—all within the eight-inch depth of the façades—is much more subtle than Corbu's treatment of a slab like the Swiss Pavilion in Paris, where he simply made both end walls of solid masonry to achieve the same effect, and thereby sacrificed possible window openings on two sides of his building.

In practical terms, the *real* reason turned out to be unexpectedly valid also. Mies had used the steel-plate covers on columns and beams as forms into which he poured the required concrete fireproofing. In most buildings prior to "860" such forms were built of wood and had to be stripped off after the concrete had been poured into the wooden mold and had hardened around the steel frame. After that, the raw concrete would, generally, have had to be finished with some facing material to make it look less crude. By making his forms of steel plate and welding the I-beam stiffeners to the steel plate before it was hoisted up into place, Mies killed two birds with one stone: he got his formwork into which to pour the concrete, and he could leave the formwork in place and let it be the finished surface of his structure. Several years later, when I. M. Pei, the young Chinese-born architect, designed his handsome Mile High Center office building in Denver, Colorado, he found that it was very difficult indeed to get away from Mies's rationale of this sort of cage building. Indeed, he deliberately discarded some of Mies's details for "860"—although he recognized that they made great practical sense—because he did not want to be guilty of plagiarism. In short, the "applied decoration" in steel on top of the true structural frame at "860" turned out to be a remarkably sensible solution.

In several other respects, too, "860" represented the clarification of Mies's views. Although the building codes forced him to conceal his real structural cage, he felt that the verticality of the structure should be clearly expressed on the façades, as it was, in a sense, the "significance" of the skyscraper. He was giving structure a *poetic* voice in his building, because prose (i.e., the building codes) did not permit his structural cage to declare itself. The "860" buildings have often been denounced as "cold" or "inhuman." They are neither. They are flights of fancy and of romance, crystal shafts rising out of a huge lake. Mies had learned the effectiveness of *pilotis* from Corbu, and so these twin towers were raised on stilts above the ground. Twenty-six stories farther up, this separation of building from earth becomes an exhilarating experience analogous only to flight itself. For here, looking out through the glass walls of "860," one feels suspended halfway between the shimmering lake and the sky, floating in a calm and dreamlike world far removed from the chaos of the city. No building by Wright has ever conveyed more of a sense of romance.

In the apartments themselves Mies once again put to a test his theory of universality. Because of the wide and regular spacing of columns, each apartment plan is quite flexible. When *Life* published a story on Mies several years ago, the editors included some remarkable photographs showing several floors of apartments at "860" lit up at night. Each apartment, it turned out, was decorated in an entirely different manner: some owners had brought in antiques and applied classical moldings to all walls and doors; others had bought Mies-designed chairs and tables. Although the building presents a uniform and orderly pattern to the outside world—because, according to Mies, an orderly building can be a powerful force for greater order in the world around it—each apartment seemed to offer a maximum degree of freedom of self-expression to those who live inside it.

Mies, incidentally, was never one of those. He did have an apartment reserved for him, and the move into "860" would not have been very troublesome, as his old apartment was located only a block or two away. But Mies is a man of slow motion; he hates travel, and hates dislocation. He finally decided to stay where he was, although Greenwald and many other friends urged him to join them in the beautiful new buildings.

"860" was an economic as well as aesthetic success, and Greenwald was soon commissioning Mies to build more of the same, both in Chicago and elsewhere. Before long, Mies completed two towers, clad in aluminum and glass, farther up along Chicago's North Shore. Shortly afterward he added two more steel-and-glass towers to the ones at "860," so that Chicago now has an impressive stretch of uninterrupted Mies-designed lake front. Greenwald was also developing projects in Detroit, Brooklyn, Manhattan's Battery Park, and Newark, New Jersey. Before long, Mies was spending almost two thirds of his working time on urban redevelopment projects financed by Herbert Greenwald.

Then, one day in 1959, Mies and an assistant were getting into a plane in Havana, Cuba, where Mies was about to start on a concrete-and-glass office building for the Bacardi Company. His eye caught a newspaper headline that said that a plane had crashed into New York's East River. "That's incredible—how can anyone crash into that little stream?" Mies said to his assistant. Upon landing in New York a few hours later, Mies read the details. Among those killed in the East River crash was his friend, Herb Greenwald, forty-two years old.

Lafayette Park, Detroit, 1960. A development consisting of tall apartment towers, and two-story row houses, all arranged in a pattern of interlocking squares. (Photo: Hedrich-Blessing)

X I I I

ONE DAY IN the summer of 1954, while Mies was working on the Architecture Building for I.I.T., a young American woman living in Paris opened the New York papers and saw there a rendering of a tall office building her father was proposing to build on Park Avenue. The lady's name was Mrs. Phyllis Bronfman Lambert, and her father was Samuel Bronfman, President of Joseph E. Seagram & Sons, the distillers. Mrs. Lambert, who had taken several advanced college courses in architecture and related arts, thought that the proposed Seagram Building pictured in the New York papers looked more like a design for a "gift decanter" than a distinguished work of architecture, and flew back to New York to have a heart-to-heart talk with her father. The outcome of this talk was that her father released his architects and authorized her to search for the best possible man to design the most distinguished sky-scraper that art and technology could produce, and money could buy.

Through a friend at the Museum of Modern Art, Phyllis Lambert met Philip Johnson, who was then the Director of the Museum's Department of Architecture, and, under Johnson's guidance, went to see every major architect in the U.S. and looked at every important building put up by leading architects, young or old. She also talked to critics, magazine editors—anyone of any standing in the world of American architecture. "It has been said that Frank Lloyd Wright was the greatest architect of the 19th. century," Mrs. Lambert wrote to a friend during those months of exploration. "To me [his] Johnson Wax [building] is a complete statement of 'Manifest Destiny,' the embodiment of all the philosophy of that period in America. It has a force and vitality that is almost cyclonic. It's crazy as hell and as wonderful as it is crazy. . . . (But) his is not the statement that is needed now."

As for Corbu, whom she considered at length, she wrote that he "has not built a building in this country. . . . Would he be a great and good influence here? I am afraid not. . . . One is fascinated by his spaces, his sculptural forms, but are not people likely to be blinded by these and skip over the surface only?" Whether or not one agrees with her judgments—especially her judgment of Corbu—it is obvious that she took her assignment very seriously and went through a great period of soul-searching. Finally, through Johnson, she met Mies and saw "860." She had heard everyone talk about Mies long before she met him. "The younger men, the second generation, are talking in terms of Mies—or denying him," she had written. "They talk of new forms—articulating the skin or façades to get a play of light and shadow. But Mies has said: 'Form is not the aim of our work, but only the result.' . . . He has articulated the skin [of his buildings] at the same time creating a play of depth and shadow by the use of the basic structural steel member, the I-beam. This ingenious and deceptively simple solution is comparable to the use of the Greek orders. . . . It is not a capricious solution; it is the essence of the problem of modern architecture that Mies had stated in 1922: 'We should develop the new forms from the very nature of the new problems.' "

Seagram Building, New York City, 1958. Designed in association with Philip C. Johnson. The façade is of bronze and gray-tinted glass. (Photo: Ezra Stoller)

So, Mies was selected to design the new Seagram Building, and he, in turn, asked Philip Johnson (who was registered as an architect in New York State) to associate with him on the project. Three and a half years later, in the summer of 1958, the thirty-eight-story bronze- and gray-glass tower on Park Avenue was formally opened. By almost any standards the building was a superlative success. Lewis Mumford, the advocate of open spaces and of more humanism in the city, wrote delightedly that the open plaza in front of the elegant tower, which represented a wonderfully conspicious "waste" of some fifty percent of the site, set an important example for others to emulate. As for the bronze finish on the building, Mumford admired its "warmth" and pointed out that Mies could no longer be considered a "cold" architect in the light of this performance. Henry-Russell Hitchcock said that he had never seen "more of less." And the British architect Peter Smithson—a leader of the so-called New Brutalist cult in England—admired the Seagram Building's elegance and *lack* of brutality. "Everything else [in Manhattan] now looks like a jumped-up supermart," he said.

Indeed, the most remarkable effect of Seagram's triumph was what the building did to some of the fine work around it: diagonally across Park Avenue stands the handsome Lever House, based originally upon Mies's glass towers of the early twenties, but now looking a little too slick, a little too much like a Cadillac next to Seagram's Rolls Royce nobility. Curiously enough, it was only the sixty-year-old Italianate Racquet Club designed by classicists McKim, Mead & White, directly across from Seagram on Park Avenue, that could look the new bronze tower straight in the eye without flinching.

This, of course, was no accident. For at Seagram, Mies built an essentially classical building—symmetrical, formal, raised on a granite-paved plaza bordered by a marble parapet and inlaid with two rectangular pools. Superficially, Seagram is quite similar to *one* of the "860" towers; but the point, at "860," is that there were first *two* towers and later four, so that the composition on Lakeshore Drive was always asymmetrical and dynamic, whereas the composition of the Seagram tower is axial, monumental, noble, and in repose. How much of this was due to Johnson—whose own glass house is so much more "traditional" and "European" than Mies's Farnsworth house—is hard to say. Of course, all the basic ideas originated with Mies. Like "860," the Seagram tower is raised on stilts, and the lobby is a volume enclosed in glass, deeply recessed behind the main façades of the tower. As a result, the ground floor of the building is surrounded by magnificent arcades, twenty-eight feet high. Above these arcades the tower soars upward to its full height of 520 uninterrupted feet, the verticality stressed by the same sort of applied I-beam mullions that give "860" its rhythm (though at Seagram the I-beam extrusions are of bronze). There is added drama in the verticality of Seagram, for the building was set back from the avenue almost 100 feet, so that pedestrians can really see the full height of this tower. By contrast, other Manhattan buildings, which tend to crowd the sidewalks, look puny because no pedestrian can really see them in their full height. Mies feels that a building deserves to be walked up to, not just driven into: for nobody dashing into an entrance lobby from an automobile portico will ever experience the full drama of a skyscaper. Actually, the Seagram Building does have canopied side entrances, for use on rainy days, as well as a large, underground drive-in garage.

Inside the glass lobby the symmetry is carried through in the arrangement of travertine-sheathed elevator stacks. At night these blocks of travertine are washed in light from coves recessed in the ceiling. Indeed, the entire building was designed with a view to night lighting: all office spaces around the perimeter have luminous ceilings that give a uniform effect to the bronze cage when the building is lit up after dark.

Rarely has a building been designed with such painstaking care all the way through. No doorknob, no lavatory or faucet, no sign, no mail chute was left to accident. All were carefully designed to make the building a unified whole. Much of the interior work was done by Johnson, and he carried Mies's discipline through into every single detail, however seemingly unimportant. Works of art were bought or specially commissioned for the Seagram Company's own floors, and much of Mies's own timeless furniture of the 1920's was used in those offices. The ultimate in perfection was probably reached in the design of the Seagram executives' men's room—a little retreat of travertine, white leather, stainless steel, and glass which would have pleased the Emperor Tiberius.

When the Seagram Building was ready to open, every architect of note in New York attended. Only Mies was absent, for his legs were almost completely paralyzed by one of his recurring attacks of arthritis. He had not been in New York very much during the months when the finishing touches were applied to the building, for apart from being hindered in his travels by his sickness, he was annoyed by a gratuitous slap administered to him by the authorities in charge of licensing architects in New York State. These gentlemen had noted that he was only licensed in Illinois, and had requested him to go through the formalities of New York State registration before continuing with his work on Seagram. When Mies tried to do so, it was discovered to the horror of New York's bureaucrats that he had never completed his high-school education! When it was suggested to him that he might take a high-school examination, Mies packed up and returned to Chicago in disgust. Johnson later managed to straighten things out, and Mies may now practice architecture in New York State without risking a prison sentence!

Seagram was an expensive building, possibly the most expensive skyscraper, per square foot, ever built up to that time. Yet it seemed to repay much of its cost in terms of good public relations and other intangibles, and the paved plaza in front of the building gave it such nobility and "prestige" that numerous banks offered large sums to the Seagram Company for the right to build branch offices on the plaza, not realizing, apparently, that the desecration of the plaza would rob the site of the very nobility the prestige-hungry bankers were willing to purchase at such high cost!

In some respects, Seagram represented the ultimate development of Mies's glass towers—the final perfection of the more or less smooth glass-and-metal curtain wall. Compared to the flat and crude curtain walls all around it in Manhattan, Seagram had the distinction of a brooch by Cartier over a piece of cheap "costume jewelry." Yet, to most architects in America, Seagram raised one obvious question. "Where do we go from here?" For Mies this question did not exist; so long as logic (i.e., existing technology) led unerringly to the rectangular steel cage, so long as the I-beam was the pilaster of our century and, hence, symbolized "structure"—so long did Truth and Beauty lie along a straight and narrow road lined by buildings like "860" and Seagram.

Yet there were many others whose convictions about architecture, truth, and beauty were less firm or rigid; and these more flexible men started to find themselves subjected to pressures from unexpected quarters—pressures intended to force them to produce "something new" regardless of whether the novelty was in any way valid. The forces that demand novelty for novelty's sake—or, rather, novelty for advertising's sake—are familiar enough in business: indeed, the U.S. economy would cease to function if it were not for the stylists who produce new models of this dress or that automobile every six months or every year, and thus force the average consumer to buy the new model or face social ostracism. During the years of plenty in America, the 1950's in particular, these pressures to produce "something new" began to be applied to artists as well, and many of the weaker ones became victims. A talented composer presented a work of music consisting of several minutes of dead silence. (It was, quite possibly, his best work; but was it art?) A talented painter began to exhibit canvases showing nothing (he was immediately hailed by the taste makers as a bright new star on the artistic firmament). And so forth. The undeniable fact was that the taste makers, like the promoters of streamlined electric toasters and automobiles with fish tails, had found it necessary to push for novelty or face professional ruin. Magazines did not want to publish anything that "looked the same," so they published buildings that looked like fish or turtles; museum directors had to keep the trustees and the public amused, so they exhibited buildings that looked like chickens or eggs. The pressure was on full blast: unless an architect was willing to face *critical* ostracism, he had to jump on the hucksters' bandwagon.

To Mies all this was not only nonsense, it was worse than that—heresy and dishonesty. "I ask myself," he said speaking of a particularly convoluted building that had just made the front page of a magazine, "what this thing would look like on Michigan Avenue. *That* is the problem of our epoch! They [the "news makers"] say they are bored with my objectivity. Well, I am bored with their subjectivity!" It was not that Mies was trying to perpetuate an old-fashioned technology simply in order to perpetuate his own form of expression. (Indeed, in 1946, when he had first become acquainted with the structural properties of reinforced plastics, Mies designed a number of compound-curved chairs very similar in form to conch shells. This was long before most architects began to play the "shell game," and it made obvious sense in terms of *chair* technology and *chair* function.) But everyone familiar with the problems of American building today and in the forseeable future knows that the rectangular frame of steel or concrete, within certain minor variations of detail, is the only logical kind of structure for most buildings in economic and technical terms. Undoubtedly this harsh fact of life imposes upon American architects a discipline—even a strait jacket —which many of them are tempted to throw off. Every issue of every architectural magazine shows one or two buildings that torture structure —buildings that reflect, with terrifying clarity, the desperate and presently fruitless struggles of certain architects to break through the limitations imposed by technology. These tortured buildings are the agonies of those who lack the stern faith of Mies—the faith that rests upon St. Augustine's "Beauty is the splendor of Truth." Mies, also, needs an outlet for creativity, and he finds it in the perfection of details. (For his Bacardi building in Cuba, Mies made more than a hundred detailed studies of the profile for the eight concrete columns that hold up the roof.) But novelty for its own sake? That, to Mies, disqualifies a man from being an architect. "I don't want to be interesting," Mies told an interviewer. "I want to be good!"

X I V

N THE ARCHITECTURAL SCHOOLS of the United States, Europe, and the Far East, Mies today reigns supreme. The unfaltering logic of his steel cage filled with glass or brick, the convincing strength of his concept of universality to serve a world of rapidly changing needs and functions, and the fact, finally, that Mies's work (as Philip Johnson has said) seems so easy to copy—these have made Miesian architecture the simplest and most flexible vocabulary available to today's architectural students. And his influence is by no means confined to the schools: in England, Germany, Japan—as well as throughout the United States— architects originally trained in a freer idiom have today accepted Mies's discipline, because they have found it the most logical way of applying the available technology to modern problems. Only in the concrete-

building countries—France, Italy, the South American countries, etc.—
is Mies's rectangular discipline challenged by the plasticity of Le Corbusier.

This does not mean that Mies's followers have invariably succeeded in translating Miesian technology into architecture. Much of
today's Miesian work is little more than a re-use, for eminently practical reasons, of Mies's details and his basic principles of planning. The
refinement of proportion, the perfection of workmanship—these are often
lacking. For Mies has only provided a vocabulary; most use it to write
prose; only a few can write poetry. Still, a coherent prose-vocabulary is
one of the most urgent needs of architecture today—just as it was when
our beautiful New England towns were first constructed from carpenters' "pattern-books."

By comparison with Corbu, Gropius, and Wright, Mies has dedicated himself to a very limited area of endeavor: where the other three
treated the whole world and all its problems as part of their concern,
Mies seemed to have drawn a tight circle in the sand and said: "Only
these things within this circle are the concerns of architecture." Outside this tight circle, Mies has placed problems of political and physical
planning on a large scale, problems of painting and sculpture, problems
of theoretical speculation. Indeed, he has even left out some problems
of functionalism which are rightly considered a part of the architect's
area of activity, and he has left them out at his own peril. To him,
architecture has always been a single, simple progression, from material
through technology to significant form and art.

His apparent narrowness when compared to far-ranging men like
Gropius, Corbu, and Wright has had several distinct advantages: for
one thing, Mies became a master of the limited field he had outlined
for himself, whereas the others became generalizers of ideas, rather than
specialists in any given area. No one in our time has built with as much
attention to detail as Mies; both Corbu and Wright have often ignored
the details of building—Mies, never. For another, Mies has never deviated from the *possible*. Others in search for new forms or symbols or
techniques to alleviate the boredom within themselves have often strayed
all over the lot; Mies, who once told his students that "education must
lead us . . . from chance and arbitrariness to rational clarity and intel-

Administration building for the Bacardi Company, Santiago, Cuba, 1958. The coffered concrete roof is supported on eight cross-shaped concrete columns. The glass pavilion on the pedestal contains a large office space; the pedestal itself holds subsidiary offices and storage spaces. (Photo: Hedrich-Blessing)

lectual order," has never been tempted to wander into the Disneyland of modern architecture. To him, there are no laws that dictate forms in architecture; but there *are* laws that demand responsibility, clarity, and intellectual order. He has often been criticized for "working with blinders on." To this Mies answers that "if it were necessary to make curves, I would make curves. [But] as long as we have this same economic and scientific structure, steel will be the essence of our cities. Our buildings need not look alike. After all, there are about 10,000 species of seashells. They don't look alike, but they have the same principle. The trouble is that most architects try to invent something every time. *The real thing is a very slow unfolding of form. We should refine what is known. And when a new problem comes along, then we'll know how to solve it.*"

A new problem came along late in 1958, when Mies was asked to design the Bacardi office building in Santiago, Cuba. The problem was concrete, and Mies solved it with tremendous verve: on a classic pedestal similar to that which supported the Barcelona Pavilion, Mies placed a structure of eight cross-shaped, tapered concrete columns that carry a concrete roof plane some 180 feet square. This roof is a five-foot deep concrete egg crate, and its column supports occur approximately fifty feet in from each of the four corners, so that the corners themselves are deeply cantilevered from the supports. The roof thus seems to float almost twenty-five feet above the paved pedestal. The gray-tinted glass walls of the great office space are recessed twenty feet from the face of the roof plane so that the interior will be shaded most of the time. As Bacardi's owners wanted a single large room in which to conduct their operations, Mies divided the great space only by three low, free-standing partitions. The pedestal on which the building stands is high enough so that many of the service rooms can be accommodated below the glass room.

"The trouble as well as the advantage of concrete is that you can do anything with it," Philip Johnson once said. "You can't rely on structural discipline as a guide." Almost anyone except Mies would have run riot with his first all-concrete building; indeed, others who profess to be influenced by Mies have abandoned all architectural restraint when they first encountered this flexible material. But Barcardi, though unmistakably a building of reconstructed stone—almost a modern version of the Parthenon set on its own formal Acropolis—remains an intensely moral building: serene, clear, unaffected, pure, and utterly self-assured. It is likely to do for modern *concrete* architecture what the Farnsworth house did for modern *steel* architecture—that is, bring its practitioners back to their senses.

By the middle of 1959 Mies was very busy indeed. He had just completed a museum in Houston, Texas, and though he had to attend its opening in a wheelchair, his arthritis had let up considerably since then and he was almost as spry as in the old days. The Bacardi Company had commissioned him to build a second structure in Mexico City; the U.S. State Department had asked him to design the new Consulate General in São Paulo, Brazil; and several of Herb Greenwald's projects would probably go ahead, despite Greenwald's death. Like all the other "Grand Old Men" of modern architecture, Mies was beginning to col-

Detail of typical column for the Bacardi building. The tapered concrete columns are topped with a stainless steel "hinge" on which the roof is supported. (Courtesy, Mies van der Rohe)

lect honors, right and left. In the summer of 1959 he went to London
to receive the Royal Gold Medal for Architecture from Queen Elizabeth
II. After that, there was a medal or two to pick up in his native Germany. And in 1960 the American Institute of Architects awarded him
its Gold Medal as well. Wherever he went, there were enthusiastic, and
curious, admirers. For Mies, the man who had swept modern architecture cleaner than anyone else, was virtually unknown as a person. And
after the embarrassment of all the publicity was over, Mies returned to
his quiet and uncluttered apartment in Chicago with a sigh of relief.

He was not in the best of health. Arthritis plagued him more and
more, and he began to spend most of his time in a wheelchair. Yet,
even though he was thus confined, he worked on numerous projects
both in the U.S. and in Canada that rank among his finest: the Federal
Center in Downtown Chicago (two office towers, and a single-story
post office between them); the Toronto-Dominion Centre on 5.5 acres

*Section through Westmount Square, Montreal, 1968. The
two buildings at left are twenty-one-story apartment houses;
the taller building at right is an office tower; and the two-
story structure between them is a low-rise commercial
building. The base on which Westmont Square stands contains a shopping concourse tied into Montreal's subway
system. (Photo: Hedrich-Blessing)*

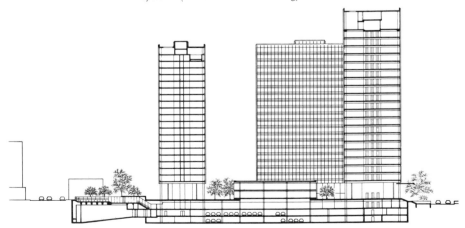

View of Westmount Square at plaza level. The two-story commercial building is at left, one of the apartment buildings is straight ahead, and the colonnade of the office tower is at right. (Photo: Peter Blake)

of land in the heart of that city (two tall towers, with a single-story banking pavilion between them); and Westmount Square, in Montreal (two apartment towers, one office tower, and—between these—a low, two-story commercial building). The last two of these projects were important in terms of city planning as well: the platforms on which they sit contain elaborate infrastructures patterned after New York's Rockefeller Center—pedestrian concourses, stores, parking garages, and connecting links to mass-transit facilities. In Westmount Square, especially, the integration of the complex with the infrastructure of Montreal is an impressive achievement.

These buildings and complexes represent subtle refinements in detail of the basic model established by Mies at Lakeshore Drive and in the Seagram tower several years earlier. When the budget permitted it, the curtain wall would be detailed in bronze, as at Seagram (and as in the as-yet-unbuilt office tower for the City of London); when the budget was tight, Mies would fall back on a roughly similar curtain wall of anodized aluminum or of painted steel. But though these curtain walls appeared to the casual observer to be identical, they did, in fact, represent subtle refinements in many details—in the integration of airconditioning grilles, in the joining of mullions to glass, in the turning of corners. Mies saw no point in changing his basic vocabulary, at least not until technology had provided significant alternatives, in materials or components, or in ways of assembling them. So he continued to build and to refine.

To revisionist critics of modern architecture, Mies van de Rohe's urban spaces—horizontal slabs of marble and water—should, almost by definition, be "urban wastelands." Oddly enough, this does not seem to be the case at all. William H. Whyte, one of the most astute critics of modern urban design, thinks that the Seagram Plaza in Manhattan is quite simply the best of its vintage—in terms of human accommodation. Philip Johnson, who was Mies van der Rohe's associate on that project, was delighted by Whyte's judgement, but also considered it something of a joke. That plaza, according to Johnson, was not designed with any thought whatsoever for human comfort—it was designed as a pedestal to set off the Seagram's bronze-and-glass shaft against the rest of the streetscape. "What all this proves, of course," Johnson has said, "is that great architecture ultimately is the thing that draws people, and moves them." Mies, one feels, rejected the condescension implied in some contemporary urban criticism—the notion that one must design "down" to people's rather pedestrian needs so as to make them feel comfortable. Mies believed that mankind does not live by bread alone.

X V

T HROUGHOUT MOST of the 1960's, Mies had worked on a scheme for a so-called New National Gallery (Neue Nationalgalerie) to be built in West Berlin, as part of a large cultural center going up in that city. On September 15th, 1968, the building was dedicated. It turned out to be one of his finest works—easily on a part with the Barcelona Pavilion and the Seagram tower.

Its basic scheme resembles that of the Bacardi Administration Building, designed by Mies for Santiago, Cuba, in 1958, but never built. It differs from the Bacardi Building in two essential respects: its great pavilion structure is of steel, rather than of concrete—and it is about fifty per cent larger in area. The huge steel-and-glass pavilion was designed to house temporary exhibitions (it is known as the Gallery of the Twentieth Century); and the pedestal on which the pavilion stands houses the permanent collection of the so-called Prussian Cultural Heritage Foundation. The two areas are administered as a single museum, but—initially, at least—the exhibition spaces were kept quite separate. As a result, exhibitions much more suitable for the low (thirteen foot) ceiling height of the galleries within the pedestal were shown under the huge (twenty-eight foot) ceiling height of the upper level, and dwarfed by it.

Apart from this, the building is a success in every respect. It has a grace, an attention to detail, a quiet repose that makes it one of the most completely self-assured structures of the century. When Dirk Lohan, Mies' grandson and close collaborator, inspected the finished building, he felt that the "grain" of the Greek marble used to clad the two vertical utility shafts within the upper floor might have been better matched. But that seemed to be the only flaw—and no one except Lohan or Mies would have noticed it.

The vital statistics are impressive: the prefabricated, steel roof measures about 215 feet square, and weighs 1,250 tons. It was raised hydraulically to a clear height of twenty-eight feet in a mere eight hours and fifty-seven minutes. (Mies was driven onto the site in a Mercedes convertible during the roof-hoisting operation, and stood under the roof as it went up, leaning against his car. Someone found him there, watching those 1,250 tons of steel poised over his head—while his chauffeur had taken cover in a safer precinct—and asked how it all looked to him. "Enormous!" he said, grinning, and puffing at his cigar.)

Like the Bacardi project, the glass pavilion of the New National Gallery is supported on eight cross-shaped steel columns, pin-connected to the roof. The roof framing consists of six foot deep welded steel girders, spaced twelve feet apart in both directions to form the grid. The frame, it was announced by the German structural engineers, was "statically indeterminate to the 36th degree," and could not have been designed without reference to computers. One major problem, in Mies' mind, at least, was how to determine the amount of camber (or upward curvature) required in the steel roof to counteract the downward deflection that occurs when the structure settles in place. This incredibly

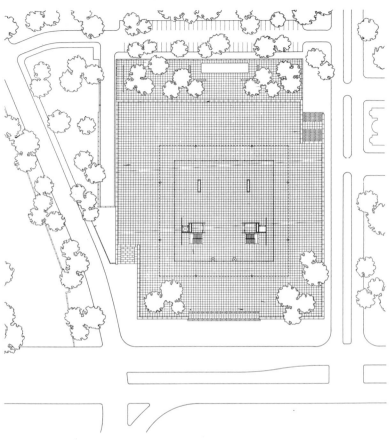

Upper floor plan, Neue Nationalgalerie, Berlin, 1968. This floor was designed to house temporary exhibitions. (Photo: Hedrich-Blessing)

subtle balance between initial upward curvature and ultimate downward deflection was here achieved to perfection.

The roof grid contains elaborate downlights, designed to be as inconspicuous as possible. Within the egg-crate of structural steel, there are recessed grilles of black aluminum that keep the glare of spotlights out of the viewer's eyes.

The platform on which the steel-and-glass pavilion stands is more conventional in construction—reinforced concrete, clad in granite, and

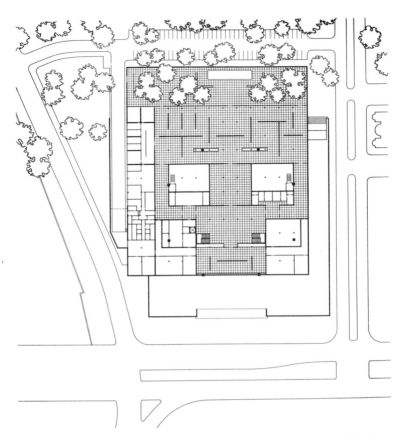

Lower floor plan, Neue Nationalgalerie, Berlin. This level was designed to house the permanent collection of the Prussian Cultural Heritage Foundation. (Photo: Hedrich-Blessing)

measuring roughly 350 by 340 feet in plan. A portion of this—a slice about sixty-six feet wide and a little more than 300 feet long—is a sculpture court, open to the sky. The rest of this handsome "basement" is a succession of spacious galleries, most of them artificially lit.

The site is next to one of West Berlin's characteristic canals—the Landwehrkanal—and has a slight slope to it; and the New National Gallery's pedestal almost touches the sidewalk on the east, and drops off toward the west so that the walled sculpture court, at the end of the building, is really on grade with its surroundings. The building not merely fits into its site—it helps define and organize it through its granite retaining walls, and the wide flights of stairs that rise to the upper level platform. That platform—the plaza on which the steel-and-glass pavilion stands—supports major works of sculpture as well.

When the New National Gallery was dedicated, Mies' doctors in Chicago pronounced him unfit to attend the ceremonies.

They were wrong, and he might have lived a little longer had he seen this splendid work. Museum directors from every part of the world attended the opening, and so did architects—including even Walter Gropius. He had not always seen eye-to-eye with Mies, nor Mies with him. An American friend who had gone to Berlin to attend the dedication talked to Mies upon his return. Mies was enormously excited: he did not care about the honors, the dignitaries who had attended (or what they had said); he wanted to know about the light and the space, and about the finish of the structure and the quality of the workmanship.

He had told the citizens of Berlin, three years earlier, during the groundbreaking ceremonies, that he hoped his Gallery would be "an

Bird's-eye view, Neue Nationalgalerie. The walled sculpture court on the lower level is at left. (Photo: Walter Sanders)

*Glass wall of the Neue Nationalgalerie. The sculpture at
far left is by Alexander Calder. (Photo: Peter Blake)*

adequate framework for a noble endeavor"; and a few days before the
dedication he had sent word from Chicago that he hoped the New
National Gallery would serve the happiness of mankind, man's spirit,
and man's art.

He seemed to sense that this would be his last work. He died in
Chicago, at the age of eighty-three, on August 17th, 1969. He had accomplished everything that an architect could accomplish in a lifetime,
and more.

FRANK LLOYD WRIGHT

and the Mastery of Space

I

FRANK LLOYD WRIGHT was, very probably, the last of the true Americans. This is not intended to suggest that he was of Red Indian origin (which he wasn't) or that his ancestors came over on the *Mayflower* (which they didn't). It *is* intended to mean that Wright was the last great representative of all the things this country once stood for in the world when "America" was still a radical concept, rather than a settled continent: a symbol of absolute, untrammeled freedom for every individual, of as little government as possible, the end of classes and castes, of unlimited and equal physical opportunities for the adventurous, of the absence of all prejudice—excepting prejudices in favor of anything new and bold; of the absence of form and of formality, and, finally, a

Frank Lloyd Wright at Taliesin West. (Photo: P. E. Guerrero)

symbol of a society of many individuals living as individuals in individual settlements—not a society of masses living in giant cities.

When Wright was born in the 1860's, America was still, to some extent, that sort of miraculous place. Only a dozen years earlier Walt Whitman had published his first edition of *Leaves of Grass*; and though Whitman believed (just as Wright was to believe in his later years) that the American idea was being corrupted by all the things that had helped sterilize Western Europe, the very existence of Whitman and Thoreau and Emerson was evidence of the continuing strength of the fundamental, anarchic dream of a community of individuals.

To understand Wright's position in American history, it must be remembered that Emerson, Longfellow, Melville, and Whitman were still alive when Wright was born. Thoreau had died only half a dozen years earlier, at the age of forty-five. Tom Paine and Jefferson were as recent a memory to Wright's family as Theodore Roosevelt is to our parents. The Civil War was barely over. America was being interpreted (and criticized) by the spokesmen of the romantic movement. Frank Lloyd Wright, the son of a Baptist preacher in Richland Center, Wisconsin, was born right into that movement and never left it until the day he died.

One of the many oddities about Wright is that the exact year of his birth is a little uncertain. During the last decades of his life Wright always gave June 8, 1869, as his birth date, but there is some evidence that he was actually born two years earlier. Why he should want to cheat the record by a mere two years is something of a mystery, unless he was, at one point, loath to admit to his real age and found himself stuck with that little white lie for the rest of his life. This is not at all unlikely, as Wright, who had the looks and talents of a spectacularly handsome matinee idol (or former matinee idol) during most of his life, was delightfully vain about his personal appearance and his youth. In his last dozen years or so he became more and more touchy about the photographic portraits that were published of him. He was particularly fond of one photograph showing him, at the age of eighty, astride an impressive charger; on the other hand, he strongly disapproved of a frontispiece photo used by the publishers of one of his last books, because the picture showed his hair to be quite long—a fact that (he claimed) made him look effeminate! Whenever he saw a copy of that book on a friend's shelf, he would quickly pull out a pencil and start blacking out the long hairline in the frontispiece picture.

These rather charming vanities were, perhaps, an important clue to Wright's personality. To the outside world he often seemed arrogant, strident, full of conceit. Yet, in all likelihood, these characteristics were little more than a "front." He was a country boy all his life: a country boy who had been sneered at as some sort of "hick" when he first emerged from the Wisconsin hills; a country boy who had spent all his life defending the simple, hick-like things he had learned about in Wisconsin against the condescension and scorn of urban sophisticates. He was intensely conscious of his clothes (he learned to dress like a king), intensely conscious of what people thought and said of him, intensely conscious of and deeply hurt by what he considered to be the insults regularly hurled at him by the city slickers. Although he liked to make a good deal of noise whenever he emerged from the brush to put in a spectacular appearance on some Big City forum, it is very likely that the noise was really nothing more than an understandable defense against the hostility he fully expected to meet in the city.

To him, the city was evil incarnate—and growing more evil by leaps and bounds. When Wright was born, there were only 38,000,000 people in the United States; when he died, there were nearly 180,000,-000. When he was born, only one quarter of his fellow Americans lived in cities; when he died, almost three quarters had moved into the big urban centers. Wright himself was a part of the minority that had not: after his death in April 1959 he was buried in Spring Green, Wisconsin, only a dozen miles or so from where he was born some ninety years earlier. It seems to have been almost a matter of principle with him that he never really left the place where he first saw the light of day.

Wright's parents were anything but ordinary: his father who, in all likelihood, was born in England, had been married once before and widowed. Sometime after that, in Wisconsin, when he was nearly fifty, he met Anna Lloyd-Jones, who was almost twenty years his junior. They were married and had three children, Frank being the oldest. Shortly after the birth of their third child, the Wrights moved to Massachusetts, where they stayed until the boy was ten, at which time they returned to Wisconsin.

Wright's father was eccentric, to say the least. There had been a tradition of preaching in his family, and so he became a preacher, too. But his real passion was music, and he literally inundated his home with music from morning till night. To make a living, he would sometimes preach, sometimes give music lessons, and never do either one of these things very profitably. When his son Frank was only fifteen years old, William Wright suddenly disappeared; he had decided to abandon his family, and neither his wife nor his children ever saw him again.

Unlike his father, Wright's mother was an extraordinarily strong personality. Although Wright used to describe much of his childhood by referring to life and work on Uncle James Lloyd-Jones's farm, the truth is that both before and after his father disappeared young Frank was his mother's favorite and, probably, a pampered one at that. His mother, according to Wright, had been absolutely sure even before he was born that he would be a great architect; she had dominated his life from the earliest years through her preoccupation with certain educational theories and systems; and she had sacrificed a great deal to enable him to enter the University of Wisconsin as a student in civil engineering. Yet, although Wright was quite possibly pampered by his mother and endowed by her with an enduring arrogance, there is no indication that he was ever a spoiled weakling. Indeed, the very opposite is true; nonetheless, he *did* rather worry about the fact that his face looked a little womanly. When Wright died, Alistair Cooke, the American correspondent of the *Manchester Guardian*, wrote that Wright used to look "like Merlin posing as Whistler's Mother. Indeed, there was always a curiously feminine grace about him," Cooke continued. "He looked . . . like a matriarch of a pioneer family." If Wright had been alive to read this charming and witty tribute, he might, conceivably, have punched Mr. Cooke in the nose—or would have, at a younger and more pugnacious age.

Wright, of course, was anything but effeminate. But it was his strong-willed mother, rather than his erratic father, who governed his early life and left her imprint on the later years as well. Grant Manson, Wright's scholarly biographer, has recorded one incident, in particular, that formed the young man's life most decisively: when the Wright family was living, briefly, in Massachusetts, the parents took a trip to Philadelphia to see the Centennial exposition being held there in 1876. Mrs. Wright, who had long been interested in various educational theories, discovered at the exposition a small display explaining the theories of the German progressive educator Friedrich Froebel, who had, before his death some twenty-five years earlier, succeeded in establishing a whole series of kindergartens throughout Germany. (Indeed, he invented the word "kindergarten.") His basic theory was that children should be taught through creative play to experience objects, colors, textures, causes, and effects. (In a sense, therefore, he had anticipated the famous Bauhaus introductory course by seventy years!) To supplement his theories, Froebel had developed several sets of toys—most of them simple, geometric blocks that children were encouraged to assemble in different ways—and these sets of blocks had become available in the U.S. as well. Mrs. Wright immediately became fascinated with these objects and the theories behind them; she began to read all she could about Froebel's ideas, got in touch with Froebelian teachers in New York and Boston, and, as it was too difficult to send Frank to the nearest Froebelian kindergarten (he was too old for that, in any case), she set up her own little Froebelian play school for her son in her own home.

In later years Wright frequently acknowledged the great impression these games made upon him. Not only did they give him an immediate, tangible acquaintance with shapes of every sort, but they also introduced him to ways of ordering related elements into larger groups of forms. Froebel's notion was that children should be brought to relate his blocks and other devices in imaginative, but increasingly *planned* compositions, and he suggested that these compositions might form furniture, or complete buildings, or even small villages and towns. In any event, Wright found these blocks a wonderful medium through which to exercise his imagination: Froebel's basic units may have been rectangular blocks (which tended to add up to rectangular structures); but beyond these blocks, there were games using folded and pleated paper, string, beads, spheres, and cones; and the young Frank Lloyd Wright found delight in all of these as well.

When the Wrights returned to Wisconsin to live in Madison, young Frank came under the influence of his uncle, James Lloyd-Jones, whose farm, located some thirty miles west of Madison, became a second home to him. There he spent a good deal of time every summer working hard and close to the soil. It was pretty rough going, but, despite the drudgery, he felt that working with nature and natural things brought him in touch with values that had changed very little throughout the history of mankind. Moreover, as he got to know life on the land more and more intimately, young Wright saw that nature was a wonderful teacher and had answers to many questions that theoretical learning could not explain nearly so well.

This is how young Frank Lloyd Wright grew up: largely dominated by an extraordinarily powerful mother who adored him and did everything possible to lead him to greatness; close to the wildly romantic traditions of his mother's pure Welsh ancestors, (whose motto, "Truth against the World," was both a defiant statement of rationalism against prejudice, and a typical *Sturm und Drang* slogan of a passionately individualistic era); and just as close to the land where his mother's forebears had worked and he, Frank, would also work and live and die. These are the names of nearby towns and villages: Lone Rock, Black Earth, Blue River. Spring Green was where Uncle James Lloyd-Jones had his farm. These names are part of the romance of Wright's life—part of what he took from the Wisconsin hills and tried to convey to the world at large as a great and lasting principle.

HEN WILLIAM WRIGHT walked out on his family, Frank decided that he had to go to work and help support his mother and his sisters. He was then only in his teens, but his preoccupation with building made it perfectly clear to him where to turn for work, and he took a job with a local contractor in Madison. As there were no architects in the town, Allen Conover, Wright's employer, designed as well as built his structures; and while their design was undistinguished, their contruction was generally very solid.

Young Wright started as an apprentice to Conover and moved on to becoming supervisor of construction on several jobs. At the same time, he spent a few hours each day at the University of Wisconsin, studying civil engineering. After some two years of this combined study and apprenticeship, Wright left Conover's office, as well as the university, and went to Chicago. To fortify him, his mother (who strongly disapproved of the move) had given him a copy of Plutarch's *Lives*, and sewn a little mink collar on his tweed coat. Wright was no more than eighteen years old; he had spent less than two years in intermittent study at the university; he had had some apprenticeship in building; he had had no chance to acquire stylistic prejudices about architecture; and he had enormous confidence in his own ability. This confidence together with whatever genius he might be able to summon from within himself were his only tangible assets.

Going to Chicago was not as much of a risk as it may appear in retrospect. One of Wright's uncles, the Reverend Jenkin Lloyd-Jones, had commissioned a well-known Chicago architect, Lyman Silsbee, to design a new church for his congregation. It was pretty well understood that young Frank could get a job in Silsbee's office to work on that church if he wanted to—and he did.

Wright stayed with Silsbee for less than a year, but the man's influence upon him was quite considerable. Silsbee, though an Easterner, had none of the growing infatuation with the neoclassicism being preached by the Beaux Arts Academy in Paris; instead, his own style was rather comfortably, informally English—a sort of early "cottage style," somewhat rambling, soft, romantic, never ostentatious, always restrained. Silsbee liked to use many elements then in fashion: shingled walls, porches with archways leading into them, hexagonal rooms or bays jutting out of rooms, picturesque combinations of chimneys, dormers, and intersecting roof planes. Although there was nothing in the least bit unconventional about Silsbee, his ground rules, if any, were so flexible when compared with those of the neoclassicists that Wright was able to pick and choose from a fairly broad range of details, forms, and expressions. Silsbee was good for Wright, not only because he opened his eyes to a number of new possibilities, but also because he did not limit Wright's growth at a critical moment by forcing him into any stylistic strait jacket.

Wright left Silsbee's office late in 1887 to take a job with the firm of Adler & Sullivan. Louis H. Sullivan was then only beginning to make his mark, though architects and draftsmen, especially in Chicago, knew that his approach differed radically from the accepted notions of polite architecture of the period. Sullivan had written and spoken of a new "democratic" architecture whose form would develop naturally out of structure, material, and function. Although he was only in his early thirties when Wright came to him, Sullivan was already looked upon as the great white hope of Chicago architecture; and just before Wright walked into his office, Dankmar Adler and Louis Sullivan had won the commission to build the Chicago Auditorium, the great opera house which was supposed to establish Chicago as the cultural center of the United States.

Although the sketches Wright showed to Sullivan when he came to ask for a job left the older man rather cold, Wright was hired and put to work on the Auditorium drawings. In those days Sullivan was still strongly influenced by the massive, Romanesque stone buildings of Henry Hobson Richardson, and the exterior of the Auditorium was to owe a great deal to Richardson's vigorous Marshall Field warehouse, almost completed at the time of Richardson's death in 1886. But inside, the Auditorium was a burst of exuberance and decorative delight that was strictly Sullivan's own characteristic ornament. This ornament, with which he liked to cover huge surfaces, consisted of intricately entwined plants—grasses and leaves forming a lacy pattern without beginning or end. Sullivan used to draw this ornament, free-hand and full-size, on endless rolls of paper which would then be turned over to the terra-cotta men or the plasterers to reproduce in three dimensions.

To work on the Auditorium was Wright's principal assignment in Adler & Sullivan's office for a year or more. It made an enormous impression upon him, and in many different ways. But most importantly, perhaps, the work on the Auditorium introduced Wright to what was, in effect, the vocabulary of Art Nouveau—for Sullivan's concept of ornament was, in most essentials, undistinguishable from the sort of thing done by William Morris and others in England and on the Continent. Like Sullivan, these artists tried to find a new "honesty" in design, and they saw in the forms of nature a complete set of principles which, if followed, would inevitably lead to this new honesty in expression. The Art Nouveau movement was given added impetus by the newly discovered decorative work from Japan which was largely based upon forms in nature and had developed a highly stylized set of images based upon these forms.

Art Nouveau, in the hands of lesser men, tended to degenerate simply into another form of surface decoration. And surface decoration is indeed what Sullivan produced with his Art Nouveau designs. But to both him and, much more so, to his brilliant young assistant, the forms found in nature seemed to hold a deeper meaning; for these were, in effect, structural forms, though of a sort that Sullivan, at least, was never able to grasp in their full implication. He remained to the end interested in the rectangular cage, the more or less modular skyscraper frame that we have come to accept as a commonplace today. He realized (unlike many of his successors in the skyscraper game) that the proportion of a structural bay was all important, and that changing the proportion as the building rose to its full height added an infinitely subtle touch to the drama of the soaring, vertical shaft. He also saw in his ornament (which really became an over-all texture whose detail was apparent only at very close quarters) a means of enriching the flat slabs his cagelike buildings must inevitably become.

All this Sullivan understood clearly, and he sensed, perhaps, that there was an inner meaning in the forms of plants, which he used as a basis of his ornament—an inner meaning that might lead to a very different kind of structure and architecture. But he only sensed it; it was Frank Lloyd Wright who, many years later, began to see through the tracery of Sullivan's ornament at the Auditorium and elsewhere, and saw through it a great architectural truth—a principle he was later to call "organic architecture."

When Wright first entered Adler & Sullivan's office, he found the going tough. He was considered something of an upstart by his fellow draftsmen. They thought he was crude, uneducated, and arrogant. They ganged up on the country hick and made life hard for him from the first day on. In many respects Wright undoubtedly provoked whatever animosity he encountered in Sullivan's office. More than fifty years later, in his *Autobiography*, he recalled his first impressions of that office in less than appealing language. Here he is, describing the draftsmen in the Adler & Sullivan office: "To the right Eisendrath—apparently stupid. Jewish. Behind me to the left Ottenheimer—alert, apparently bright. Jew too. Turned around to survey the group. Isbell, Jew? Gaylord, no— not. Weydert, Jew undoubtedly. Directly behind, Weatherwax. Couldn't make him out. In the corner Andresen—Swedish. Several more Jewish faces. Of course—I thought, because Mr. Adler himself must be a Jew. . . ." Finally, one day the animosity engendered by the cocky youngster from Wisconsin exploded into a fist fight. Wright recalls this, too, in his *Autobiography*: "I laid down my pencil, swung around on the stool and looked at him," Wright remembered, many years later. "He sat at his table, a heavy-bodied, short-legged, pompadoured, conceited, red-faced Jew, wearing gold glasses. . . . I got up and walked slowly over to him and without realizing he was wearing glasses, or hesitating, struck him square, full in the face with my right hand, knocking him from his stool to the floor, smashing his glasses. I might have blinded him. . . ."

These passages from Wright's *Autobiography* sound as repellent as a Nazi tract; but the man who is speaking is a rather primitive country-man by instinct, and this includes the usual run-of-the-mill prejudices. Undoubtedly, to a Wisconsin farm boy, Jews were "Big City" crooks, and had to be handled accordingly. Many years later, when Wright had his Fellowship of young apprentices in Wisconsin and Arizona, he demonstrated again and again—and not publicly at any time—his utter lack of prejudice in the conventional areas of race, color, or creed. Indeed, it almost seems as if he included these faintly nauseating paragraphs in his *Autobiography* as an act of penance; for even while he was writing these sentences, he was busy demonstrating, by his private actions, that he had no hatred for anything in life except cruelty and sham.

Wright won his fist fight in Sullivan's office, and soon after, he was accepted as an equal by the men in the drafting room. The fact that Sullivan saw great promise in the young man naturally helped: within two years after Wright had joined the firm, he was given his own private office next door to Sullivan's. By this time Wright was just twenty-one years old, but Sullivan had seen in him so great a talent that he was willing to turn over to this young man an increasing amount of work and responsibility.

Like many architectural offices doing large buildings, Adler & Sullivan were not properly organized to take on the design of private houses. However, there were frequent occasions when an important businessman-client asked to have a house designed for his own family, and the firm could not afford to turn him down. These jobs were handed to Wright, who, in turn, did most of the drawings at home in his spare time and only occasionally brought his designs to Sullivan for criticism. This arrangement became so routine that Wright was, in effect, almost solely responsible for all domestic work in Adler & Sullivan's offices from about 1888 on. These houses represent Wright's earliest independent work, and one of them—the Charnley house, built in 1891—revealed Wright's independent genius for the first time.

The Charnley house had many extraordinary facets, but in retrospect its most important characteristic is its extreme "modernity"—a kind of modernity which was not to be emulated by the pioneer European architects until twenty or thirty years later. For the Charnley house was an entirely smooth, geometric block, three stories high, rendered in precise brickwork (Wright used a flat, elongated brick known as "Roman brick" to the trade), and composed in an absolutely classical, symmetrical way. The windows were unadorned rectangles cut out of the masonry wall, and the roof appeared to be a thin, flat slab projecting out beyond the face of the building. The composition was severe in the classical manner: there was a base, a truncated masonry shaft, and then the slab roof. (Sullivan, who treated his skyscrapers much as the Greeks and Romans handled a column, generally used a base, a shaft, and a projecting roof cap to balance his tall buildings.) In short, the Charnley house was Wright's first completely disciplined and unromantic statement. When he attacked the International Style architects in later years and criticized the boxiness of their buildings, he liked to mention, casually, that he had done *his* box a few decades earlier and grown out of it. The Charnley house was that box.

As a matter of fact, the house did show certain romantic, Art Nouveau touches, which Wright had obviously acquired from Sullivan. Over the main entrance door there was a projecting balcony, whose parapet was ornamented in a typically Sullivanesque manner; and the edge of the flat, projecting roof was decorated with a continuous frieze that is reminiscent of Sullivan's decorative treatment of the roof fascia of the Wainwright building in St. Louis, completed in 1890 while Wright was working in the Adler & Sullivan office. Wright was never able completely to throw off the delight in ornamentation which he acquired from Sullivan; and this fact, more than any other, made him often seem old-fashioned in later years. Actually, the ornament on the Charnley house was extremely graceful, whereas much of Wright's later applied ornament on roof fascias and wall panels became embarrassingly crude and even "jazzy." The reason may have been that Wright tried to modernize what he had learned from Sullivan in the field of decoration, rather than copy it or give it up entirely. However that may be, the decorative friezes on the Charnley house are among the best Wright ever achieved.

Inside, the Charnley house was just as simple as its elevations suggested. Yet it was still very definitely "inside"; there was none of the interpenetration of interior and exterior spaces which Wright learned to handle to such perfection in later years. However, many of his later details are first suggested in these interiors, particularly the use of strong, linear, horizontal bands that create distinct levels within rooms and along walls. Except for a profusion of ornament in a few scattered areas, the Charnley house interiors were as simple as anything done by the Austrian pioneer, Adolf Loos, and others twenty years later.

While Wright was doing Adler & Sullivan's houses in his spare time, he spent the days working on some of the large projects then in the office. Among these the most important one was the Transportation building for the World's Columbian exposition held in Chicago in 1893.

The Chicago Fair, as a whole, has been described by Wright and others as a serious setback to the independent architectural movement just getting under way in Chicago. For various, complex political reasons, the Chicago Fair was turned over almost in its entirety to the

Eastern architects who represented the neoclassicist party line of the Beaux Arts. This fact did, indeed, constitute a severe blow to Sullivan and a few others who had broken away from the snobbish "upper class" architecture being imported from Europe, and had tried to create a genuinely American, "democratic" expression. What Sullivan meant by this was never made completely clear by him, though Wright made it abundantly clear later in his own words and works. Basically, the conflict lay between the Beaux Arts men on the one hand, who could forget architectural "honesty" and apply false fronts designed according to preconceived, neoclassical standards to any building regardless of its function; and those like Sullivan and Wright on the other hand, who believed that "honesty" was a function of function—that no building could be true to itself, that no building could be a true expression of the aspirations of those who built it, unless its exteriors clearly declared its purpose.

Sullivan was severely hurt by the rejection of "democratic" architecture and the espousal of "autocratic" neoclassicism at the Chicago Fair. The Transportation building, which he was asked to design, was located on the edge of the Fair grounds, the central areas being occupied entirely by neoclassical palaces of equal cornice height (sixty feet) and related arcades. These same rules applied to the Transportation building as well, so that Sullivan could not really make this an honestly expressive structure either. But in applying the great, monumental front with its huge archway to the steel-framed exhibition hall in back of that front, Sullivan and Wright tried to make a statement about the potential power and verve of "honest" architecture which would be unmistakable even though it was only a symbolic act, rather than a true architectural solution as they saw it.

They made their statement in two ways: first, they substituted for the colonnades of the Beaux Arts a huge arch reminiscent of Richardson's Romanesque arches, but rendered in lacy, decorated terra cotta rather than massive stone. The decoration was, again, a collection of natural forms, intertwined in the Auditorium manner. To Sullivan and to his young disciple, the symbolic images of nature began, more and more, to represent images of America and of democracy as well. America was space, and landscape—Europe was crowding and formal, urban life. . . . The ornaments on the Transportation building were symbols of honesty, of down-to-earthness, just as Mies's steel pilasters of fifty years later were to become symbols of order and technological progress.

The second aspect of the Transportation building which made it distinctly different from its Beaux Arts neighbors had to do with its dominant line—the horizontal. The dominant line of classicism (and neoclassicism) is the vertical, the image of man standing up against nature. The dominant line of Sullivan's and Wright's down-to-earth architecture was the horizontal, the image of man in love with nature. If these images seem too mystical, it should be remembered that both Sullivan and Wright were mystics; and, indeed, Wright's mysticism was to become more and more dominant as he further developed his basic principles.

The horizontals that characterized the Transportation building were slabs and planes somewhat in conflict with the great Richardsonian arch of the main entrance. Indeed, it is possible to isolate, on this single façade, the elements that were contributed by Sullivan and those contributed by Wright. Still, the ensemble was splendid—the only building of the great Columbian exposition still remembered by anyone today.

It has long been argued as to whether Sullivan largely directed Wright, or whether Wright influenced his first, true, and only master. There is little point in speculating upon the exact degrees of influence: without Sullivan, Wright could not have achieved half of what he did achieve; Sullivan was his springboard. Yet, without Wright, Sullivan, in later years, created nothing that went very far beyond the Auditorium, the Wainwright building, and the Transportation building. In short, theirs was a near-perfect association as long as it lasted; and the Transportation building, more than any other structure they designed together, was evidence both of the rich vocabulary Sullivan could supply and the dynamism and verve his young disciple injected into the master's work.

I I I

A FEW MONTHS after Frank Lloyd Wright arrived in Chicago, his mother moved down from Madison to join him. Their means were very modest and they had to live in small furnished rooms. A year or so later, mother and son moved to Oak Park, a suburb of Chicago, to live with a friend of Mrs. Wright's. Meanwhile, Frank had fallen in love, and by 1889 he was engaged to be married to Catherine Tobin, a nineteen-year-old girl he had met at a church social. His mother was opposed to the idea in view of their youth; but, by this time, Wright had attained so considerable a standing in the offices of Adler & Sullivan that they were willing to give him a five-year contract under which he could draw upon funds ahead of time to enable him to start a family and build his own house. So, in 1890 he and Catherine were married.

Their first house in Oak Park was quite small and looked, from the outside, not very different from the pleasantly shingled cottages Wright had seen in Silsbee's office. However, in several respects the house differed radically from Silsbee's polite "cottage style." To start with, it was much simpler, much less rambling than a Silsbee house; indeed, it was rather severe by comparison. Next, the Oak Park house showed a sense of interior organization which had nothing to do with Silsbee's rather unimaginative plans. There were few doors between rooms on the main floor; instead, adjoining spaces were allowed to merge into a single, continuous space modulated by more or less free-standing partitions. At the level of a normal door head (approximately seven feet above the floor), Wright carried a continuous band all around the walls of the rooms. All openings in the walls were kept below this band; above it was an additional height of wall treated rather like a frieze, and then came the second horizontal line, the ceiling. This little detail is one that Wright perfected and made an essential part of his vocabulary in later years. It is an extremely helpful device of spatial organization, for the lower horizontal band at door level brings the height of any room down to the scale of the human figure, without, at the same time, making the ceiling itself oppressively low. (The standard door height of seven feet corresponds roughly to the height of a man standing with upraised arm—the basic Modulor figure that Corbu was to adopt as the point of departure for his proportionate scale some fifty years later!)

Finally, the little Oak Park house contained various details that were either Sullivanesque or, for the first time, originally "Wrightian." There was a brick fireplace with an arched opening reminiscent of Richardson's and Sullivan's great arches; there were decorative friezes (though only a very few of them) not unlike Sullivan's; and there was the hint of an important idea that Wright was to perfect in years to come: the idea of the "utility core," a central, compact arrangement of fireplace and kitchen, back to back. This was, of course, a standard feature of every Cape Cod house; but in Wright's vocabulary this core became not only a central-heating system, but a sort of mystical life-giving element in the heart of his houses, from which all spaces expanded and radiated toward a distant horizon. The Oak Park house had none of this drama—or, for that matter, the setting necessary for such a dramatic composition. But even this small project contained the seed of Wright's later, powerful radial plans.

Under Wright's contract with Adler & Sullivan, he was expected to continue to do the firm's residential work in his spare time. As this domestic practice grew, people began to come to Wright directly, and he designed a number of private houses on the sly, sometimes using a pseudonym to hide the fact from Sullivan. These "bootlegged" houses, as he called them, may, in retrospect, seem to have involved some sort of breach of faith on his part; however, the chances are that these commissions started to come to him directly in a rather casual way, and, as Sullivan was not particularly interested in such work, Wright probably did not want to bother him with it. Soon, however, the houses began to take up an increasing amount of Wright's time, and, as he was always short of cash (a chronic state of affairs throughout his life), he welcomed the chance to increase his income. He was obviously embarrassed by the subterfuge all this involved, but he was soon too deeply involved in this clandestine practice to extricate himself. One day in 1893 Sullivan discovered what Wright had been up to. There was a terrible row, and Wright walked out of Adler & Sullivan's offices. He did not see Sullivan again until many years later.

The only influence on his work which Wright ever acknowledged was that of Louis Sullivan. Yet it seems, in retrospect, as if it was Sullivan's *idea*, rather than Sullivan's actual work, that gave Wright some of the impetus he needed. Sullivan's notion, poetically expressed in many writings, such as his famous *Kindergarten Chats*, was that American democracy could not be built upon pretense, that a democratic architecture must be an honest architecture in the sense that it must express its contents and intents on the face and in all details of its buildings. Yet Sullivan never for a moment believed that buildings that expressed their structure and their function must therefore, inevitably, be beautiful. All he did believe was that honesty of expression was the ethical basis of a democratic architecture—the only basis upon which things of true beauty could be built. His dictum—"form follows function"—has been one of the most widely misunderstood statements of

aesthetic principle of all time: what he meant was *not*—or not *only*—
that form must grow out of function, but that form, *beautiful* form,
could only be created after functional expression had been satisfied. In
one of the dialogues between "The Master" and "The Student" in his
Kindergarten Chats, Sullivan wrote: "THE MASTER: I am endeavoring to
impress upon you the simple truth . . . of the subjective possibilities
of objective things. In short, to clarify for you the origin and power of
beauty: to let you see that it is resident in function and form. THE
STUDENT: So is ugliness, isn't it? THE MASTER: To be sure . . ."

Here is the crux of the matter: when Wright, in later years, attacked the functionalists and declared that they had misunderstood
Sullivan and him, he meant that the functionalists had taken the wrong
turn at the fork in the road, where there appeared at least two alternative "subjective possibilities of objective things." To Sullivan and to
Wright, beauty was only *"resident"* in function and form. It was never
the inevitable by-product of function and form.

Wright was deeply attached to Sullivan, to whom he always referred as the "*Lieber Meister,*" a touching if not quite idiomatically
correct appellation. Yet there is good reason to think that Wright's
affection for Sullivan was caused as much by Sullivan's paternalistic
attitude toward his young disciple (who was happy to find a father
substitute) as it was by any great revelation of architectural truths supplied by the master. Sullivan's buildings were, without doubt, the finest
of the Chicago School; they had a strength and beauty unequaled by
any of his contemporaries. Yet the greatness of Sullivan's Wainwright
building in St. Louis and his Guaranty building in Buffalo lay in an
ordered structural rhythm that Wright himself did not emulate for very
long. Curiously it was Mies, rather than Wright, who learned the lessons
of Sullivan's skyscrapers; Wright received from Sullivan a great idea and
a hint of truths to be learned from things in nature. He did not receive
from his "*Lieber Meister*" any important, formal architectural concepts.

Sullivan's emotional break with Wright was perhaps as much the
former's fault as it was the result of Wright's "bootlegging" activities.
Before long, Sullivan was to become a hopeless alcoholic, and the weak-
nesses that finally caused this disease—a disease that, in the end, brought

him poverty and a lonely death—were apparent even in the early days when Wright worked for him. In any event, though Wright felt intensely unhappy and somewhat guilty about the break with Sullivan, he never ceased to honor this great man to the very end.

During the months of the Chicago exposition of 1893, Wright saw on the exhibition grounds a model of a traditional wooden Japanese temple, reproduced at half its full size. This was the official Japanese contribution to the fair. Wright was intrigued. He had become quite familiar with the Japanese prints that were such an important source of Art Nouveau ornament, but this was probably his first direct contact with Japanese architecture in the flesh. For some reason he always denied, quite furiously, that there was any influence of Japanese architecture upon his work at all: but this is obvious nonsense; he was much more strongly influenced by Katsura Palace than by the Auditorium, and only his increasing arrogance could obscure the fact to his own eyes.

The black wood posts and beams, the deep roof overhangs, the white plaster panels between the darkened framework, and the intimate relation of house and nature—all these made a profound and lasting impression upon Wright. So did the open spaces within, lightly divided by sliding screens and separated from the gardens by still more transparent and translucent sliding panels. And so did the strong, modular organization of the buildings, the horizontal emphasis (the door-height horizontal that Wright used at Oak Park had long been a standard Japanese device). Indeed, it is highly unlikely that Wright's Prairie houses, built in the first decade of this century, would have looked even remotely as they did if Sullivan's young apprentice had not seen the Japanese exhibit at the much maligned fair of 1893.

Wright's presentation drawing of a house built during the first decade of the century. Even the graphic technique is reminiscent of Japanese prints. (Courtesy, Taliesin Fellowship)

I V

As WRIGHT's PRACTICE and his family grew, the Oak Park house was expanded several times until it was a rambling complex of buildings, designed both for work and for living. The Wrights had six children, in more or less rapid succession, and Wright found himself, as usual, pressed for money. For this reason he had to accept several commissions for "traditional" houses that he might well have turned down if his finances had been in better shape. Among these was a large Colonial villa in the neo-Palladian manner, several cottages à la Silsbee, and one or two rather severe and classical houses somewhat similar to the Charnley house. But however conventional these houses may appear today, each showed—especially in its interiors—a highly individual style;

Winslow house, River Forest, Ill., 1893. The second floor is ornamented in the characteristic Sullivan manner. (Photo: Aaron Siskind)

and the inevitable ornament in friezes and in glass panels was becoming increasingly geometric and very different from Sullivan's curvilinear patterns. Here, in these angular, geometric lines is the first powerful evidence of the influence of Froebel's games upon the formation of Wright's aesthetic preferences.

Wright built his first really extraordinary house in 1893 for a wealthy businessman called William H. Winslow, who had bought a large piece of land in River Forest, a suburb of Chicago close to Oak Park. The Winslow house was an extremely simple, somewhat severe, symmetrical structure two stories in height, topped off with a pitched roof of terra-cotta tiles with deep overhangs all around. The first floor of the house was treated much like the base of any classical building:

it was of Roman brick, with simply framed windows of rather horizontal proportions cut into the brickwork. The central, main entrance was set into a panel of decorated tiles, and reached across a flight of low, horizontal steps and a wide terrace. The second floor was expressed quite differently from the first: instead of Roman brick, Wright here used an intricately ornate tile as the finished wall surface, and the horizontal windows were again set into this tile wall. The sweeping roof plane completed the composition.

Anyone looking at the Winslow house today would be struck by the quiet distinction and good taste of its façades, and by the excellence of the workmanship. Less obvious would be those elements that Wright himself has, since 1893, made part and parcel of the vocabulary of American architecture. Yet in 1893 these elements were radical in the extreme; but, unlike much first radical work in the arts, the Winslow house showed such a self-assured handling of proportion and detail that it appears to be the work of an architect who had been doing this sort of thing for many years.

In two respects, particularly, does the Winslow house appear quite masterly: first, in the handling of its horizontal composition; and, second, in the handling of its scale.

To Wright the horizontal had by this time become the most important architectural line: it was not only that he had been impressed by the dominant horizontal of the traditional Japanese house; rather, he had begun to feel that there was some affinity between nature and architecture—an affinity not as yet quite clearly defined—and that a horizontal architecture tended to suggest harmony with nature, rather than opposition to nature.

Still, here was a two-story house—not an easy thing to make appear horizontal. Yet that is exactly what Wright set out to do, and succeeded in doing. The first device (starting from the top) was to make his roof a wide, low-slung, low-pitched lid, with a deep brim all around. The roof became a sort of flattened-out tent and dominated the rest of the house completely. Moreover, Wright was able to swallow up some of the height of his second story within the roof shape, so that the second floor of the Winslow house looks much lower than it really is.

Below the roof, there is the device of stratification, of dividing the building into distinctly different horizontal bands. The second floor was a low and long band faced with ornamented tiles; the first floor was a somewhat higher band made to look long and low because it was faced with Roman bricks, whose shape is long and flattened-out. Finally, Wright set his house down, ever so gently, on the lawn, by surrounding it at the base with a continuous step of limestone that projects out beyond the edge of the wall, and by placing a flat terrace in front of the main entrance. Indeed, wherever you look in this house, the horizontal line is the dominant detail: two urns flanking the entrance are horizontal in shape; the double-hung windows are divided horizontally into two long and flat rectangles of glass; and even the entrance door is kept low and squat, rather than tall, simply to accent the dominant line of the composition.

Wright's handling of scale in the Winslow house is just as successful. One of the eternal rules of great architecture is that it must stand up, visually, from two vantage points: from far away, and at close quarters. All great buildings of the past looked well at a distance; their over-all form tended to be simple, somewhat diagrammatic, clearly understandable. At closer quarters, however, the importance of the over-all silhouette would be diminished and the eye would search for new points of interest—smaller-scale detail. The masters of the Acropolis, of the Gothic, and of the Renaissance all knew this truth. Only in recent years has it been forgotten, for much modern architecture looks simple and clear at a distance, but only flat and somewhat dull at close quarters.

In the Winslow house, Wright showed how clearly he understood this principle. For the over-all silhouette of this house is sharply defined, clear, and simple. Only as you approach its front door do the different wall surfaces reveal something new—an intricate play of ornamental detail, a richness of texture quite unexpected from so severe-looking a block. Sullivan, of course, knew the secret of scale-giving ornament and applied it to perfection in his Guaranty building. But even Sullivan never applied it better than Wright did in the Winslow house.

In plan, the Winslow house was as simple and bold as the Charnley house, though there was a much greater play of related, open spaces and of changing floor and ceiling levels. This constant change in the quality of interior spaces was to become an increasingly important aspect of Wright's work; but even more prophetic than the interiors of the Winslow house was a secondary building Wright designed for the Winslow estate—a building to house the stables. Like the main house, the stables were symmetrical in composition (indeed, Wright did not break away completely from classical symmetry until 1908 or 1910). And, like the main house, the Winslow stables were strikingly horizontal in expression, with great, sheltering roof tents holding the structure down to the ground. In fact, while the main house was still rather staid and formal, the stables were quite dynamic in appearance and suggested a degree of integration between architecture and landscape which no one had achieved before. (One of Wright's amusing and favorite tricks was employed here: to leave an existing tree undisturbed, he simply left a hole in one of the deep roof overhangs and allowed the tree to continue to grow through it.)

In the sixty-five years after the Winslow house was completed, Wright did much to extend and elaborate upon the basic concept stated there in River Forest, in 1893. But the germ for almost every great idea Wright brought into domestic architecture was contained in that extraordinary house. No architect of the past hundred years was able, in a single work, to produce so complete, so independent a creative statement. When the Winslow house was built, it became clear that Wright was capable of leading American architecture into a new age.

For some years after the completion of the Winslow house, Wright was busy designing large and small homes around Chicago. Some of these were quite traditional (because the client insisted, and Wright needed the money), and there was, in fact, one "half-timbered" Tudor house of huge proportions which many of Wright's potential clients liked, but which he himself despised. As a matter of fact, the half-timbered theme—a kind of blend of the Japanese post-and-beam frame and the Tudor expression—seems to have left a notable mark on Wright's sense of detail; for it reappeared in some of his most beautiful houses of the early twentieth century. Other designs of the immediate,

Hickox house, Kankakee, Ill., 1900. One of the first rather "Japanese" houses, rendered in near-black and white. (Courtesy, Museum of Modern Art)

post-Winslow era were as daring as their precursor at River Forest, though sometimes in rather different ways: for example, Wright began, slowly but quite noticeably, to throw off the strait jacket of symmetry; and though symmetrical elements remained in his houses for many years to come, the over-all composition became increasingly free and dynamic. Finally, some of the post-Winslow houses showed an increasing use of blocky compositions reminiscent of Froebel's geometric games, and of overlapping folded roofs that may be traced to Froebelian exercises with folded paper. But in his domestic work Wright did not really advance radically beyond the Winslow house until the turn of the century. When he finally did, the breakthrough was so complete that American architecture is still trying to catch up.

V

―――――――――――――――――――――――――――――――――

THE AMERICAN NATION has a heart and a backbone and a pattern of its own and is rapidly forming a mind of its own," Wright told an audience at the Chicago Art Institute in the year 1900. What he meant was soon to be revealed in a series of houses whose "pattern" was a reflection, not only of an entirely new kind of architecture, but of an entirely new way of life.

During the first decade of this century Wright probably built the greatest houses of his lifetime. One of these, the Robie house, completed in 1908, may someday be considered the most influential house of its era. At least half a dozen other houses of the decade are of such extraordinary strength and spirit that each, taken alone, would have

Coonley house, Riverside, Ill., 1908. A palatial Prairie house with definite "Japanese" overtones. The projecting roof beams were sheathed in copper. The large planting urns in the foreground were among Wright's favorite devices in this period. (Photo: Aaron Siskind)

assured its architect a prominent place in the history of his art and his time.

The houses of this decade are now known as Wright's Prairie houses, for reasons which are quite apparent: for all have the dominant, earth-hugging horizontal plane, which, in Illinois, means the plane of the prairie. Indeed, these houses have so many things in common that they must be considered elements of a single, great work: the creation of a new, American domestic architecture.

The horizontality of the Prairie houses was foreshadowed by the dominant lines of the Winslow house. Yet the Winslow house seems monumental and tightly, vertically self-contained by comparison with the sweeping horizontal volumes of the Willits and the Isabel Roberts houses a dozen years later. For here Wright had at last broken completely with symmetry and substituted for it a dynamic asymmetry, a balance-in-motion infinitely more complex and infinitely more poetic than the formal disciplines of past civilizations.

Horizontality was Wright's response not only to the earth and to the things that grew out of it, but also to the great spaces of America. The Winslow house and, even more so, the Charnley house—these were still, in a sense, "European" houses; for they reflected the tight discipline required by a densely settled continent. The Prairie houses were all space and motion, all dynamism, all America. For this, after all, *is* (or, at least, *was*) the chief characteristic of the New World: space, freedom to move about, an ever expanding frontier. From Walt Whitman to Jack Kerouac the recurring *American* theme is the open road, the man on the move, the limitless spaces, especially of the Middle West. When Wright built his Prairie houses, he no longer built "boxes" containing so much usable cubage; he built spaces sheltered under great, sweeping, intersecting, low-slung roof planes—spaces that were open to one another within, and open to the prairie landscape without. Each great horizontal plane would extend from the center of the house out, beyond the line of windows, into deeply cantilevered overhangs that lead the eye toward some distant horizon, some expanding frontier. These houses were the first dramatization, in three dimensions, of what Whitman meant when he said: "I inhale great draughts of space, the east and west are mine, and the north and the south are mine . . . The earth expanding right hand and left hand . . . O highway . . . You express me better than I can express myself . . ." This, the central American theme, was first made architectural in these magnificent horizontal planes-in-motion that Frank Lloyd Wright built around Chicago during that first decade of the century.

Everything somehow evolved out of this central theme: if the road was to be open, then the space within had to be open, and the outside walls had to be open, too. The interiors (except, of course, in areas where privacy was required) consisted of interlocking spaces separated not by doors, but by carefully developed angles of vision. As you moved through those interior spaces, they would unfold in dramatic and ever changing vistas: everywhere there would be elements of surprise; a sudden, unexpected source of light around a corner, a glimpse of the landscape, a low ceiling after a high ceiling (to be followed again by a high one), a succession of experiences so varied and yet so continuously re-

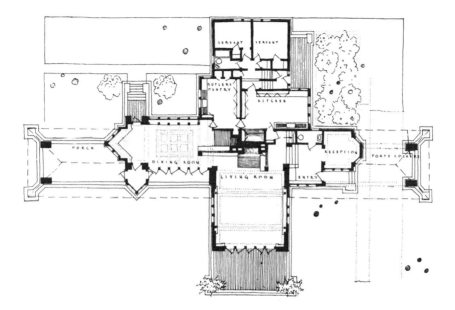

Plan of Willits house, Highland Park, Ill., 1902. The core
of the house is the hearth, and all wings extend outward
from it. (Courtesy, Taliesin Fellowship)

lated that the interior became a symphony of space and light. The boxy,
self-contained spaces of the traditional European house were demolished
in one fell swoop by a simple, dramatic device: the abolition of closed,
interior corners. Such corners were simply dissolved in glass, or else
resolved by free-standing walls at right angles to one another which
never actually met, but, instead, seemed to slide past each other in
space. And the theme of space-in-motion was not confined to the insides
of the Prairie houses; for each vista from inside out was picked up and
continued in terraces and retaining walls that surrounded the house and
helped merge the interior, visually, with the surrounding landscape.
Every detail of the Prairie house was designed to support this powerful,
central theme: the roof overhangs were deep and thin-edged; the windows were continuous ribbons of glass, starting directly at the underside

of the roof and continuing down to a common, horizontal sill line; the parapets of the terraces beyond had continuous horizontal copings of concrete or limestone, and these parapets often would become planting boxes or planting urns which brought elements of nature directly into the architectural composition. As he did in the Winslow house, Wright set his Prairie houses down on the ground with infinite tenderness, stepping down the house around its base until base and lawn were one, or surrounding the house with terraces at gradually descending levels that finally brought the floor line down to natural grade.

In most of the Prairie houses, there would be a central element somewhat taller than the rest—often a two-story living room. From this tall, central mass, wings would extend in all directions—first roof planes, then the planes of parapets, finally the low slabs of terraces—so that the entire house seemed, in the end, to have grown out of the landscape like some geological formation of horizontal strata of masonry and glass.

Many of the Prairie houses used the devices of Japanese architecture to achieve their poetic effects. As in the traditional Japanese house, there was, generally, a dominant horizontal band inside at approximately the height of a standard door opening. This band continued all the way around the walls and finally emerged on the exterior as the roof fascia. All added heights were developed above this low plane, so that many rooms would have intimate, low ceiling areas (generally around the fireplace) whose height would be just about that of a standard door, and dramatic, high areas at the center where the ceiling would suddenly be formed by the underside of a pitched roof. In other ways, too, the Japanese tradition came into play: many of the Prairie houses had a sort of "turned-up" roof edge that gave the roof a broken silhouette very similar to that found in traditional Japanese houses.

In only two respects did the Prairie houses reflect some influence of half-timbered Tudor: first, in the black-and-white façade with its darkened posts and beams and its stucco fill-ins, which was somewhat reminiscent both of Japanese and of half-timbered tradition; and, second, in the matter of small, leaded windowpanes. Wright very rarely used large sheets of glass in any of his buildings, and in these early houses his windows were completely broken up into patterned panes of

Roberts house, River Forest, Ill., 1908. The tall living room at the center and the low, extended wings around it are typical of Wright's early compositions. (Courtesy, Museum of Modern Art)

glass. Much of this mania for leaded glass was undoubtedly due to Wright's preoccupation with ornament, but there was another and much more significant reason: Wright realized that large sheets of glass looked blank, black and dead from the outside, and tended to reflect only a single image of nature; a leaded window or a broken-up expanse of glass tended to look like a glittering mosaic of many facets and colors when seen from the outside, for no glazier has ever succeeded in setting two adjoining sheets of glass exactly parallel to one another. As a result, each little pane of glass reflects a different part of the sky or the sun or the trees, and, instead of appearing dull and dead, a fragmented glass wall becomes a rich mosaic, constantly changing in the light.

"Air, soil, water, fire," Whitman wrote, "my qualities interpenetrate with theirs . . ." In the Prairie houses, Wright established a sort of atavistic principle of planning, which remained apparent throughout his work. For at the heart of every Prairie house, there was a fireplace, often of rock, always broad and firmly anchored at the center of the composition. From this hearth all spaces would extend, radiate into the landscape. This was the source of all life within the house. Beyond that heart, there would be airy spaces, then, quite frequently, pools of water, and, finally, the earth. These primitive elements—water, fire, earth—be-

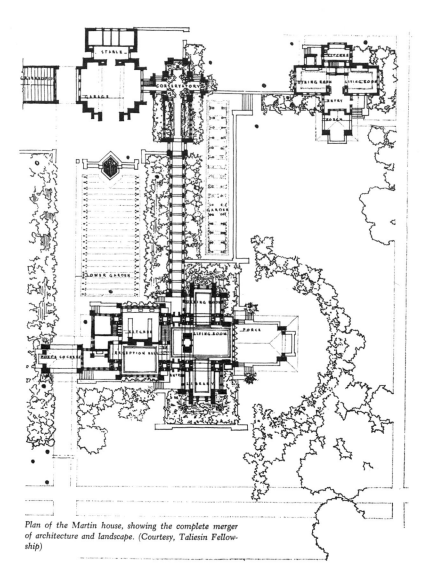

Plan of the Martin house, showing the complete merger
of architecture and landscape. (Courtesy, Taliesin Fellowship)

Martin house, Buffalo, N. Y., 1904. One of the finest Prairie houses, with all the best characteristics of this prototype: low-slung roof planes, ribbon windows, terraces that extend the house into the landscape. (Courtesy, Museum of Modern Art)

came a sort of obsession with Wright from the days of the Prairie houses onward. Some thirty years later, when he built his famous Bear Run house over the waterfall in Pennsylvania, Wright succeeded in making the hearth of his central fireplace an existing rocky ledge protruding up through the floor; and the third element, water, was, of course, the great theme of that house.

Many of the Prairie houses were not built on the prairie at all, but on suburban sites around Chicago—in River Forest, in Wilmette, in Riverside, and in Oak Park. One of the most beautiful Prairie houses, the one for Darwin D. Martin, was actually built in Buffalo, New York. Others were built in Rochester, New York, in Wisconsin, and in Ohio. Although their sites were often restricted, Wright succeeded in making the indoor and outdoor spaces seem large by extending interior walls into the landscape, then turning them to form terraces and courts outside the line of the glass.

Fortunately, many of the Prairie houses have survived real-estate "progress." The Martin house in Buffalo was restored, and the Robie house, which was almost demolished to make room for temporary dormitories, was saved by William Zeckendorf, the New York realtor, and put back—almost—to its original state. The Coonley house in Riverside,

Illinois, a magnificent complex of buildings designed in 1907 and built of stucco and ornamental tiles, looks bedraggled but beautiful. Several of the houses of the period have changed ownership and type of occupancy: one, on the North Shore of Chicago, is now a pleasant restaurant, its double-story living room a very effective dining area. But most of them are still in use as residences, and occasionally come on the market to be bought by a growing band of admirers.

It is almost impossible to catalogue the infinite number of innovations in residential architecture which accompanied Wright's development of the Prairie house. Apart from the ribbon window and the corner window, Wright developed a window unit that was a casement opening out, rather than in; he began to plan his houses around a "utility core"; he dramatized his rooms with "cathedral ceilings"; he built concrete slab floors directly on the earth without basement, and set the radiant heating systems into that floor. He designed an infinite number and variety of built-in furniture, including storage walls and built-in tables. He employed built-in lighting, including some of the first geometric modern lighting fixtures (which, however, were invariably ornamented with some fairly hideous Art Nouveau frills). He developed the "carport" (beginning as the *porte-cochère*). The list could be continued indefinitely, but enough has been said to make it clear that most ideas that characterize the modern American house grew out of the Prairie houses of the first decade of this century.

A good many architects in the history of the art have staked their claim to fame upon much less radical creations than are reflected in the Prairie house. Indeed, very few architects of any time have contributed more than is represented in this work. Yet, incredible though it may seem, the Prairie house was only the beginning, only one facet of Wright's creative genius. For while the Prairie houses were going up, he created an entirely new commercial and industrial architecture as well; and after these two phases of his work had been completed, he began to think in terms of a new kind of structural principle which, in turn, was bound to produce an entirely new kind of architectural expression. So, the Prairie house was only Step One in what was to become the most prolific creative career this country had ever seen.

Robie house, Chicago, Ill., 1909. This is probably one of Wright's most famous works, and shows all the elements of the Prairie style to perfection: low-slung roof planes, interlocking volumes and masses, sweeping horizontals. (Photo: Hedrich-Blessing)

V I

DURING THE FIRST DECADE of this century, which saw the creation of the Prairie house, Wright was busier than he would again be for a long time. His home in Oak Park was expanded to incorporate a studio; apprentices came to work under Wright's guidance; and more and more clients came to commission nonresidential buildings, as well as private houses.

Among the nonresidential commissions, there were four or five projects and completed structures of a brilliance and inventiveness as great as any Wright displayed in the creation of the Prairie house. The first of these was merely a sketch: in 1894 or thereabouts, almost thirty years before Mies van der Rohe was to conceive of his glass skyscrapers, the American Luxfer Prism Company asked Wright for a design to help promote its new "directional" glass block. Wright's answer was a project for a slab building, ten stories in height, whose street façade was to be entirely of glass block and movable, glazed sash! This was the first suggestion of a true "curtain wall" of glass and metal ever made, and the sketch looks as modern today—except for its occasional frills—as any glass-fronted office building put up in any large U.S. city. As the American Luxfer building was designed for a typical site in the middle of the block, it had only one façade—the one fronting on the street. Its side walls were blank (they were presumed to be party walls), but its rear façade was probably meant to be of glass also. Largely because of the great, rectangular simplicity of the design, and because of its blank side walls, the American Luxfer building is remarkably similar to Corbu's Swiss Pavilion of 1932. Indeed, the façade expression of the structural cage is almost identical with that used by Corbu, and there is a suggestion of some kind of penthouse that breaks the over-all façade pattern not unlike the roof treatment that Corbu used in the Swiss Pavilion. The *pilotis* at the ground-floor level were, however, absent.

Although it is doubtful that Mies or Corbu ever saw the drawings for the American Luxfer project, there is no doubt that Sullivan did see them; and the Schlesinger-Mayer store in Chicago (now Carson, Pirie, Scott), which Sullivan designed and built around 1900, was clearly influenced by Wright's American Luxfer designs. After that, of course, the glass-walled slab building was very much in the air; and it was Frank Lloyd Wright who had put it there.

The second nonresidential building of outstanding importance during this period in Wright's life remained a project also: this was a design for the Yahara Boat Club to be built in Madison, Wisconsin, in 1902. Wright had done several boat- and country-club structures in earlier years, including a rather massive and ungainly Municipal Boathouse, which was built on Lake Mendota in Madison in 1893. (He had won the job in a competition.) Like the American Luxfer project, the Yahara Boat Club was astonishingly "modern": it consisted of a simple, rectangular block, topped by a long band of glass, and finished off with a deeply cantilevered, flat, slablike roof. The entire composition sat on an extended base of retaining walls that continued far out beyond the limits of the building itself.

This was undoubtedly the simplest, most strikingly geometric design put on paper by Wright up to that time. Quite clearly, its blockiness owed a great deal to Froebel's games; just as clearly, there was evidence of that same horizontal driving force—the driving force of the open road—that dominated Wright's dramatic Prairie houses. But nowhere else until that time had Wright (or anyone else) reduced architecture to so simple and uncompromising a statement. Perhaps the Boat Club would have shown some of Wright's weakness for finicky ornamentation had it been built. However that may be, the Boat Club stands as a prophetic statement of a great deal of modern architecture which was to be developed by Wright and others in the decades to come: it was prophetic of Mies's Barcelona Pavilion, of much of Willem Dudok's work in Holland after World War I, and also of Wright's own Usonian houses of the 1930's—especially the beautiful Winkler-Goetsch house of 1939. In this single, powerful sketch, modern architecture was given a new and decisive direction.

In the Boat Club—just as in the Prairie houses—the predominant, in fact the *only* movement of space was in the horizontal direction. "I see this extended horizontal line as the true earth-line of human life, indicative of freedom," Wright said many years later. The Yahara Boat Club sketch was a really stunning exposition of the extended horizontal line and the extended horizontal space. If one thinks of "space" as a sort of invisible but ever present vapor that fills the entire architectural volume, then Wright's notion of space-in-motion becomes more clearly

Project for the Yahara Boat Club, Madison, Wis., 1902.
One of the most remarkably "modern" designs among
Wright's early work. (Courtesy, Taliesin Fellowship)

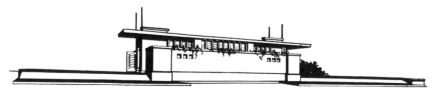

Coonley playhouse, Riverside, Ill., 1912. A small, symmetrical, monumental structure quite similar to the Yahara Boat Club project of ten years earlier. The curious geometric pattern in the stained glass antedates similar Cubist work in Europe. (Courtesy, Museum of Modern Art)

understandable: the contained space is allowed to move about, from room to room, from indoors to outdoors, rather than remain stagnant, boxed up in a series of interior cubicles. This movement of space is the true art of modern architecture, for the movement must be rigidly controlled so that the space cannot "leak" out in all directions indiscriminately. The controlling element in the Boat Club was the sweeping horizontal roof plane and the long side walls; both directed the movement of space horizontally outward, in a single plane. A few years later, as Wright's mastery of the art of manipulating space became more profound, he began to play with space moving in all directions. In the Yahara Boat Club, the manipulation of space was much less complex and thus, perhaps, all the more dramatic.

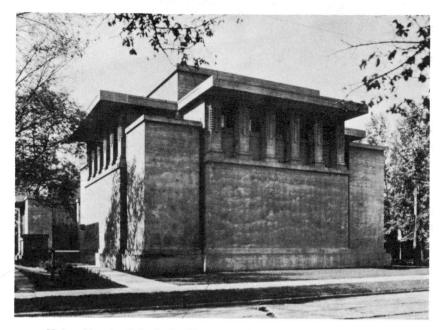

Unity Church, Oak Park, Ill., 1906. A monumental, poured-concrete structure of great force. (Courtesy, Museum of Modern Art)

Unity Church, which resembles the Boat Club in many respects, was actually built in 1906, in Oak Park. It is one of the most important buildings in Wright's career, and one of the best. Basically, the building consists of two separate blocks: an auditorium, more or less square in plan, and a parish house, which is rectangular and linked to the auditorium by the narrow "neck" of an entrance loggia. The entire building was of poured concrete—Wright's first use of this material—and its composition was even blockier than that of the Boat Club. However, Unity Church was not nearly as horizontal in emphasis as the Boat Club: both of its elements were at least two stories in height, with different levels and balconies projecting out from the walls into the tall, central spaces. Like the Boat Club, Unity Church had a solid base, topped by a band of windows which, in turn, were held down by the projecting lid of a flat roof slab. Like the Boat Club, Unity Church was also very simple and modern in composition, and all small-scale texture and ornament was restrained and noticeable only at very close quarters: there was only a little ornamentation on the window mullions, and some textural pattern in the concrete, achieved through the use of a coarse, pebbly aggregate.

These are, however, relatively superficial characteristics of the building. Its true importance lies in three specific aspects: the organization of its plan and all that this implied; the organization of its spaces; and the quality of its linear, geometric, interior ornament.

The plan of Unity Church looks familiar to us today simply because it is the prototype of thousands of eminently successful modern plan types, from houses to city halls. Here, for the first time, we find an absolutely clear-cut demonstration of the articulated, "binuclear plan," or "H plan"—the plan that every functionalist, from Le Corbusier to Marcel Breuer's young American students, has found an eminently satisfactory solution to the organization of a multifunctional building. What the H plan does, in effect, is to separate the two principal, opposing functions of any given building—in a house, the daytime living areas

Plan of Unity Church. The two principal wings are separately articulated, and joined by an entrance link. This plan diagram has since become a standard in modern architecture. (Courtesy, Taliesin Fellowship)

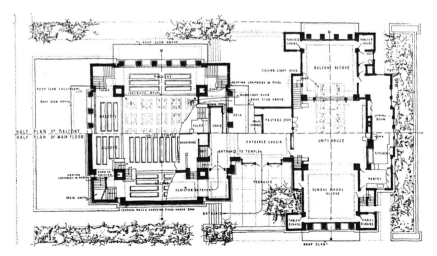

versus the bedrooms; in a city hall, the administrative office block versus the council chamber—and link these opposing functions with a narrow "neck" that also serves as the principal entrance to both elements of the building. This arrangement works beautifully because the entrance link, being at the center, makes each part of the plan equally and independently accessible.

Some critics have claimed that the functionalists' preoccupation with separating functionally different elements from one another grew out of Cubist tradition—or, specifically, out of the tradition of Russian Constructivism after World War I. Possibly so, but the evidence of Unity Church, built in 1906 and widely publicized throughout the world, suggests an earlier source for the principle of separate articulation —one of the really fundamental principles of modern architecture.

The second important aspect of Unity Church is the manner in which Wright handled the space within. In the Boat Club this space was conceived of as a horizontally moving entity; here, at Unity Church, the volumes are tall and complex in their height. Balconies intrude into the auditorium and the parish house at various levels. And, more importantly, light intrudes from the sides *as well as from above,* for the roof is no longer a solid, horizontal lid, but a giant "egg crate" of skylights, so that the space within is drawn upward, sideways, and, indeed, in all directions.

Here, for the first time, Wright developed an entirely plastic space. (The Larkin building, in Buffalo, which was built in 1904, showed some of these possibilities, but did not come as close to realizing them as does Unity Church.) Before long, Wright would be completely fascinated by the possibilities of truly plastic, multidirectional movements of space, and would come to the recognition of an entirely new concept of structure through this understanding. "Unity Church is where I thought I had it," Wright recalled in later years; "this idea that the reality of a building no longer consisted in the walls and roof. So that sense of freedom began which has come into the architecture of today and which we call organic architecture."

Finally, there was the linear, geometric ornament used throughout the auditorium in particular. This linear ornament consisted of long

Interior detail of Unity Church. Everything about it suggests De Stijl Cubism—which did not come along until a dozen years later! (Photo: Richard Miller)

bands of flat trim, occasionally forming squares and rectangles in dynamic and asymmetric compositions. Each of these linear patterns was closely related to the architectural element to which it was applied: the balconies, the pulpit, the lighting fixtures, the skylights. What it all added up to was simply this: in the interiors of Unity Church, Wright—almost casually, almost as an afterthought—laid the foundation for one of the most important movements in modern design, the movement formed in Holland a dozen years later and known as De Stijl. Where-ever one looks in the auditorium, he can see Mondrian's paintings in the flesh—a dozen years before Mondrian! There can be no question whatever that the Dutch De Stijl painters and architects had seen the exhibition of Wright's work in Holland in 1910 and that they were familiar with his Unity Church. Thus we find Wright giving birth, almost absent-mindedly, to one of the most influential and one of the most powerful groups in the entire history of modern art.

The curious and amusing aspect of all this is to be found in the twists and turns that aesthetic influence will take: Wright's geometric ornament in Unity Church was intimately, "organically," related to the structure, to the different volumes within the space, and to the manner in which these volumes might help him manipulate the space within. Then De Stijl came along and took the *surface* patterns of Unity Church, ripped them off the architecture that had produced them to begin with, and began to play with the patterns for pattern's sake, to make them a discipline of graphic design. Indeed, van Doesburg, in particular, later used the geometric pattern to *destroy* certain architectural spaces, rather than help underline the architecture! Finally, the young International Style men in Europe, finding Mondrian and van Doesburg more "modern-looking" than Wright, with his slightly Victorian fussiness, took over De Stijl, reinterpreted it as a three-dimensional discipline (relating it again to structure, mass, volume, space), and presented the whole thing to the world as a new sort of architecture! In one sense, of course, it was; for Wright was rarely able to get away completely from the stigma of nineteenth-century taste, and the International Style did succeed in doing that. But when Wright said, in 1928, that "all Le Corbusier says or means was at home here in architecture in America in the work of Louis Sullivan and myself, more than 25 years ago, and is fully on record . . ." he may, perhaps, be forgiven for his vast arrogance: for Unity Church, in its plan, in its spatial organization, and in its linear ornament, was indeed one of the most fertile sources for all of twentieth-century architecture.

Two years before Unity Church was completed, Wright built several important structures in Buffalo, New York, for Darwin D. Martin, whose own beautiful Prairie house in that city has been mentioned earlier. Through Martin, Wright got the job of designing the Larkin Company administration building, the first entirely air-conditioned modern office building on record. In some ways the Larkin building resembles the Boat Club and Unity Church: like them, it is blocky and extremely simple in its forms, and has very little ornamentation. But here the similarity ends; for the Larkin building was as decisively vertical as the Boat Club was horizontal. Indeed, it was the first consciously architectural expression of the kind of American structure which Europeans were beginning to discover to their delight: the great clusters of grain silos and similar industrial monuments that men like Corbu and Gropius found so exciting in the early 1920's. Indeed, the Larkin building was, in a sense, a squared-off silo—monumentally simple and powerful. But it was a great deal more than that, for the space within—the "reality" of the building, as Lao-tse put it centuries ago—was very different from the space within a silo.

It was a very dramatic and simple space: in the center, a four-story well, topped by a huge skylight; and around this well, galleries of office space open to the center shaft of light and air. Here the movement of space was entirely vertical, and every detail helped accent that fact. But the walls of the Larkin building were not tight enclosures by any means. "I think I first *consciously* began to try to beat the box in the Larkin Building," Wright said years later. "I found a natural opening to the liberation I sought when [after a great struggle] I finally pushed the staircase towers out from the corners of the main building, made them into free-standing, individual features." Suddenly, the enclosure—the need for enclosure—melted away, and it was possible to develop the space within the building in all directions without fear of hitting a blank wall.

For this building, Wright designed lights, desks, office chairs, and other fixtures and furnishings of metal and glass—extraordinary, spidery, Constructivist-looking objects (fifteen years before the Constructivists came along)—objects that seem occasionally odd and complicated in retrospect, but, when squinted at, suddenly appear remarkably similar to today's articulated furniture designs produced by the spearheads of our current *avant-gardes*. As for the office-planning techniques em-

*Larkin Company Administration building, Buffalo, N. Y.,
1904. A monumental block owing little to anything except,
perhaps, to the spirit of American industry as expressed by
silos and similar structures. (Courtesy, Museum of Modern
Art)*

Interior of Larkin building. Like most of Wright's urban structures, this one was lit primarily from above, thus shutting out the surrounding townscape. All fixtures and furnishings in the building were designed by Wright. (Courtesy, Museum of Modern Art)

ployed, these must have seemed radical in the extreme in their day: all steel files, for example, were built flush into walls and into partitions in modular combinations; and all secretarial spaces were treated as open, flexible "pools" that could be subdivided at will if need be.

Every book on modern architecture published in Europe in the 1920's carried pictures of the Larkin building. It was probably the most widely admired American structure (apart from the Robie house) of the first decades of this century. Yet the City of Buffalo, in 1949, sold the building for a few thousand dollars to a wrecking firm, for salvage. It seems that nobody at Buffalo City Hall knew very much about that old pile of bricks in their midst, and so it was sacrificed to progress.

V I I

By 1909 WRIGHT WAS, in all probability, one of the best-known architects in America. Nowadays this fact is not very widely understood, for there has grown up a myth about Wright to the effect that his great, native genius was ignored by his own countrymen and only recognized by Europeans for what it really was. This is nonsense; between 1889, when Wright built the first section of his house in Oak Park, and 1909, twenty years later, when his two most beautiful Prairie houses—the ones for Avery Coonley and Frederick C. Robie, respectively—were completed, Wright had actually built something like 140 houses and other structures! In addition, he had completed nearly fifty projects for various clients, and many of these were widely published and exhibited. Indeed,

Wright's work took up an increasing share of the annual exhibitions at the Chicago Architectural Club from 1894 onward; so much so, that an entire room was set aside for his work alone in the Club's annual show in 1902, and a special and major section of the show's catalog was devoted to Wright's work. There was, as a matter of fact, a good deal of grumbling over the growing prominence given to Wright by the Club's "Hanging Committee," and because of this, Wright withdrew from the Club's annual exhibitions for a period of time. Nevertheless, he and his work either sought the limelight, or the limelight sought him: his houses were published everywhere (the *Ladies' Home Journal* actually commissioned him to design one of the first Prairie houses for its readers); and he was asked more and more often to speak before professional and lay audiences.

One of the most significant lectures Wright gave during that period, the "Hull House Lecture," was entitled *The Art and Craft of the Machine*. Wright first delivered this lecture in 1901, then revised it several times for later delivery before various other audiences. The Chicago Architectural Club, in 1901, reproduced the lecture in full in its catalog (*in lieu* of showing any of Wright's work that year), and its influence was therefore widespread and, probably, strong. Here, almost twenty years before the Bauhaus, Wright stated certain principles of art in an industrial civilization—and, specifically, in an industrial democracy— which are as valid today as when they were first formulated. "The machine is here to stay," Wright announced. "There is no more important work before the architect now than to use this normal tool of civilization to the best advantage—instead of prostituting it as he has hitherto done in reproducing with murderous ubiquity forms born of other times and other conditions. . . ." (Words always tended to roll off Wright's tongue in great, melodic torrents. He was a true disciple of Whitman, in every way!) "Genius must dominate the work of the contrivance it has created," Wright continued. In other words, unlike the latter-day functionalists, Wright never believed that the machine look was an essential result of machine fabrication. "This plain duty (of dominating the machine) is relentlessly marked out for the artist in this, the Machine Age."

This was perhaps Wright's most important pronouncement at Hull House, but it was by no means his *only* important statement of principle. Although most of the functionalists against whom he would wage war in later years were still in their knee pants, Wright seems to have had a premonition of some of the theories that were bound to spring up sooner or later—theories he would have to fight as vigorously as Sullivan fought the systems of the neoclassicists. "I believe that only when one individual forms the concept of the various projects and also determines the character of every detail in the sum total . . . will unity be secured which is the soul of the individual work of art," Wright said at Hull House. This is, of course, in diametric opposition to the theories later to be propounded by Gropius and others, who believed that architecture in the modern world (a world of 3,000,000,000 human beings) must be the product of teamwork. It is true that Gropius felt that the architect was the only "specialist" equipped to be a universal man, and that he should, therefore, head the team and co-ordinate its work. But, even so, teamwork was the key slogan of Gropius's kind of society; whereas "unity through individual creativeness" became, as early as 1901, the key slogan in Wright's theory of a democratic architecture.

In all likelihood, Gropius and Wright were not nearly as far apart as it may have seemed at various times in their lives. But to Wright the issue had to be drawn with the utmost precision, without compromise. "Genius and the Mobocracy" was the title he gave to his later biography of Sullivan. The true danger in a time of mass populations was, in Wright's mind, that democracy would become ruled by the mob; whereas the American ideal, to him, implied the dominance of the free individual—free to act creatively and to live creatively within a minimum of necessary limitation. In later years, when Wright became identified increasingly with "liberal" politics (he was so "liberal," in fact, that the Communists were able to dupe him on occasion to lend his name to causes they wanted to see promoted), other "liberals" found it very difficult to understand why, for example, he opposed Roosevelt's New Deal with such passion. The reason was simple. Roosevelt, in Wright's mind, had done two things that were alien to the American democratic ideal: he had centralized and strengthened governmental power (instead of decentralizing and weakening it in the direction of the anarchist ideal); and he had handed this power to "the mob" (rather than depend upon individual genius to act creatively and on a large scale). That much of this was nonsense (for Wright's theories of how to run *any*thing, from a school to a nation, were somewhat dubious) did not detract from the purity of Wright's nineteenth-century principle; indeed, he was considerably more liberal than most of his latter-day "liberal" admirers.

The version of the Hull House lecture delivered to a gathering of the Daughters of the American Revolution, in 1904, contained some passages on the American city which form a permanent and beautiful contribution to the literature of the United States. "Thousands of acres of cellular tissue, the city's flesh outspreads, layer upon layer, enmeshed by an intricate network of veins and arteries radiating into the gloom, and in them, with muffled, persistent roar, circulating as the blood circulates in your veins, is the almost ceaseless beat of the activity to whose necessities it all conforms. . . . If the pulse of this great activity . . . is thrilling, what of this prolific silent obedience? Remain to contemplate this wonder until the twinkling lights perish in groups, followed one by one, leaving others to smother in the gloom; until the fires are banked, the tumult slowly dies to an echo here and there. Then the darkened pall is lifted and moonlight outlines the sullen, shadowy masses of structure deeply cut here and there by half-luminous channels; huge patches of shadow, shade, and darkness intermingle mysteriously in blocklike plan and skyline; the broad surface of the lake beside, placid and resplendent with a silver gleam. And there reflect that the texture of the tissue of this great machine, this forerunner of the democracy we hope for, has been deposited, particle by particle, in blind obedience to law —the organic law to which the great solar universe is but an obedient machine, and marvel that this masterful force is as yet untouched by art or artist. . . ."

From the day of his arrival in Chicago, when young Frank stood outside Wells Street Station in a drizzle, with "sputtering white arclights in the station and in the streets, dazzling and ugly . . . crowds. Impersonal. Intent on seeing nothing"—from that day on, Wright both hated and loved the city: hated it for its money-grabbing ugliness; loved it for its brute vigor. In all his life he was never able to cope with the city successfully. Unlike Corbu, he could never approach it rationally. Where his country buildings seemed, literally, to melt into their environment, his city buildings were, invariably, a kick in the teeth of their surroundings. Yet all through his life he wanted to try to find a way to make the city mesh.

During these successful years of Wright's professional life, his family grew up close to his Oak Park studio: the two oldest children, Lloyd and John, were destined to become architects; next there was a girl, Catherine; after her, another boy, David, now an executive with a firm manufacturing concrete blocks; then another girl, Frances, and another son, Llewelyn. Mrs. Wright, in effect, operated a sort of kindergarten; Wright insisted that each child should learn to play a musical instrument (a heritage of William Wright's preoccupation with music). He himself would often sit down at the piano to play Beethoven's music. "His eyes closed, his head and hands swaying over the throttles, I think he imagined he was Beethoven," John Lloyd Wright recalled many years later. "He looked like Beethoven. . . ." As a matter of fact, Wright was extremely handsome in a romantic sort of way, and knew it. (The only picture of him taken during those years was one *he* took by means of squeezing a long rubber tube while sitting in front of his own camera!) Wright was very much of a ladies' man, and he was attracted to some of his clients' wives as much as the wives were to him. He liked to dance, and to go out riding on horseback and, later, in a roadster that he himself had redesigned. "I think this car had something to do with Papa's leaving home," John Lloyd Wright has written. "I know it added new values to his life, for it was at that time that an attractive young woman fell in love with him, or he with her, or both with each other. They went riding often."

The attractive young woman was the wife of a neighbor, Edwin Cheney, for whom Wright had built a small house in 1904. "Everything, personal or otherwise, bore heavily down upon me," Wright said later. "Domesticity most of all. What I wanted I did not know. I loved my children. I loved my home." Yet he no longer loved Catherine, and marriage without love seemed to him a crime. He asked for a divorce, but Catherine refused. Finally he took the decisive step: in the fall of 1909 he abandoned his family as his father had abandoned his. With Mrs. Cheney, Wright took off for New York and Europe, leaving his practice behind in something close to chaos. Their first stop was Berlin, where the publisher Ernst Wasmuth was preparing the great publication of Wright's work up to that time. After spending some time with Wasmuth on this volume, Wright and Mrs. Cheney went on to Florence, where they rented a little villa to escape the newspaper publicity their flight from Chicago had caused. "I now sought shelter there in the companionship with her who, by force of rebellion as by way of love was then implicated with me," Wright wrote in his *Autobiography*. They stayed until 1911, and then returned to the United States. By that time the Wasmuth edition of Wright's work had been published in Berlin, and a parallel exhibition of his work had been shown throughout Europe. Overnight he had become the most widely discussed architect of the day. Every young European architect tried to find out all he could about Wright's work and principles. Only in America, where the scandal press had used Wright's private life as a means of attacking his work, did he seem to be losing ground.

V I I I

U NHAPPILY, the publicity resulting from Wright's affair with Mrs. Cheney was only the beginning of a whole series of private disasters that were soon to be turned into public scandals. For the moment, however, Wright's life seemed to be settling down to something close to normalcy. Upon his return from Europe, he decided that he wanted to build a new home for Mrs. Cheney and himself. "I suppose that faith carried . . . me through the vortex of reaction, the anguish and waste of breaking up home and the loss of prestige and my work at Oak Park," Wright recalled. "Work, life and love I transferred to the beloved ancestral Valley where my mother . . . had bought the low hill on which Taliesin now stands and she offered it to me now as a refuge. . . . I began to build Taliesin to get my back against the wall and fight for what I saw I had to fight." Taliesin is the name of a mythical (or, at least, legendary) Welsh poet. The word actually means "shining brow," and it was around this shining brow at Spring Green, Wisconsin, that Wright began to build a new home for Mrs. Cheney and himself.

Taliesin East (as it was to be called later) has undergone many transformations—some of them, as we shall see, violent in the extreme. Today it is a vast, rambling complex of buildings with many courts—several houses, in fact, rather loosely joined together. The original Taliesin East was rather small—a Prairie house in the best tradition, joined to a drafting room wing that, in turn, was linked to stables, a barn, and a garage. It had all the beauty of the typical Prairie house and most of its characteristic detail: low-slung, pitched roofs with deep overhangs; and ribbon windows that created an intimate relationship between the interior spaces, the surrounding gardens, and the rolling Wisconsin landscape beyond. The scale was established by the low eave height inside and out, which, in turn, was dramatically contrasted with the high roof ceilings in less intimate spaces. Most of the furniture was built in; all of it was of the blocky, geometric variety Wright had come to like and to build especially for his houses whenever possible. The décor throughout was Oriental—Japanese prints, figures of Buddha, valuable Chinese vases, etc. But Taliesin East showed the influence of the Orient in a more profound way as well: the classical, European approach to a building is direct, straight, monumental; the Parthenon is approached that way, and every European building of the classical tradition has been approached in this straightforward manner. But the typical Japanese house or temple is approached quite differently: there may be a gate, and then a hedge or fence that forces one to turn, and then a walk through gardens, up a few steps and down a few steps, more turns through smaller and larger gardens, past pools and so forth—until suddenly a corner of the building is visible behind some planting. And only after the final turn does the visitor see the building revealed, more or less in full. Taliesin East was designed in exactly that way—not on paper, not diagrammatically, but by a great artist capable of visualizing a progression of spaces and forms, a changing of vistas, a play of surprises, and of light and shade from unexpected sources. (Medieval European architecture has some of these same characteristics, and this is the only European tradition Wright ever admired.)

Wright had made his first trip to Japan in 1905 and had become completely enchanted with the traditional architecture of the islands. He had actually donned Japanese dress and traveled through many of the smaller towns and islands to see, in their native setting, what he had first come across in the small Japanese Pavilion at the 1893 exposition. Despite his furious denials, it was quite obvious that the Japanese house had long influenced his own work to a high degree; and his love for Japanese prints—the only decorative art (excepting his own ornament) he ever tolerated in his buildings—dates from that trip. So, Taliesin East became an American house in the Japanese tradition.

Still, it was a very radical reinterpretation of that tradition. For one thing, Taliesin East, like the Hillside Home School that Wright had built in Spring Green for his two maiden aunts, Nell and Jane Lloyd-Jones, in 1902, was constructed largely of local stone, in massive piers that seemed to grow right out of the earth. For another, the plan of Taliesin East, though entirely open in the living areas, was compartmented for privacy in the sleeping areas. Finally, the floor of Taliesin East was virtually on a level with the surrounding land to facilitate the "marriage" of indoor and outdoor space, whereas the traditional Japanese house, for practical reasons of flood and earthquake resistance, is elevated on short stilts.

Yet the principles of planning were very similar, and there was no particular reason for Wright to deny this, except that he insisted upon denying all influence upon his work other than Sullivan's. The latter's influence upon Wright did, indeed, crop up about this time in a remarkable project Wright prepared for the *San Francisco Call*: the twenty-four-story Press building to be built on Market Street in the downtown area of the city. Two versions of the Press building were designed by Wright; the more interesting of the two was a free-standing tower, a thin and wide monumental slab of Sullivanesque proportions. Here were Sullivan's base, shaft, and cap rendered with tremendous

*Midway Gardens, Chicago, Ill., 1914. A fantastically orna-
mented structure that shows the first influences of Mayan
architecture upon Wright. (Courtesy, Museum of Modern
Art)*

verve. This was to be a soaring skyscraper, with strong vertical piers
growing straight out of the sidewalk and continuing all the way up to
the top floor. A sweeping roof overhang, much deeper than the one at
the Wainwright building, topped off the skyscraper. Like the American
Luxfer building, this project, though unbuilt, was remarkable in its modernity. Except for the treatment of its cap, the building resembled many
of the finest slab structures by Mies and others developed in later years.

Shortly after the Press building project was completed, Wright was given one of the largest and most spectacular commissions of his career; the design of the Midway Gardens restaurant in Chicago. In many respects this group of buildings represents a new point of departure in Wright's work, in the direction of greater ornamentation and greater complexity. The program for the Midway Gardens suggested some of this: it was to be a combination casino, a resort-restaurant, and a place for outdoor concerts.

What Wright produced here was, in effect, a huge complex of terraces and turrets, of masses and volumes on intersecting levels so playfully manipulated that a new kind of spatial experience seemed to be suggested by them. These intersecting levels raised the horizontal into the third dimension, suggesting a movement of space upward and downward, as well as parallel to the plane of the earth. In a sense the Midway Gardens are an urban, architectural elaboration of the terraced gardens at Taliesin East; indeed, Midway Gardens, as its name suggests, was largely outdoors, a spacious central court surrounded by ascending terraces and buildings.

Perhaps the most remarkable fact about Midway Gardens was the nature of its ornament—both that designed by Wright (generally of patterned concrete block) and that by the sculptor Ianelli, whose figures were placed on pedestals and parapets all around the central court. This ornament, done in 1914 quite independently of any Cubist developments in Europe, was almost entirely abstract in character. Just as Wright had, in a sense, invented De Stijl at Unity Church, so he anticipated much of the later Cubist work in painting and sculpture at Midway Gardens. Again, this significant innovation was merely incidental to the architecture; it was certainly a necessary part of the volumes and spaces—an organic part in that each abstract turret or figure helped underline the movement of space and the ascent of the brick masses— but it was not at the heart of the architectural problem, which, as usual, was one of manipulating space. In short, Wright had once again, almost casually, given the other arts a helping hand. Unfortunately, this masterpiece was soon to be torn down: for various reasons the enterprise was never very successful, and Prohibition gave it a final blow from which it could not recover. The Gardens were replaced by what Wright called an "auto-laundry."

"When the Midway Gardens were nearly finished," Wright recalled in his *Autobiography*, "my son John and I . . . were sitting quietly (one day) eating our lunch in the newly finished bar." Suddenly there was a long-distance telephone call from Taliesin East. There had been a terrible tragedy: a Barbados Negro, a servant at the house, had suddenly gone berserk, killed seven of the inhabitants of the house, and set fire to the buildings. Mrs. Cheney and her two children were dead, and so were four apprentices and workmen. The living quarters were demolished; only the working areas survived. It was a tragedy of such monumental proportions that Wright was completely numbed. He buried Mrs. Cheney himself, "and no monument yet marks the spot where she was buried," he wrote later. "All I had left to show for the struggle for freedom . . . had now been swept away. Why mark the spot where desolation ended and began? . . . The gaping black hole left by the fire in the beautiful hillside was empty, a charred and ugly scar upon my own life."

For days Wright himself seemed hardly to be alive. He slept, or tried to sleep, in the studio wing that had been untouched by fire. Armed men searched the hills for the madman, who was finally caught. The numbness that had overtaken Wright probably spared him some of the horror of the newspaper publicity that grew out of the tragedy—for, of course, the scandal sheets loved the whole affair. Here was this mad architect, this freethinker, this radical who had run off with a married woman and left his own family in the lurch; the man had obviously received his just desserts. And wasn't this sort of scandal just what you would expect from people who lived in crazy-looking houses? The yellow journalists tried to destroy Wright, not only as a man, but as an architect as well. "As one consequence of the ugly publicity . . . hundreds of letters had come to me from all over the country," Wright recalled. "I tied them up together in a bundle now and burned them. Unread. I went to work. The salt and savor of life had not been lost." And Wright performed a supreme act of courage: he went on living.

I X

S OME TIME AFTER the Taliesin tragedy, Wright received a very sensitive and understanding note of sympathy from a complete stranger —a sculptress called Miriam Noel—and he answered it gratefully. Shortly thereafter, Miss Noel turned up in Chicago. She was a striking woman of great sophistication and elegance, quite unlike anyone Wright had ever known before. In his loneliness he felt drawn to her, and they became intimate friends.

Meanwhile Wright had obtained one of the best-known commissions of his career—the job of building the new Imperial Hotel in Tokyo to replace an earlier Imperial Hotel that had burned down during an earthquake. The manager of the hotel and a commission of advisers had made a trip through Europe and the United States to find an architect to do the job, and when they saw Wright's houses around Chicago, they were instinctively drawn to him. By 1915 Wright and Miriam Noel were in Japan, and Wright, especially, loved every moment of it. He felt that here was a civilization complete in every detail: from prints to clothes, from music and poetry to architecture, there was not a single false note. "How can anything human be so polished and clean?" Wright asked. And, for the first time, he was willing to admit that "if Japanese prints were to be deducted from my education, I don't know what direction the whole might have taken. *The gospel of elimination of the insignificant preached by the print came home to me in architecture.* . . ." Thirty years later, when Wright attacked Mies's credo of "less is more," he seemed to have forgotten some of those earlier words.

Yet his stay in Japan was not pure bliss by any means. There were serious financial and political difficulties in connection with the planning of the Imperial Hotel; but, more disturbingly, there were difficulties connected with Miriam Noel. It turned out that she had had a fairly long history of mental instability, and there were serious emotional crises of the most morbid kind. Wright blamed himself; he was still unable to marry her, because Catherine would not agree to a divorce, and his self-recriminations hardly added to his own happiness.

The planning of the Imperial Hotel took many months. It was to be an extremely complex building—complex not only in its plan, but also in its structure. In plan Wright tried to do something similar to what he had achieved at Midway Gardens—an infinite variety of spatial experiences, surprises, and delights, all scaled to the small size of all things Japanese. In structure he tried to solve the terrible, traditional problem of Japan—how to combat earthquake tremors.

This problem was complicated by the fact that the site on which the Imperial Hotel was to be built consisted, as Wright put it, of "eight feet of cheese-like soil that overlay . . . liquid mud." There seemed to be no way of getting any kind of solid support for the building, so Wright determined to "float" its foundations on this bed of mud, rather than try to find some solid support deeper down. The next problem was how to keep the building from cracking up like hard icing on a base of jelly once the jelly begins to shake. Wright decided that there was only one way, and that was to make the building itself of many small and independent parts to start with, rather than wait for the next earthquake to do it for him in an unpredictable way. Thus the Imperial Hotel was made of many sections with "expansion joints" between them—sections that could move independently of each other if the need to do so ever arose.

Still, such sections were often as much as sixty feet in length. A fair-sized earth tremor could easily crack this, so Wright developed a system of structural supports that were a stroke of pure genius. "Why not carry the floors as a waiter carries his tray on an upraised arm and fingers at the center—balancing the load?" Wright asked. Why not indeed? It was something the Japanese had *tried* to do in their wooden houses supported on individual posts (the idea being that if one or two posts were lifted up or lowered by the earth tremors, the wood frame of the house could absorb the strain and would eventually return to its original shape as the tremors subsided). But in the traditional Japanese house the posts were around the perimeter of the building, so that an earth tremor *anywhere* under the house would be bound to affect its structure. A wooden structure might be able to resist such strains, but the monolithic concrete-and-steel buildings going up around Tokyo were bound to crack under the impact.

So, Wright put his concrete "posts" or "fingers" under the center of each section of the Imperial Hotel, and then cantilevered the floor slabs out from that pin-supported center in all directions, letting the slabs touch the perimeter walls only very lightly. These walls, in turn, were supported on systems of pins or fingers as well, so that each part of the building was allowed, in effect, to move independently and then to return to its original position.

Wright's clients thought he was utterly mad, but his persuasiveness carried the day for him again and again. On one occasion, when the building was almost completed, a severe earthquake shook the structure —and left it completely undamaged. After that, Wright was given his way in almost every respect. However, one of the conditions imposed

Imperial Hotel, Tokyo, 1916-22. A rich blend of Mayan ornament, Japanese scale and detail—all drawn together by Wright's picturesque genius. (Courtesy, Museum of Modern Art)

upon him was that he would stay in Tokyo until the building was finished. So, he and Miriam Noel remained in Japan until 1921, with only a few trips to Taliesin in between. Wright was thus able to control every detail, every decorative touch, every single item of cabinet work put into the Imperial Hotel. The result was an unparalleled bit of fantasy— delightful, charming, and slightly unbelievable.

To begin with, on its surface the Imperial Hotel was one of the least "Japanese" buildings Wright had done up to that time. Why this was so is hard to explain: perhaps he was trying to prove to someone (possibly himself) that he had not been influenced by Japanese tradition at all. In any event, the Imperial Hotel is one of his first faintly Mayan temples—an astonishingly ornate and rich structure strongly reminiscent of the temples at Chichen Itza in Yucatan. It is as if Wright had tried, subconsciously, to return the compliment by bringing something beautiful of the Western Hemisphere to the Japanese Islands.

But in its scale, and in its play with surprise elements, the Imperial Hotel is completely Japanese. Wright was apparently so struck by the smallness of Japanese things that he made everything in the Imperial Hotel tiny: in some of the rooms the glazed doors leading out to little balconies are hardly more than five feet high; elsewhere, windows overlooking gardens and courts are so low that one must get down on all fours to enjoy the view. (On the other hand, the doorknobs on guestroom doors are so high that the small Japanese maids must stand on tiptoe to reach them—possibly an intended effect, as Wright liked the grace of Japanese women.) There were little terraces and little courts, infinitely narrow passages suddenly opening out into large two- or threestory spaces; big and little pools (both for ornament and to provide water for fire-fighting during earthquakes, when the municipal water system tended to collapse). And there were many different levels, both inside the rooms and outside the buildings, including connecting bridges between the two long, parallel wings of guest rooms. Finally, Wright achieved something almost unheard of in hotel design: in this most standardized of all fields of cubicle architecture he succeeded in making almost every guest room different from every other. In short, he created a hotel that would be an efficiency expert's nightmare, and a pure delight for any guest.

Two years after he left Japan, a terrible earthquake struck Tokyo and destroyed much of the city. One hundred thousand people perished. There was utter confusion in the press reports reaching the United States; for several days the papers said that the Imperial Hotel was completely destroyed. Wright could not believe it. Finally, there arrived the famous telegram that is now part of architectural history:

HOTEL STANDS UNDAMAGED AS MONUMENT OF YOUR GENIUS HUNDREDS OF HOMELESS PROVIDED FOR BY PERFECTLY MAINTAINED SERVICE CONGRATULATIONS.

Banquet hall in the Imperial Hotel. The ornament is largely derived from American-Indian themes. (Courtesy, Museum of Modern Art)

It was signed by Baron Okyra, Wright's great friend, the Chairman of the Board of the Imperial Hotel. The virtually untrained, untutored country hick from the Middle West had shown himself to be one of the finest engineers of his time.

In spite of this and other professional triumphs, Wright's life remained complicated and unhappy. Miriam Noel's condition had gone from bad to worse; finally, Wright was able to persuade Catherine to grant him a divorce so that he could marry Miriam. He hoped that this would help her emotional balance, but, if anything, her health deteriorated after their marriage. Suddenly she left Taliesin—where the Wrights had gone after their return from Japan—to live in Los Angeles. After consultation with a psychiatrist, it became obvious to Wright that their marriage, too, was beyond repair. They were divorced in 1927; she died in a sanitarium a few years later.

X

ON THE SURFACE, Wright's work was becoming more and more ornate; in plan and spatial organization, it was becoming increasingly complex. Compared to the Yahara Boat Club of twenty years earlier—that unbelievably modern, clean-cut composition of sweeping, flat planes—the Imperial Hotel looked old-fashioned and fussy. What exactly was happening to Wright? Was he simply growing old?

What was happening had been suggested here and there by details found in his work for a couple of decades: he was beginning to discover a new kind of space entirely, and with it a new kind of structure. To all great architects, the "reality" of a building is the space within and around it, not in its plan and elevations. Wright was always fond of quoting (or paraphrasing) Lao-tse and pointing out that "the reality of the vessel is the void within it." To Wright the walls, roofs, floors, frills, and all the rest were merely tools of the trade—the raw materials with which an architect must work. But the potential greatness of architecture was the quality of the space within and without.

In his early buildings—the American buildings that paralleled Whitman's "open road"—Wright had felt that his kind of space should be a horizontally moving entity, always controlled in layers parallel to the earth. Such spatial movement tended to produce an architecture of soaring, flat slabs, all directing the eye toward some distant expanding frontier, some distant prairie horizon. But somewhere along the line— at the time of the Larkin building and of Unity Church—Wright began to sense the possibilities of space-in-motion up and down, as well as sideways. He began to sense the excitement inherent in changing levels, in light appearing not only through horizontal bands of glass but also through huge skylights above, of progressions through architecture involving not only turns and twists, right and left, but ascents and descents as well.

Something of all this had been in the back of his mind from the days when he first saw Sullivan's ornament for the interiors of the Auditorium. "The magic word *plastic* was used by the Master in reference to his ornament, and the room itself began to show the effects of this ideal," Wright wrote in his *Autobiography*. "The ideal began to enter the Auditorium interior. Not consciously, I believe. Subconsciously . . . while no advantage was taken of the arched elliptical form (of the theater) to carry the loads above . . . still the form was appropriate, suitable to its purpose and prophetic."

Just how prophetic it was, Wright himself did not realize until several years later. But Sullivan's ornament had two tremendously significant characteristics, which eventually led Wright to a new architectural concept: the ornament was "plastic" and it suggested "continuity." The most characteristic form in Sullivan's ornament was a spiral form, generally made up of bent and twisted grasses or twigs, with no beginning and no end. This form in nature is, of course, the snail—a structural organism of extraordinary sophistication completely unmatched by man, at least until Wright began to try to match it.

His first attempts in that direction were relatively crude: the low ceiling planes of the roof overhang carried into the house, contrasting with high ceilings formed by the pitched roof itself; the steps up and down within open spaces; and the occasional hidden slot of glass somewhere inside the folded roof structure which permitted streaks of sunlight to move, like long fingers, across walls and floors as the earth rotated. This sort of thing had been done before, though rarely with such subtlety and art. But now Wright tried to create a new kind of structure to enclose and enfold the continuous spaces that, he felt, were suggested by structures in nature—structures like sea shells, cobwebs, and cocoons.

From Unity Church onward, Wright had sensed the enormous potentials of concrete reinforced with strands of steel. "Concrete is a plastic material," he wrote. "I saw a kind of weaving coming out of it. Why not weave a kind of building? Then I saw the shell. Shells with steel inlaid in them . . . Lightness and strength! Steel the spider spinning a web within the cheap, plastic material." To describe the special characteristics of reinforced concrete, Wright liked to fold his hands tightly and then try to pull them apart. "The steel strands are there to resist tension," he would say, "and the concrete resists compression. Together, the two can resist any stresses from any source." The plasticity of concrete, he went on, inevitably opened up an entirely new world of form. Not only did it make the right angle and the box obsolete, it actually made them inefficient. The great thing was to let the stresses in floor, walls, and roof flow into one another without any dividing line at any of the traditional corners—to allow the plastic concrete to work together just as in a sea shell, making it both the structure and the enclosing skin.

How radical this concept was can be understood only when one looks at the "skin and bones" architecture of Mies and of most classical architecture of the past. Wright liked to demonstrate the (to him) old-fashioned character of post-and-beam structures by holding up the index finger of his left hand and placing his other index finger on top of it horizontally, to form a T. "You see, this is the old post and beam principle," Wright would say, wiggling the two fingers to show the inherent instability of such a structure. "It is only as strong as its connection. But in a continuous structure of concrete," he would go on, now folding his hands and trying to pull them apart, "the strength is in the organic form itself."

So, the natural forms of Sullivan's Art Nouveau ornament led Wright to a re-examination of the structural (rather than ornamental) qualities of forms in nature. And he came up with a principle—continuity—which, for the first time in the history of architecture, represented an effort to conquer the problems of structure by the use of forms found in nature for millions of years. To the list of his masters— a list bearing only Sullivan's name to date—Wright added that of Nature herself.

One of the tragedies of Wright's life is that technology never quite caught up with him in his own lifetime. Indeed, not until the last few years of his life did engineers and other architects begin to grasp the possibilities of shell structures in which there were no longer skin and bones, but only a thin, reinforced skin so warped and twisted as to give it tremendous structural strength. One engineer—Professor Mario Salvadori at Columbia—used to demonstrate the principle to his students by picking up a thin and flat sheet of paper, holding it at one end, and making it flap up and down. "You see, the skin has no structural strength at all now," he would explain. Then he would pick up the same sheet of paper at one corner, give it a warped shape by twisting it between his fingertips, and try again to make it flap around. But now the sheet had become quite rigid and was capable of supporting itself without trouble. Wright grasped this principle from the early 1920's on, but he did not have the technological tools to demonstrate it properly until many years later. As a matter of fact, at the time of his death in 1959, certain plastics engineers were just beginning to experiment with reinforced and irradiated plastics that promised the kind of structure Wright had prophesied during the latter part of his life.

Wright's first conscious attempts to create such continuous, plastic structures were made in the year after he returned from Japan. One of these was a house he designed for Mrs. Alice Millard, in Pasadena, California. Here he tried to use concrete—a specially and ornately patterned concrete block—and a mesh of steel reinforcing rods to create a strong

"Hollyhock" house for Miss Barnsdall, Los Angeles, Calif.,
1920. A fantastic "Mayan Temple," rendered in exposed,
poured concrete. (Photo: Ezra Stoller)

'fabric for all floors, walls, and roofs, strong in tension as well as compression. This sense of an interwoven structure was expressed on the
outside by a gridlike ornament—again very Mayan in character, and very
geometric. Within, the spaces were on several interlocking levels, with
fingers of sunlight penetrating the space from many secret and surprising sources. In the following year, 1923, Wright built two more of these
"woven fabric" houses, both in Los Angeles—one for Dr. Storer, and

the other for Charles Ennis. Here again the ornament and exterior composition were Mayan; and while the Millard house was still rectangular in its silhouette, the Ennis house had several walls and masses that tapered upward, creating an effect of greater plasticity in form than was apparent in the rectangularity of the Millard and Storer houses.

Wright's preoccupation with reinforced concrete block continued throughout his lifetime, and three of his sons were involved in these experiments in one way or another. Lloyd and John Lloyd Wright, both architects, were helping him directly on the early California houses. David became an executive with a company manufacturing concrete blocks, and continued his interest in his father's experiments throughout

Ornament in "Hollyhock" house. (Photo: Ezra Stoller)

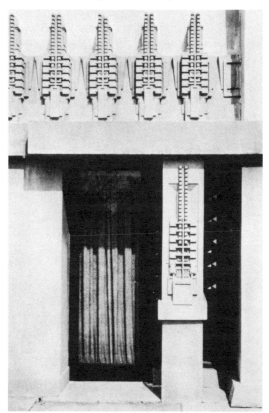

the latter's life. Actually, the idea of reinforcing modular concrete blocks with steel rods, vertically and horizontally, and then pouring concrete into the hollows of the blocks to "weld" the steel to the concrete makes considerable sense and is used frequently in more run-of-the-mill construction. But by its very rectangular nature the concrete block did not really lend itself to the sort of plastic expression Wright was trying hard to achieve: a building of concrete blocks was almost bound to be rectangular in its over-all shape. (Many years later, when Wright built his extraordinary concrete-block house for his son David, he probably "bent" and "twisted" the block as much as it can possibly be bent and

Living room in Ennis house, Los Angeles, Calif., 1924. One of several concrete block houses of the period, using a specially designed, ornamented block, and a mesh of reinforcing rods to tie the masonry together. (Photo: Ezra Stoller)

First Unitarian Church, Madison, Wis., 1950. A folded-roof structure designed on a diamond-shaped module. The peak is meant to represent hands raised in prayer. (Photo: Ezra Stoller)

twisted. But this was strictly a *tour de force,* and not a serious attempt to find a widely applicable solution.)

By the same token, Wright was severely handicapped in his attempts to introduce plasticity into wood-framed houses. The straight wooden stud or joist is a very hard thing to bend, and Wright never quite succeeded in bending it. What he did do was try to fold it. Some of his designs of the early 1920's—particularly the cabins he designed for a projected summer colony on Lake Tahoe—look very much like the folded paper games that were part of his Froebelian upbringing. While a folded plane is not as inherently strong, structurally, as a molded sheet, it does possess a structural strength much greater than that of any post-and-beam-and-skin building. Still, it was only the beginning, and Wright was quite obviously frustrated by the terrible limitations imposed upon him by the straightness of available building materials.

Yet the twin notions of continuity and plasticity obsessed him for the remainder of his life. He saw that here was a principle so new, so tremendously important to the future of architecture that all those who seemed to stand in its way were on a par with the Beaux Arts academicians who had barred the way to Sullivan in 1893. What the International Style men were building in Europe was, to Wright's way of thinking, another kind of box—stripped of neoclassical ornament, but still a box with straight posts and beams, straight sides that ended up being just another sort of strait jacket. There was no chance for a free, democratic architecture, Wright felt, until man could make buildings unbend, until the building could be shaped by the desired flow of space in any and all directions. Such buildings would be truly "organic," for not only did they express the aspirations of free men to free space, but they also expressed a kind of structure that had within it all the elements of living things in nature—muscles, tendons, fibers, skin—all woven together into a single organism acting in unison. "Nature is right, but man is straight," Thoreau had written. "She erects no beams, she slants no rafters, and yet she builds stronger and truer than he." To Wright, American architecture had to be Nature's architecture—organic, flexible, free. Conversely, he felt, all straight, post-and-beam architecture was, in effect, an expression of a straight-laced, autocratic, European concept of society.

Much of this sort of argument was, of course, rather far-fetched. The Japanese post-and-beam house, in which the walls were literally dissolved into the garden landscape beyond, had seemed to express a concept of freedom to Wright only a few years earlier. And in his later Usonian houses Wright himself frequently returned to rectangular geometry closely related to the post-and-beam concepts of the traditional Japanese house. Yet the obsession with fluidity and plasticity of structure remained; if he was not always able to express it in his houses, in particular, the reason lay in the straightness of available American build-

*Auditorium of Madison Unitarian Church. The diamond-
shaped space creates an intimate enclosure, lit from various, unexpected sources. (Photo: Ezra Stoller)*

ing materials. Indeed, most of Wright's truly "plastic" designs prior
to 1945 remained projects on paper. Only in a few of the last, great
buildings of his career did he finally and completely break through the
grid of rectangular geometry to demonstrate what he meant by an
"organic" architecture.

In later years, as part of his attempt to break through "the box,"
Wright discovered that a hexagonal, diamond-shaped or triangular
module might work almost as well as a square one, and produce an

infinitely greater variety of spaces. This fascination with polygonal shapes may be traceable to Wright's experience with Silsbee's informal cottages, whose inevitable bay windows were, generally, half a hexagon or half an octagon. Indeed, Wright's first experiment with nonrectangular forms came not long after he left Silsbee: this was a 60-foot-high windmill and water tower built at Spring Green for his two aunts —a structure that, for somewhat far-fetched reasons, Wright insisted upon calling Romeo and Juliet ever after. The structure, in plan, consisted of a diamond-shaped spine being "embraced" by a somewhat shorter, polygonal tower—hence (apparently) "Romeo and Juliet." In any event, this very charming structure contained within it not only a suggestion of future modular patterns in Wright's work, but also a prophesy of folded-skin structures not very different from the Lake Tahoe cabins of several decades later.

When Wright returned from Japan and built his handful of California houses, he was well past fifty. His fame was completely assured. His work was published everywhere; and though most of the publicity surrounding his unhappy personal life was not conducive to making him widely accepted or respected by conventional society, his name was revered among imaginative young architects everywhere. He had built or projected hundreds of structures, each more inventive than the ones preceding it.

Meanwhile, in Europe, Le Corbusier and Mies van der Rohe were just beginning to make names for themselves. Neither had built more than a couple of houses, or designed more than half a dozen "ideal" projects. Wright, in short, had a tremendous head start over those who would soon begin to challenge him. On the other hand, in the eyes of the new European modernists he remained somewhat tainted with the excessive frills and finnicky tastes of the nineteenth century. He was never quite able to overcome this handicap, never quite able to become "more modern" than he had been in the Yahara Boat Club project and in Unity Church. But despite his tendency toward fussiness in detail and ornament, he held firm to his great central convictions about the nature of space and of structure; and in these areas he remained ahead even of younger generations until the end of his life.

X I

THE 1920'S WERE YEARS of recurring disaster and unhappiness for Wright. Shortly after his separation from his second wife, Taliesin East once again caught fire, and the living areas were once again destroyed. "During the terrible destruction," Wright wrote, "the crowd stood there on the hill-top, faces lit up by the flames. . . . Some were already sneering at the fool who imagined Taliesin could come back after all that had happened there before." Yet Wright went back to work, rebuilding his home once more.

Then his mother died at the age of eighty-three. She had been very close to him throughout his life, and had come to visit him in Japan during the building of the Imperial Hotel. And Louis Sullivan died, destroyed in part by public indifference and neglect, in part by alcoholism. Wright and Sullivan had met again and resolved their quarrel before his death, and Sullivan gave his disciple the first copy of his own autobiography, with a dedication. The copy was destroyed in the fire at Taliesin, in 1924.

And whatever happened, and wherever it did, the press was there to cover the event. Wright was hounded by Miriam Noel and her lawyers, and he was hounded by creditors. There were fewer and fewer clients. Except for a couple of old and faithful friends, like Darwin D. Martin, or a relative like Richard Lloyd-Jones, almost no one came to Wright. It was not that he was not sufficiently well known (indeed, he hired a newspaperman to keep his name *out* of the papers, but the effort was a failure); it was, simply, that there was an air of instability about him and his life, and few potential clients were willing to risk their money with him.

And things continued to get worse: Wright was still in debt over the rebuilding of the first Taliesin when the second version burned down. To build Taliesin III, he went into debt more deeply than ever; everything he owned was mortgaged to the hilt. Moreover, there had been a further complication: in the early days of his separation from Miriam Noel, Wright had met Olga Lazovich, the daughter of an aristocratic, Montenegran family, and they had fallen in love. Olgivanna, as he called her, had been married before and had a daughter by that first marriage. Her former husband teamed up with Miriam Noel's lawyers and, before long, Wright—now married to Olgivanna—found himself a fugitive from justice, being arrested under all sorts of warrants sworn out either by Miriam Noel's lawyers or those of Olgivanna's former husband. Moreover, he was unable to meet his obligations under the mortgages on Taliesin III, and the banks foreclosed. Wright found that the only way to save Taliesin was to incorporate himself and to sell shares on his potential earning power to his wealthy friends. This he did, and the Taliesin Fellowship was founded.

During these nightmare years Wright managed to build or project a few things of lasting value. How he did it is almost incomprehensible in retrospect; he was constantly in and out of the headlines, in and out

Taliesin, Spring Green, Wis., 1925-59. Many levels, many courts, and many unexpected vistas make this one of the most subtle spatial compositions of our time. (Photo: Ezra Stoller)

of the courts. In all likelihood, it was the quiet strength of Olgivanna which saw him through. One of his finest works of these years was Taliesin III, rebuilt from 1925 onward, and still partly under construction when Wright died thirty-four years later. At Taliesin III Wright created one of the most beautiful rooms of his career—a living room of many spaces, all flowing together under the great central roof ceiling. Here were most of the finest elements that Wright had brought into domestic architecture: the heart of the house, a great, rocky fireplace with a huge boulder for a lintel; a skylight so placed as to allow a streak of sunlight animate this rugged chimney breast; a symphony of roof levels, some low and intimate over sitting areas, others high and spacious over places where people might gather at a party; a play of many differ-

Guest room at Taliesin. The streak of sunlight moves across the chimney breast in the course of the day and makes the space come to life. (Photo: Ezra Stoller)

ent materials and textures—stone from the Wisconsin hills, natural wood, plaster in a natural sand color; built-in furniture of every sort, with the characteristic, horizontal blockiness that had become Wright's personal idiom; and planting everywhere, indoors and out. There is hardly a more romantic room than this in America.

The 1920's were, of course, the great skyscraper-building years in America; and though Wright did not get a chance to build one until after World War II, the seeds for his various skyscraper concepts were sown in this difficult period.

Wright had two major difficulties of a philosophical sort in designing a skyscraper: first, as a believer in an architecture close to nature, he had a hard time justifying a tall, upright, seemingly antinature building; and, second, his obsession with the twin concepts of continuity and plasticity—a preoccupation that had led him to the sea shell and the cocoon as ideal structural prototypes—made it difficult to approach the design of a tall, multicellular building (there are no really tall sea shells). He solved this dilemna in a characteristic fashion, by going to the one source in nature which did indeed suggest a way of building a tall structure: the form of a tree.

In structural terms a tree is a vertical beam cantileverd out of the ground. Most of its mass is above the ground, and most of the stresses applied to a tree—such as wind pressures and snow loads—are applied to it high up, close to its crown. The structural force that keeps a tree

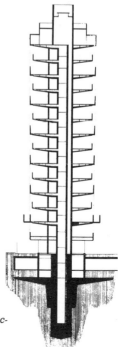

Section through Johnson Wax tower, showing the structural system employed. (Courtesy, Taliesin Fellowship)

from toppling over is, of course, the restraint applied to its roots by the earth in which they are embedded; and any time a storm blows up, the wind pressures are counteracted by pressures applied by the earth.

This sort of cantilever is, as a matter of fact, one of the simplest and most dramatic expressions of continuity, for it represents a delicate balance of forces, each restraining the other through an infinite number of strands and fibers which make the tree a continuous organism. To Wright, the cantilever was also the "most romantic, most free, of all principles of construction," and so he again applied a natural principle he had grasped by intuition, and demonstrated its eminently practical aspects in terms of engineering. Instead of designing a cage of columns and beams as Sullivan had done (with the outer row of columns practically in a plane with the outer walls), Wright designed a skyscraper prototype whose central, vertical core was the only structural support! This was a kind of tree trunk, deeply anchored in the soil; and floor slabs were then arranged to spread out like horizontal branches from this central trunk, so that the outside skin of the building had to carry no loads at all and could be made of glass, metal, plastic, or any other light and thin material. The central trunk was to be of reinforced concrete, and would contain all services as well—elevators, ducts, wiring, and piping.

Wright first explored this principle in a project for the National Life Insurance skyscraper, in 1924. Here, however, the core was not a single trunk, but rather a series of trunks spaced apart on a regular module. The chief difference of this system from Sullivan's typical, cagelike structure was that there were no columns in the exterior walls. The walls were to be simply of glass set in copper strips.

By 1929, however, Wright had really designed his concrete-and-glass tree just the way he wanted it: the vertical service core was the trunk, and all utilities were contained within this vertical shaft. All floors were cantilevered out from it, and the exterior skin was simply sheathed in glass and metal. This project—the famous apartment tower for the vestry of St. Mark's-in-the-Bouwerie in New York—was never built, but Wright returned to the basic concept again and again; finally, in 1954, in Bartlesville, Oklahoma, Wright was able to build his St. Mark's tower—twenty-five years after it was first designed.

Johnson Wax tower, completed in 1950. The building was constructed much like a tree, with a central trunk and with floors branching out from that trunk. As in the main building, all natural light enters through a curtain of glass tubing. (Photo: Ezra Stoller)

While Wright was developing his concrete-and-glass trees in America, Mies was designing his own glass skyscraper on an exactly parallel principle in Germany. Indeed, the 1920 skyscraper by Mies was considerably further advanced in concept than Wright's first sketches of the same year for the National Life Insurance building, and not until the St. Mark's tower, nine years later, did Wright come close to Mies's bold concept.

Whether or not Wright was influenced by Mies's widely publicized sketch and model is difficult to reconstruct; needless to say, Wright would have denied such influences, and Mies would, in all likelihood, prove too modest to make any such claims. Yet the two projects are so similar that it is very tempting to compare them and to discover what, exactly, makes them so very different in ultimate expression.

It should be said from the start that Mies's glass skyscraper was a brilliant but rather abstract sketch, whereas Wright's tower was a very detailed proposal, full of practical suggestions for such things as movable metal partitions, built-in cabinets, mechanical equipment, and so on. By necessity, therefore, Mies's sketch seems bold and simple, whereas Wright's appears a little overly complicated. Granting all this, however, Mies's glass shaft was sleek, slender, vertical, and utterly modern, whereas Wright's tower was full of fussy ornamental touches and conflicts between vertical and horizontal articulation. (He obviously still preferred the horizontal, but knew from Sullivan that a horizontally accented skyscraper will always tend to look like a candy stick.) Both Mies's and Wright's towers were irregular in plan outline, but Mies's was completely free-form in a very modern and, incidentally, very "plastic" way, whereas Wright's tower was based upon a diamond-shaped module, and its silhouette therefore looked rather jagged, almost in the manner of the Italian Futurists of the pre-World War I era. Yet the principle that motivated Mies's and Wright's designs was identical; the only difference was that Mies happened to be a generation younger and very much "in the swim" of the new ideas in the plastic arts then current in Europe; whereas Wright was something of a cultural isolationist, with an eye only for what was happening in the Far East—rather like the political isolationists in America between the two wars.

The increasing jaggedness of Wright's forms and details was the direct result of his use of triangular or polygonal modules. One reason why he used these modules was that they seemed to him to relate to geometric formations found in nature. "Crystals," he said, "are proof of nature's matchless architectural principle." What he tried to build was a crystallic architecture—at least in the cities. "Imagine a city irridescent by day, luminous by night, imperishable! Buildings, shimmering fabrics, woven of rich glass; glass all clear or part opaque and part clear, patterned in color . . . to harmonize with the metal tracery that is to hold all together . . . I dream of such a city." It was a lovely picture. But when these words were spoken, Corbu and Gropius were trying to solve the problem of the huge, urban center in very different terms. Their approach was based upon certain social convictions that were far removed from Wright's thinking, and they were based, also, upon a concept of civic art which remained unintelligible to Wright throughout his lifetime. What he was really trying to do was to make the city look more like a natural organism. "The gleam of mineral colors and flashing facets of crystals. Gems to be bought and set; to forever play with light to man's delight, in never-ending beams of purest green, or red or blue or yellow, and all that lives between. Light! Light in the mathematics of form . . ." He was describing the romance of jewels, but he might as well have been describing the romance of the sort of crystal city he liked to dream of in his studio at Taliesin.

Did this crystal city make as much sense as Corbu's Ville Radieuse? Probably not. But it did have something Corbu's city did not have—at least not in the northern, "Gothic" sense of Wright's Wisconsin. "Why should architecture or objects of art in the machine age . . . have to resemble machinery?" Wright asked. "Modern architecture . . . will become a poor, flat-faced thing of steel bones, box-outlines, gas-pipe, and handrail fittings, as sun-receptive as a concrete sidewalk or a glass tank." (This was twenty years before Mies built the Farnsworth house.) "Without romance the essential joy of living as distinguished from pleasure is not alive. The new romance is that reality." Wright may have been a cultural isolationist, but he knew exactly what he was isolating himself from.

X I I

WRIGHT'S FOUNDING of the Taliesin Fellowship in the late 1920's was not merely a way of escaping his creditors by selling shares in his own practice. It was also the start of one of the most extraordinary schools of architecture in the modern world. For many years young people from various countries had approached Wright and asked to be allowed to serve an apprenticeship in his studio. This sort of thing has always been standard procedure in the training of young architects, and Wright accepted these apprentices in ever growing numbers. Finally, in 1929, with the founding of the Taliesin Fellowship, the arrangement was made more formal: young men and women could come and work at Taliesin under Wright's direction for a fee, and many did.

The Taliesin Fellowship has often been criticized on two grounds: first, because (it is alleged) the young people who came to study there were, in effect, exploited and forced to do all sorts of housekeeping and farm work, rather than learn something about architecture. And, second, the Fellowship has been criticized because it did not produce any very talented "Wrightian" architects.

To some extent both criticisms are justified. The young men and women who came to Taliesin were required to do everything from peeling potatoes to sweeping the floors. But to Wright this did not seem to be a form of exploitation at all. For one thing, he despised formal education and felt that all it could teach was formulas—not principles. (His own education had, of course, been of the most informal sort.) It seemed to him that there were only two or three things one could teach: first, a basic understanding of nature, and he could think of no better way of teaching that than to make his apprentices work on a farm as he had done in his own youth. Second, he believed that it was important to convey the need for utter dedication to work, for architecture is no dilettante affair. And, finally, Wright believed that all you could really teach was a *principle*, and even that could only be hinted at in talks, in music, and in working on things that seemed to express that principle.

It is fair to say that through the years the Taliesin Fellowship has produced no great architects. One of the problems was that Wright tended to be resentful and sometimes even jealous of any young upstarts who dared to question ideas or actual projects under development at Taliesin. In this respect he was, however, no more intolerant than Mies, who felt, while he was director of the School of Architecture at I.I.T., that no young student had the equipment to challenge fundamental ideas until he had absorbed some of the principles of architecture through hard, preparatory work. But Wright's Taliesin, being inextricably tied to a great individualist, produced only "yes men"; whereas Mies's I.I.T., under the leadership of one who had made a fetish of anonymity, gave an occasional chance to those who held ideas very different from Mies's own. Thus the only Taliesin apprentices who have shown any great promise in their independent careers are found among those few whom Wright expelled from the Fellowship for what he considered to be their youthful arrogance!

Wright's thoughts on education were somewhat unusual, as they began with the assumption that the basis of architectural education was to reject just about every precedent. In 1930, when the Fellowship was just getting under way, he said that "any architect should be radical by nature because it is never good enough for him to begin where others have left off." At the same time, he never cared much for "radicals" in his own Fellowship, and any young man who dared challenge Wright's ideas was in danger of expulsion. His own justification of this apparent contradiction was that there *were* a few precedents that should be adhered to under all circumstances. "The workings of principle in the direction of integral order is your only safe precedent, now or ever," he told his young apprentices. "The circumference of architecture is changing with astonishing rapidity, but its center remains unchanged, the human heart." Still, the apprentices insisted upon copying the details and the mannerisms in Wright's work without apparently understanding the basic principles of spatial and structural organization beneath the often fussy detail. Indeed, it is fair to say that Wright's influence was considerably greater upon those who never went to Taliesin, for some of these younger architects saw through the Art Nouveau trappings a great and shining ideal, and explored it further in a more modern idiom. Shortly after the end of World War II, a group of apprentices got together to create a community of Usonian houses near Pleasantville, New York. The result was depressing: except for one singularly beautiful house by Wright himself, located (of course) on the highest point of the development, there were only near-caricatures of the master's own earlier houses—sadly distorted, lacking in scale, utterly unrelated. A French lady visitor whose English was not fluent, and who was taken to Pleasantville by a U.S. State Department guide to get a glimpse of what the American *avant-garde* was up to, returned somewhat baffled by the whole experience, stating to a friend that she had been to a community called, she thought, Insomnia Homes. It was an unwittingly accurate commentary, not only upon this settlement, but upon much of the work produced by former memebers of the Fellowship.

Slowly, very slowly, Wright's fortunes began to improve after his own personal disasters and after the Wall Street crash, which had hurt him as much as it hurt every other architect. In the early 1930's his work was again being exhibited, first at the Chicago Art Institute (whose Wright exhibition was widely circulated); and next at the Museum of Modern Art in New York, where, in 1932, Wright was one of the architects included in the now famous International Exhibition of Modern Architecture. The work of Corbu, Mies, Gropius, and others of the "younger" generation was shown next to Wright's, much to his chagrin. He had by this time begun to consider himself in a special class entirely, and he had made no secret of this or of his contempt for the architects of the International Style—although he had, earlier, expressed his admiration for Corbu, Mies, and Gropius on many occasions. "I believe Le Corbusier [is] . . . extremely valuable, especially as an enemy," he had said. And, later, in speaking of Corbu's delight in proportional systems: "Le Corbusier, hard as nails and sane as a hammer up to this point, goes as superstitious as a milkmaid lost in the mist of a moonlit night" when speaking of systems such as the Golden Section. Moreover, Wright had made it perfectly clear to Henry-Russell Hitchcock, one of the organizers of the Modern Museum show, what he considered his own position in architecture to be. "I warn Henry-Russell Hitchcock right here and now that, having a good start, not only do I fully intend to be the greatest architect who has yet lived, but the greatest who will ever live. Yes, I intend to be the greatest architect of all time." That, it would seem, just about settled that.

Yet despite his anger at having his work exhibited next to that of Corbu, Mies, and others, Wright benefited considerably from the experience. For he was forced, much against his will, to *look* at what the younger men had been up to in Europe; and this look did him quite a bit of good. For the next six or eight years much of Wright's work suddenly became as "modern" as any done by Mies or Corbu: the Art Nouveau ornament disappeared, flat, undecorated surfaces and sweeping planes took the place of the filigree of the Imperial Hotel and the concrete block houses in California, and there were even some buildings with large, uninterrupted panes of glass. For a relatively brief moment Wright became almost an International Style architect himself! Then one day he appears to have heard a comment to this effect, and he angrily turned his back upon the International Style forever. Still, during the few years after the Modern Museum show, Wright produced some of the greatest buildings of his long and fruitful career.

X I I I

DURING THE 1930's Wright built four structures of a beauty unexcelled in America before or since. The first of these, in 1936, was the famous Kaufmann house at Bear Run, Pennsylvania—the house that was cantilevered out over a waterfall. The second, completed in 1938, was the administration building for the manufacturers of Johnson Wax, in Racine, Wisconsin. The third, a group of buildings begun in 1938, was Taliesin West, Wright's winter headquarters in Paradise Valley near Phoenix, Arizona. And the fourth was really a structural prototype: the so-called Usonian house, a dwelling Wright developed in the late 1930's and executed, in several variations, during those years. Wright was now in his sixties; and while his fortunes were gradually improving, he was denied any part in the three most important building projects of the decade: the construction of Rockefeller Center in New York, the building of the Chicago Fair of 1933, and that of the New York World's Fair of 1939. Yet, in retrospect, it was Wright's work in those years that did most to advance American architecture.

The Kaufmann house built for the head of a Pittsburgh department store, is probably the most poetic statement Wright ever made—and the most complete statement of his romantic beliefs. Here all the ancient, atavistic elements have been invoked to create a temple dedicated to nature: the rocky ledge on which the house rests; the massive boulder that is allowed to penetrate the floor of the living area to form the hearth; the fire at the center of the house; the waterfall below; and the great, sweeping cantilevers, almost incredible in their daring, that extend from this core of rock, fire, and water and thus carry the eye to the landscape beyond.

The Kaufmann house is remarkably simple by Wright's standards: a geometric composition of horizontal concrete planes (the cantilevered balconies) played against vertical stone planes (the walls and fireplace). It is so simple, indeed, that the influence of the International Style can hardly be denied. Yet it has no boxiness whatever: all interior corners are dissolved in glass, all interior spaces extended across broad balconies into the landscape. In short, the spatial continuity is assured by much the same means Wright had perfected since the days of the Prairie houses. And the structural plasticity—which, to Wright, must inevitably go hand in hand with spatial continuity—is more dramatically expressed than ever before in the great reinforced-concrete cantilevers balanced on the small rocky ledge above the waterfall.

While the Kaufmann house was nearing completion, Wright began work on another structure, which demonstrated even more clearly what he meant by continuity and plasticity. This was the Johnson Wax building, a horizontal version of Wright's Larkin building of thirty years earlier. Here again there was a great space—a secretarial pool—lit almost entirely from above, with mezzanines cutting into the central space at various levels and containing more important, individual offices. Yet where the Larkin building was Wright's architectural version of the

Kaufmann house, Bear Run, Pa., 1936. This dramatic structure is cantilevered out over a natural waterfall. The core of the house is a rocky ledge which forms the hearth of the fireplace. (Photo: Hedrich-Blessing)

vertical grain silo, the Johnson Wax building was a flattened-out structure of great horizontal bands of brick alternating with glass tubing; and where the Larkin building was all squared-off and blocky, the Johnson Wax building was softly rounded, its module being the circle.

Here, as at Bear Run, Wright produced a structure of startling modernity, as sleek and undecorated as anything built by the International Style. But while this seems particularly striking today in view of his earlier and later fondness for ornament, the sleekness of the Johnson Wax building is only a surface manifestation. Its true importance lies again in what Wright achieved here in terms of structure and in terms of space.

The basic structural unit designed by Wright was a very slender, tapered, tall concrete mushroom, a little like a giant golf tee. This elegant column was delicately balanced on a small brass shoe embedded in concrete at the main-floor level. There were more than eighty of these concrete tees, and each carried either a mezzanine floor level, or the roof, which, like the bands of glass in the exterior walls, consisted entirely of glass tubing welded together. As a result, the great central room, a space about 230 feet square, looks like a lovely grotto lit mysteriously from above, and inhabited by a forest of graceful stalactites. Here again the cantilever principle is employed in all its grace, for each of the concrete tees is, in effect, a balanced structure whose great circular crown is cantilevered out from the tapered shaft. No one believed that

S. C. Johnson & Son, Inc., administration building, Racine, Wis., 1936-9. All structures are curvilinear, as their plan is based on a circular module. Window ribbons and the roof of the main office space are of glass tubing. The supporting columns are of concrete, shaped like huge golf tees. The laboratory tower was completed in 1950. (Photo: Ezra Stoller)

Interior detail of Johnson Wax building, showing the supporting columns and the roof of glass tubing. Like the Larkin building and Unity Church, this urban structure is largely lit from above. The curved galleries give a hint of Wright's later Guggenheim Museum. (Courtesy, S. C. Johnson & Son, Inc.)

this structure would stand up, for there were then no rule-of-thumb methods of calculating any structure other than a post-and-beam cage. To get even a conditional building permit, Wright had to erect a test column on the site and load it with sand bags to the point of ultimate failure. The Racine city engineers were as baffled as everyone else (except Wright) when the test column proved to be capable of carrying many times the loads it would ever be required to bear.

Structural plasticity and spatial continuity here again went hand in hand. The space enclosure looked very thin-shelled—as, indeed, it was—because by alternating bands of brick with bands of glass tubing, Wright made clear in the exteriors that this wall was merely a screen and carried no loads. Meanwhile, the bands of glass tubing gave the interiors a recurring rhythm of light, much of it from unexpected angles. Even at the intersection of roof plane and exterior wall, where "box architecture" would inevitably have a cornice or a sharp, dividing beam, Wright destroyed the corner by creating a soft and rounded transition of glass tubing. In fact, the building has no corners at all; every space flows into every other, gracefully, naturally, without a moment of hesitation. It is one of the finest demonstrations of space-in-continuous-motion which Wright or anyone else has ever achieved. "To enumerate in detail or even catalogue the innovations to be found in this one building," Wright announced airily, "would require more time and patient attention on your part, and mine too, than either of us care to give it. So let's say here that it is technically, and in the entire realm of the scientific art of Architecture, one of the world's remarkably successful structures. I like it. They like it. Let it go at that." Just for once, Wright was not exaggerating one bit. The building, moreover, attracted so much attention—and, hence, free publicity—that the advertising man for the Johnson Wax people estimated that his company received more than $2,000,000 worth of free advertising at the opening of the structure alone! And the company has been using the building in its advertising ever since.

Taliesin West was begun by Wright in 1938, and, like Taliesin East, it was still growing at the time of his death, twenty years later. For several years he had taken the Fellowship down to Arizona in the winter months, as Spring Green was generally snowed in for that part of the year. At first he had built a temporary camp in Chandler, Arizona —a series of wood-and-canvas structures only a little more rigid than tents. Then, in 1938, Wright had a little bit of money (for a change) and managed to acquire some 800 acres of land in the Paradise Valley which nobody else seemed to want. He bought the necessary materials— redwood, canvas, rock, cement—and, with the young men of the Fellowship, went to work building one of the most colorful, most romantic groups of buildings erected since the passing of the Mayas.

"Taliesin West is a look over the rim of the world . . . magnificent—beyond words to describe," Wright wrote. In this beautiful setting, on what he considered to be America's last frontier, Wright built

Taliesin West, Phoenix, Ariz., 1938-59. The great wooden girders at left span the drafting room and support its canvas roof. The masonry is "desert concrete"—i.e., a mixture of huge rocks and cement poured into wooden forms. (Photo: Ezra Stoller)

a structure of something he called "desert concrete"—cement and large chunks of rock, all poured into slanting ramparts—topped with super-structures of redwood and canvas. Through the canvas, light would filter and fill the interior with a lovely glow; just under the deeply cantilevered roof rafters, there would be viewing slots that opened up the great desert horizon; and all around the base of the concrete-and-rock para-pets, there would be stepped-down terraces, pools, and gardens that made the entire group of buildings a dreamlike oasis in the desert.

The buildings to start with, contained only the most necessary accommodations for the Fellowship, plus a spacious, canvas-topped drafting room. At the heart of each major structure, there was a fireplace of desert concrete, and everywhere was evidence of the materials and the vegetation of the desert. In over-all plan Taliesin West had all the subtlety and delight of Taliesin East—the calculated progression through various kinds of spaces, the sudden surprises, the dramatic building silhouettes, the feeling of oneness with its natural setting. But where Taliesin East seemed a little frilly and, hence, old-fashioned, Taliesin West was a composition of rich and bold forms, shaped by a master sculptor. What ornament there was seemed to emerge from the structure itself—or else from the landscape in terms of planting, lighting, and vistas. Taliesin West was probably influenced by the spirit of Mayan architecture, but it was so original in expression that the Mayas could have provided little more than a point of departure.

A curious fact about Taliesin West (and about some of Wright's houses built nearby) was that it seems to be destined to make as fine a ruin as well! For all the perishable materials—wood and canvas—formed a sort of light-weight superstructure on top of the massive ramparts of

Kitchen area at Taliesin West. Using the most primitive means and materials, Wright succeeded in creating a magic play of light and shadow, mass and volume. (Photo: Ezra Stoller)

Terrace and Loggia behind Taliesin West. Wright kept adding to these structures—and changing them around—until his last days. The massive masonry blocks were probably intended to make a spectacular ruin if and when the wood-and-canvas superstructure might be gone. (Photo: Ezra Stoller)

desert concrete. If this superstructure were ever to be destroyed, the chances are that the ramparts of Taliesin West would remain standing and last forever. Indeed, one of Wright's Arizona houses—the Pauson house in Phoenix, built in 1940 with a core of desert concrete and a superstructure of wood and glass—burned several years after it was constructed; and the great masonry bulk that survived the fire made a more beautiful silhouette than the house in its entirety had made when it was still standing.

The Usonian houses Wright built during these years represented, in a sense, a modernization of the Prairie-house concept. Both in their greater simplicity and in their plan (which took cognizance of the fact that servants had become a vanishing breed), the Usonian houses were

Rosenbaum house, Florence, Ala., 1939. One of the most elegant Usonian houses, with sweeping roof planes separated by slots of glass. (Courtesy, Museum of Modern Art)

realistic and beautiful solutions to living in America in our day. Wright developed several of his Prairie-house ideas further: the car port, the floor slab with integral radiant heating, the built-in furniture, the open kitchen, the utility core, the modular plan, the pinwheel growth of that plan out of a central fireplace, the two-level roof—all these were simplified, modernized, made more economical in construction. But most importantly, perhaps, Wright began to make the Prairie house *look* more modern as well; the Rosenbaum house in Alabama, one of the finest Usonian houses built, has the dramatic sweep and simplicity of Mies's Barcelona Pavilion—or, possibly, of Wright's own unbuilt Yahara Boat Club. The same is true of the Winkler-Goetsch house of the same period—a wood, brick, and glass version of the Barcelona Pavilion in many of its details. It may be argued that Wright did not need Mies to remind him of his early Boat Club project; yet the fact remains that until Wright saw the International Style work in the 1932 exhibition at the Modern Museum, he was well on the way toward forgetting his own magnificently simple projects of the first decade of the century.

In the Usonian houses, Wright laid the foundation for much modern, domestic architecture in America during the two decades that followed. These houses were not as dramatic or romantic as Bear Run: but in their modest dignity they solved a problem that needed solving in America, and they solved it to perfection.

Through most of the period between 1910 and 1930 Wright had

been receiving the sort of publicity which scandal sheets thrive on: there had been love affairs, murder, fire, foreclosure, courts, and jail. The general public had come to think of him as something of a crackpot, a wild eccentric not to be taken very seriously. In the 1930's all this began to change: Wright's house at Bear Run became the best-known modern house in the world, for pictures of it were published everywhere. Its wild, romantic beauty appealed to everyone, regardless of whether they were familiar with modern architectural theory or not. *Life* published pictures of the Johnson Wax building on the week of its formal opening, and considered the story so important that the editors gave it the cover and the "lead" in the issue. In January 1938 the *Architectural Forum's* editor and publisher, Howard Myers, devoted an entire issue of the magazine to Wright's work. This special issue, virtually designed and written by Wright himself, soon became a collector's item. During the months of preparation of this issue, a close friendship sprang up between Wright and the charming and enthusiastic Myers, and thereafter Wright "allowed" the *Forum* to publish anything of his that the magazine wanted to print. (In actual fact, this arrangement made it possible for Wright to control closely what was said and written about his work in the professional press, with the result that no really critical evaluation of his work ever appeared in America during his lifetime.) In the same year, 1938, *Life* commissioned Wright to design a small Usonian house for its readers, and this, too, gave Wright's name and work wide and serious currency.

Wright always enjoyed this sort of publicity and became very adept at generating it in his final years. He was an extremely witty and incisive

Winkler-Goetsch house, Okemos, Mich., 1939. Another Usonian house of tremendous elegance and simplicity. In these houses, Wright—briefly—became as "modern" as Mies van der Rohe, in the sense of dropping all ornament and other complexity. However, his window openings remained narrowly subdivided. (Courtesy, Museum of Modern Art)

commentator on the passing parade and its various participants, and his sayings became famous everywhere. He soon became a sort of Alexander Woollcott of modern architecture, and, indeed, Woollcott and Wright were close friends. After Woollcott first saw the Usonian house for Lloyd Lewis, he wrote to Wright that he "told Lloyd that this one makes even a group of *his* friends look distinguished," a note which Wright cherished. When another owner of a Usonian house telephoned Wright in desperation because the rain was pouring in through a leak in the roof, the master calmly suggested: "Why don't you move your chair a little bit to one side?" He told Eliel Saarinen, the late, great Finnish architect, that after he had seen one of Saarinen's designs, he had thought "what a great architect—*I* am!" Wright's magnificent arrogance really blossomed forth in those years, a delight to him and to all who knew him. When the late Philadelphia architect George Howe told a fictitious parable, in which Moses was meant to represent Wright in the latter's efforts to lead his fellow architects out of bondage, Wright calmly informed Howe that "in this story, I am God." As for his fellow architects, Wright generously allowed that he admired them all, but, regrettably, did not feel the same way about their work.

Wright had a good deal of fun making his contemporaries squirm, and he was entitled to every bit of it. He also lived on a scale far beyond his means (as he always had), and enjoyed every minute of buying expensive Japanese prints and Chinese vases, magnificent silk pajamas, exquisite ties that must have been specially tailored for him to trail flamboyantly, royal capes of the handsomest tweed available, and so forth. He was generally broke, for he liked to spend whatever he earned as soon as he had earned it. He lived beautifully, tastefully, magnificently. Whenever he came to New York to deliver a short blast, he made an arresting figure striding down Fifth Avenue, pointing out the (to him) most deplorable sights with his elegant cane. As he grew older, he seemed to grow more beautiful also: his flowing silver hair, his erect figure, looking much taller than he really was, his weathered and bronzed face—he put on quite a show. "Early in life," he once explained, "I had to choose between honest arrogance and hypocritical humility. I chose honest arrogance and have seen no occasion to change. . . ."

X I V

N O MERE MANTRAPS; no more landlords. No life imprisoned on shelves of vertical streets, above crowds on gridirons down below. No hard faced poster façades . . ." This is how Wright described his project for Broadacre City—the ideal "living city" developed in the 1930's by the Taliesin Fellowship as a kind of summation of all of Wright's beliefs about how man could exist with dignity in a crowd. From 1934 on, the members of the Fellowship worked on huge models of this ideal city, incorporating various buildings designed by Wright for specific clients and specific needs, but related, by way of underlying principle, to the central themes of his life. Just as everything Corbu designed had some reference to his concept of a Ville Radieuse, first stated by him in the early 1920's, so everything Wright had designed

3 9 1

before 1934 (and was to design in later years) was incorporated in the notion of Broadacre City. This, however, is where all similarity ends between Broadacre and Radieuse.

Where Corbu's city was a collection of vertical towers, free-standing in a park, Wright's city was largely a horizontal expanse, with about an acre of land for each family. It is true that there were a few tall apartment houses also (generally based upon Wright's 1929 project for St. Mark's-in-the-Bouwerie), but these towers were really something of an afterthought, and never very clearly related to the rest of the city fabric. In essence, Broadacre was a decentralized, horizontal, close-to-nature city. Indeed, by today's standards it was no city at all; its population densities were those of a village; its economic pattern was that of a self-contained, self-sufficient community of religious (or political) eccentrics, intent upon showing the rest of humanity how some sort of "ideal" society could be established on earth; and its functional details were often startling, to say the least—as in a multilevel traffic intersection that seemed about as complicated as a Chinese mousetrap. But despite all its nineteenth-century idealism, despite all its lack of economic and political "realism"—or, perhaps, because of all these things—Broadacre City was a marvelously engaging flight of fancy. It was a sort of modern Garden of Eden, complete with vineyards, baths, facilities for physical culture, a circus, stables, and an arboretum. There was an area devoted to "universal worship," containing—according to Wright's specifications—a "columbarium, cemetery, nine sectarian temples surrounding a central edifice devoted to universal worship." There was an establishment housing "crafts and county architects," and another identified simply as a "Taliesin equivalent." In short, Broadacre City was the home of a society devoted to leisure and pleasure, and dominated by the pursuit of the arts. The whole thing was made entirely feasible—in Wright's eyes—because new methods of rapid transportation had annihilated distances. His own contribution to this process of annihilation was a fantastic automobile designed somewhat along the lines of a paddle-wheel steamer, and a helicopter shaped rather like a flying saucer. (Wright was always something of a fanatic about cars: his own favorite automobiles, in later years, were two classic 1940 Lincoln Continentals, painted terra-cotta red—the Taliesin color. He had nothing but contempt for most other Detroit models.) Finally, he supplied a design for a gas station whose pumps were suspended, upside-down, from deep roof overhangs so that cars could be serviced from overhead.

In some respects the notion of Broadacre City was influenced by the teachings of the religious mystic Gurdjieff, whose pupil Mrs. Wright had been in Paris before her marriage to Wright. Gurdjieff's beliefs, which Mrs. Wright communicated to her husband and to the entire Taliesin Fellowship, were not far removed from Wright's own thoughts about man and nature: they were based upon the conviction that man's life was a simple cycle, originating in the earth and returning to it, and that all artificial interference with this cycle must be avoided. In addition, Gurdjieff believed in the importance of rhythm—music and dance —as a means of bringing body and spirit into harmony, and Mrs. Wright, who had always been a dance enthusiast, transmitted her enthusiasms both to her own family and to the Fellowship as a whole. Partly because of these Gurdjieff concepts, Broadacre City became an intensely agrarian sort of place—an agrarian place, that is, replete with facilities for music and dance.

What Wright was really trying to say with Broadacre City is that the modern metropolis, as we know it, should be destroyed and that the only way to save America from "mobocracy" (his term) was to give everyone enough land and air and light to enable him to live as an individual, rather than a cipher. Wright liked to quote Emerson, who had said that "cities force growth and make men talkative and enter-taining, but they make them artificial." Wright, though a country boy, was never exactly uncommunicative or dull; but neither was he artificial. Artificiality was the result of living in an unnatural way, Wright thought, and the great, noisy, industrial metropolis was fundamentally unnatural. "We cannot achieve our democratic destiny by mere indus-trialism, however great," he wrote. "We are by nature gifted as a vast agronomy. In the humane proportion of those two—industrialism and agronomy—we will produce the culture that belongs to Democracy organic. . . ."

During the 1930's and 1940's the Communists got the impression that Wright's rejection of the money-centered metropolis, together with his other radical ideas, made him a natural ally. Wright went to Russia in 1937 and reacted to the standard party line and the standard conducted tours in a rather naïve way. He read into some of the plans of the Soviet regime—the development of agricultural centers, for example—a meaning they did not have at all: for Wright's own ideal society was completely *de*centralized, whereas the Stalin state was more centralized than any political organism before or since. Still, the *professed* objectives of the Soviet state—particularly when explained in ways that were likely to appeal to Western idealists—seemed not too far removed from Wright's own, and he developed considerable affection for his hosts. Upon his return to the U.S., he had some second thoughts about the role of the individual in a collective society, and decided that his own views were diametrically opposed to those of the Communists. As he told a group of Wisconsin Communists: "[We need] a genuine system of private ownership, a system of capital with its broad base on the ground in the lives of the whole people, instead of standing precariously on its apex for the few. . . ."

Nonetheless, when World War II broke out in Europe, Wright again found himself, briefly, on the same side as the Communists. By nature (and because of his special liking for Germany and Japan), Wright became an ardent pacifist—a line the Communists also followed, of course, until the German attack on Russia. Needless to say, Wright's pacifism had nothing to do with any party-political notions; he was opposed to killing human beings and believed that absolute pacifism was the only way to stop wars, just as he thought that absolute Broadacre Cities were the only means of saving individualism. "War itself," he once said, "is a denial of Civilization." Several members of the Taliesin Fellowship became conscientious objectors, and Wright supported their stand fully. His pacifist position during the war years did not get him into any particular difficulties: everyone by this time expected him to act in unorthodox ways, and, in any case, the popular mood during World War II was not very bloodthirsty. After the war was over, and the threat of Soviet power first became apparent to most

Americans, Wright again, briefly and naïvely, thought that the way to get along with Stalin's Russia was to be kind to it. He became a sponsor of a cultural conference arranged, in 1948, at the Waldorf-Astoria Hotel in New York between a group of official Soviet "intellectuals" and a group of fairly notorious American fellow travelers. That, however, was one of Wright's last major excursions into politics. Except for campaigning for the election of Adlai Stevenson in 1952 and 1956 (partly because he was extremely fond of Stevenson), Wright kept his hands off politics as such. It wasn't that he had been burned; he was simply bored, and thought that most issues as formulated by political parties had nothing to do with the central problems as he saw them—the problems of how to recapture dignity for the individual.

Like other architects not directly involved in the war effort, Wright tried to keep busy, between 1939 and 1945, doing projects that might someday be realized. The most intriguing aspect of these projects is their insistence upon exploring and expanding Wright's notions about plasticity and continuity of space and structure. More and more, Wright got away from straight-lined architecture altogether; his module—if that is the word—became the *circle*, rather than the triangle or polygon; his characteristic vertical form became the outward taper (a narrow base growing into a wider crown—i.e., a kind of tree silhouette); and his favorite structural shape became the spiral or snail. Again and again he would return to these basic themes: in the houses for Herbert Jacobs, Gerald Loeb, and V. C. Morris; in the spa proposed for Elizabeth Arden; in the great laboratory tower for the Johnson Wax building; in the drive-in laundry for Benjamin Adelman; and in the fantastic, multisaucer country club proposed for Huntington Hartford (and meant to be placed on top of one of the Hollywood hills), Wright made the never ending circle and the outward taper his central themes.

Most of these projects were never built; but the circle pattern remained in Wright's work and dominated it throughout his final years. Indeed, his feelings against the square as a harsh, inhuman, artificial thing became so strong that he actually laid out whole developments for Kalamazoo, Michigan, and Pleasantville, New York, in which the individual building lots were circular plots, one acre in size. It was never

*Friedman house, Pleasantville, N. Y., 1950. A house based
on a circular theme, rising like a small fortress out of its
hilltop. (Photo: Ezra Stoller)*

very clearly explained what was to happen to (and who was to own),
the space *between* the circles—the part of the Swiss cheese that isn't
holes—but Wright was never very much concerned with problems of
this sort, which, he felt, were the creation of bookkeepers and others of
their ilk. It seemed to him that no one who had any love for landscape
could ever impose a rectilinear, geometric pattern upon the face of the
earth, as such a pattern was fundamentally alien to nature. (Wright,
incidentally, had gone in for contour plowing at Spring Green long
before this became accepted farming practice in the United States!)

The spiral was the next logical step; it is the circle brought into the
third and fourth dimensions. One of the first spiral structures proposed
by Wright was the (unbuilt) planetarium project for Gordon Strong,
done in 1925. Strong had come to Wright wanting nothing more than
a place from which to gaze at the skies; by the time Wright was
through, he had redesigned all of Sugar Loaf Mountain, in Maryland,
by turning its top into a kind of broad, corkscrew shape providing a
spiral automobile approach to the planetarium on top. (Wright was a
perfectly good driver, but some of his notions of traffic patterns were,
to say the least, eccentric.)

From the planetarium project on, Wright kept coming back to the idea of the snail shape until, during the later war years, he developed two projects in which the spiral ramp became the central theme: the San Francisco store for V. C. Morris, and the New York museum for the Solomon Guggenheim Foundation. Both were built after the war.

The Morris store is really a remodeling job, though this is hardly evident: for if anything at all remained of the original building, Wright managed to conceal it completely. In a sense the store is two kinds of

Morris store, San Francisco, Calif., 1948. A spiral-ramp structure—the first of its kind actually built by Wright— under a glass dome. As the visitor ascends on the ramp, the space around him seems to revolve gently and take on an infinite number of changing aspects. (Photo: Maynard Parker)

architecture: a remarkable façade, and an equally remarkable interior space. The façade is simply a blank wall of brick—no show windows whatever—penetrated by a single, bold arch, very much like a façade by H. H. Richardson translated from stone to brick. The trick, of course, was to make the store front inviting by making it mysterious and quite different from any other store front in any other street or city: as, from the sidewalk, you can see none of the vases, candlesticks, and other accessories for sale inside, you are irresistibly drawn into this strange store that refuses to advertise its wares. In a sense Wright had taken a leaf from those ancient shops in St. James Street whose owners believe in leaving the windows murky and the displays decrepit. It works like a charm.

Inside, however, there is no trace of Richardson whatever. Here the entire space is filled with a lovely two-story spiral ramp that curls up gracefully toward a huge, circular glass dome that fills the store with light. Everywhere the details are in harmony with the circle theme: tables are circular, as are lighting fixtures, suspended planting trays, stools, and the glass bowls that make up the great skylight. The whole thing has a unity and strength rarely seen in a building, and a poetic loveliness that makes up many times over for the fact that, as a sales machine, the store probably is not as efficient as it might have been. But the most extraordinary thing that happens in this space is the tangible movement in evidence everywhere: as you walk down the graceful spiral ramp, you become strangely unconscious of your own movement; instead, the space itself seems to be slowly revolving around you. There may be some potential buyers who have been discouraged by this strange sensation; but most visitors to the store undoubtedly sense that here, in this little "unimportant" gem of a building, Frank Lloyd Wright added a new dimension to space.

In the Morris store Wright used the ramp simply as a means of getting from the street floor to the mezzanine level. There are only token displays on the ramp itself. But in the Guggenheim Museum, he made the ramp the actual gallery space, and paintings are supposed to be hung on the spiraling walls. The spiral ramp makes five complete turns around a central circular well; as it makes these turns, the spiral becomes slightly wider, so that the form of the building tapers outward in the characteristic Wrightian fashion. The light for this great circular well comes from two sources: from a large skylight dome above, and from strips of glass above the spiraling walls which follow the curvature of the structure all the way to the top. "They're going to try and figure this one out for years to come," Wright would say with glee as the Museum went up on Fifth Avenue.

In many curious ways the Guggenheim snail resembles the main entrance hall to the museums of the Vatican in Rome, which was built some twenty years earlier. But the Vatican spiral hall (though also skylit through a glass dome) is used only as a means of getting visitors upstairs and down, whereas the Guggenheim snail was meant to be the museum itself. In rationalizing this form, Wright made three points: first, that the slow descent would help visitors avoid "museum fatigue" (they are carried upstairs in an elevator); second, that the outward-slanting walls of the spiral ramp resembled easels and thus permitted a more faithful presentation of paintings than vertical walls would; and, third, that "the rectilinear frame of reference in a painting," as the *Architectural Forum* put it, "has more to do with the frame than with the painting."

Now, with all due respect—indeed, with supreme respect—for Wright, this is unmitigated nonsense. The Guggenheim Museum is almost impossible as a museum in the normal sense: if it had not been for certain changes made after Wright's death, a gallery-goer would have had to stand on an incline, look at a wall sloping away from him—a wall, moreover, that is curved so that any *large* paintings would have had to be fitted to its contours—and, while doing all this, he would have had to avoid being blinded by a continuous band of light from above, which appears aimed directly at his eyes! It is probably untrue to say, as one ex-Taliesin man suggested, that Wright hated the paintings in the Guggenheim collection and built a building to destroy them. He *did* dislike most modern art and had very little knowledge of or interest in it. But the chances are that the Guggenheim collection was far too unimportant to him to try to demolish it in such an elaborate manner. The fact is, quite simply, that Wright just *had* to build one great, wonderful spiral before he died,

Guggenheim Museum, New York City, completed in 1959. This is the view from the downtown end of Fifth Avenue. The big spiral in the foreground contains the galleries; the smaller, circular structure to the rear contains administrative offices. (Photo: George Cserna)

and he managed to sell the Guggenheim Foundation on the idea that it would make a good museum. (In 1947 he tried to sell Edgar Kaufmann, the Pittsburgh department store owner and client for "Falling Water," on the idea of building a spiral parking garage in downtown Pittsburgh—and, later, in the great Pittsburgh Point project. This suggestion made a good deal more sense than using the spiral for a museum gallery, although the parking attendants would have had to get their schooling in a hamster cage.) In short, the Guggenheim Foundation got a fabulous piece of architectural sculpture—the only completed work of uncompromising plasticity and continuity achieved by Wright—and should now make plans to build a place in which to show its paintings.

In several respects the Guggenheim Museum is an extension of earlier Wright buildings. When compared with the Larkin building of 1904, for example, it becomes quite clear what Wright had been driving at over the years. The Larkin building is really the Guggenheim Museum done in rectangular geometry: it has the same central well (but the well is a rectangle); it has galleries overlooking the well (but the galleries are level floors); it has a great skylight illuminating the well (but the skylight, again, is rectangular); and it has a simple, over-all form with stair towers, etc., pushed out beyond the central mass (but the form is squared off, as are the stair towers). In short, the road from Larkin to Guggenheim is the great avenue of Wright's creative development over half a century—from an architecture that was monumentally simple (but still boxlike) to an architecture that was fluid, plastic, continuous, and has utterly changed our ideas of the nature of space and structure. In between these two great buildings there were many others that are milestones along the way: Unity Church in 1906, with its great, skylit space of many levels; Johnson Wax of 1936, with its fluid forms, its glass roof, and its mezzanines; and the Florida Southern College buildings from 1938 onward, with their suggestion of *folded* planes à la Froebel, their many surprising levels, their astonishing play of light from above.

The Guggenheim Museum was almost finished when Wright died in April 1959. Apart from its importance as a plastic statement, it is important as Wright's last slap at the city. No building could be designed to fit less well into the established urban pattern—and that, in Wright's view, was about as great a compliment as you could pay a building. Both in form and in its clay color the Guggenheim Museum looks like a growing organism in a graveyard—not pretty, but certainly alive and kicking. Its exterior is perhaps a little too plain and crudely

Project for a parking garage, Pittsburgh, Pa., 1947. Here the spiral ramp was used to solve an eminently practical problem. This project was designed while the Guggenheim Museum was on the drawing boards. (Courtesy, Taliesin Fellowship)

Chapel at Florida Southern College, Lakeland, Fla., 1940.
The folded planes that form this hexagonal structure are
part of Wright's attempt to get away from boxy architec-
ture. The resulting forms are remarkably similar to those
of Froebelian games, on which Wright was brought up in
his childhood. (Photo: Ezra Stoller)

finished—one of the few *un*ornamented Wright buildings, perhaps because Wright wanted nothing to distract from the boldness of the
principal statement. But the chances are that when the planting begins
to trail over the curved parapets, the Guggenheim Museum may look
a good deal softer than it did on its opening day—almost mellow toward
its surroundings, as its creator grew to be toward *his* surroundings in the
last days of his life.

X V

LIKE LE CORBUSIER AND MIES, Wright had more work after World War II than he had ever had before. In addition to the Guggenheim, the Johnson Wax tower was built; the Florida Southern College campus at Lakeland progressed at a rapid pace—the sixteenth building nearing completion at the time of Wright's death; in Bartlesville, Oklahoma, Wright at long last found a client who was willing to build the tower originally designed, in 1929, for St. Mark's-in-the-Bouwerie; and all over the country there were new houses, big and small.

In addition, Wright worked on a vast number of projects that never went beyond the paper stage. Like Le Corbusier, he produced a seemingly endless flow of these detailed studies. One reason was that he was

Price tower, Bartlesville, Okla., 1953-6. A small skyscraper containing offices as well as apartments. In this tall structure, Wright at last realized a concept that had intrigued him for 30 years. (Courtesy, H. C. Price Co.)

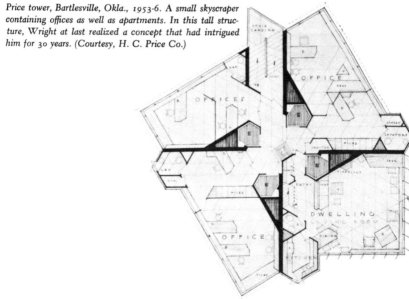

Plan of typical floor in Price tower, showing the cross-shaped "spine" that supports the building. All floors were cantilevered out from this "spine." (Courtesy, Taliesin Fellowship)

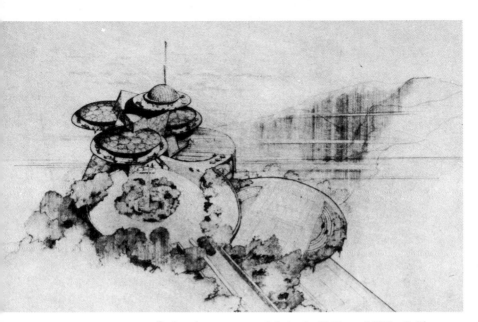

*Project for a country club in the Hollywood Hills, Calif.,
1947. Saucer-shaped platforms were to have been cantilevered out from a mountain top to carry restaurants, ten-
nis courts, etc. (Courtesy, Taliesin Fellowship)*

willing to jump into any situation that seemed even faintly promising,
to get his foot into the smallest crack in any door; another was that his
students at Taliesin represented a large, enthusiastic (and cheap) labor
force, delighted to try anything that might advance the cause of organic
architecture. Among the most impressive studies of the postwar years
was the country club for Huntington Hartford mentioned earlier—a
jagged pyramid of stone growing out of a mountain top, with half a
dozen circular concrete saucers or trays cantilevered from the central
mass of rock to carry restaurants, gardens, and pools halfway between
Hollywood and heaven. There was a towerlike hotel for Dallas, sheathed
in magnesium and glass, and tapered outward in the characteristic tree
silhouette. (Unfortunately, the client died before the project could go
ahead.) There was the plan to develop one of the most dramatic sites
in the U.S.—the Pittsburgh Point Park, the triangular tip of the city
formed by the Allegheny and Monongahela rivers. This study was

financed by a group of prominent Pittsburgh businessmen under the leadership of Edgar Kaufmann, but, unfortunately, came to nothing: instead, several real-estate promoters perpetrated an act of singular architectural barbarism on this beautiful site, and a great opportunity was lost.

As Wright passed his eightieth birthday and approached the age of ninety, he became, if anything, more, rather than less, prolific. The tower in Bartlesville for the H. C. Price Co. was completed in 1956—an eighteen-story structure containing both offices and apartments, and making up for a rather impractical layout by its success in turning a multicellular building into a statement of individualism (rather than a giant file cabinet). In 1955 Wright's occasional home town of Madison, Wisconsin, voted to have him design a magnificent civic center on Lake Monona. (The project—an extravaganza of circles and ramps—was shelved because local politicians were afraid of its cost.) In 1957 Wright heard that the State of Arizona was about to put up a new State Capitol building. Preliminary plans showed that the proposed structure would be just another "box," looking like the head office for a drugstore chain, rather than a center of democratic government. Wright decided that there was still a chance to prevent this particular act of official idiocy, and submitted a proposal of his own: a huge, romantic, teepee-shaped structure of hexagonal concrete grilles ("a vast lath house," Wright called it), surrounded by lower structures, gardens, fountains, and easy, pedestrian approaches. (He felt that a seat of government deserved a more leisurely and dignified approach than that suggested by a limousine tearing down a six-lane highway.) Despite a great deal of public agitation in behalf of Wright's lovely design, there was no stopping the bureaucrats, and the drugstore box was built instead. Finally, in that same year, Wright began work on a fantastic project for King Feisal II of Iraq—a fabulous opera house and civic auditorium for Baghdad, to be located on an island in the middle of the Tigris River. (While he was working on that design, he decided that he might as well also create the new University of Baghdad, although that commission had been given to Walter Gropius.) Wright's cultural center was to have been a circular structure, rather like a big musical top; it was to have been approached by means of a spiral-ramp highway leading up to the central complex, and guaranteed to chill the blood of any but the most experienced motorists. The building itself was to have been topped off by a glass-and-gold spire, which Wright referred to as "Aladin's Wonderful Lamp." And the whole thing would, indeed, have made Haroun Al-Rashid (or any of his Victorian admirers) goggle-eyed. Unfortunately, the revolution in Iraq and the murder of young King Feisal put an end to this project as well.

Meanwhile Wright received many honors, in the U.S. as well as abroad: the City of Florence awarded him its Gold Medal in 1951, and Wright (who had, in earlier years, said some unkind things about the classicism of the Renaissance) allowed that the great architects of that period in Florence did, after all, seem to have known what they were doing. However, he also felt, upon seeing his work exhibited in one of the great Florentine *palazzi*, that he did not have to worry about the judgment of history. Two years before the Florentine medal, in 1949, the American Institute of Architects had, rather belatedly, decided to award him *its* Gold Medal—only to detract from that honor a few years later by naming one of its "safe," conservative members the "Architect of the Century" (the century in question being the one dominated, for more than half its span, by Wright's genius). Wright's own reaction to these honors was predictably sarcastic: what really worried him was that he seemed to be becoming acceptable and even fashionable—a terrible fate for *any* radical! To keep the opposition opposed, Wright made a point of being outrageous in public as often as he could. His public pronouncements on such matters as the modern metropolis, the International Style, modern art, cigarettes, automobiles, clothes, TV commercials, Washington, D. C., and on all other architects became increasingly biting. He discovered that one way of making people sit up and take notice of what he had to say was to start by dropping a bombshell or two, and then to talk quietly (and often sensibly) in the ensuing silence. This is, of course, one of the accepted techniques employed by publicists of every stripe, and it contains certain dangers: for example, Wright occasionally produced designs that were so fantastic as to border on the preposterous—simply because he seemed to feel that this was an effective way of making a point. His 1956 Mile High building for Chicago's lake front was an example of this; if this giant needle-shaped tower with its 130,000 daytime inhabitants had ever been built, the problems of moving people, supplies, and services in and out of the structure would have been insoluble without razing the entire center of Chicago (which was, of course, precisely what Wright had had in mind).

This sort of thing hardly endeared Wright to his more "practical" fellow men, and it is probably for this reason that Wright was denied so many important commissions during the last years of his life. It is nonetheless unforgivable that the U.S. government never awarded a single commission to Wright, while lesser architects were asked to design new American embassies, consulates, military academies, post offices, and memorials all over the world. It is just as unforgivable that the states of Wisconsin and Arizona never awarded a commission to their illustrious citizen. And it is deplorable indeed that the American Institute of Architects, which often forms committees to recommend men for important public commissions, did not once remember its own Gold Medalist of 1949. Admittedly, Wright did not make it easy for bureaucrats to approach him; but, then, no one ever really made the effort. The result, in any case, is that the various governments of the U.S. do not possess a single building by America's most creative architect!

Wright never seemed to grow old. When he celebrated his eightieth birthday, he talked about moving farther out into the Arizona desert in ten years or so because the lights and telegraph lines of civilization were beginning to intrude upon the views from Taliesin West. Whenever he came to New York to stay in his (Wright-decorated) red-and-gold suite at the Hotel Plaza—from which he supervised the construction of the Guggenheim Museum—he seemed easily as spry as any of the bellboys, and a great deal more alert. And on the rare occasions when his work was exhibited next to that of younger men, he generally made his juniors look rather timid and stuffy by comparison with his own daring flamboyance.

Because he *was* the great Patriarch of architecture, no one ever really challenged him, however outrageous he might appear in some of his pronouncements. Le Corbusier and Mies van der Rohe might be

Walker house, Carmel, Calif., 1952. The house sits on a promontory overlooking the Pacific Ocean. (Photo: Ezra Stoller)

"Corbu" and "Mies" to every architect the world over, but Wright was always "Mr. Wright." He was the King—unchallenged, unchallengeable. At times, when he was staying at the Plaza (which he considered to be the Royal Residence in New York), he would take friends on a tour of the building, calmly walking into board meetings and similar gatherings in the hotel's private rooms and interrupting the proceedings to point out (with his Malacca cane) a decorative detail here or a flaw there. It never occurred to anyone to stop him: his presence was far too commanding. On TV and radio programs to which he had been invited as a guest, he would soon take over and run the show, and the cameras and microphones seemed irresistibly drawn to his face and voice as if by some sort of magnetic force. All of this Wright found exceedingly pleasant; indeed, one of his favorite stories in later years was about a lady who had asked Adlai Stevenson whether all the public adulation to which he was subjected was doing him any harm. "Adlai answered that it was all right so long as he didn't inhale," Wright would recall, grinning wickedly.

As a matter of fact, Wright inhaled deeply and with great satisfaction. After all, this was the pay-off, in a small way, for the poverty and the early struggle, for the condescension toward the country hick in Sullivan's office, for the innumerable projects left unbuilt and derided, for the years of yellow-journalist persecution, for the meanness of his fellow professionals and the grudging slowness of their recognition. Still, though he did enjoy the honors that came his way late in life, he managed to do so without any loss of dignity. To some he even seemed to grow rather mellow: when the National Institute of Arts and Letters awarded its Gold Medal to him in 1953, he stated, in mock alarm, that "a shadow falls . . . I feel coming on me a strange disease—humility." But the bitterness over much of the past was never far below the surface. "Although all may raise the flowers now, none have become trees," he wrote to a friend shortly before he died. "Why so late and why never the least gratitude from those who took heed? As the years have rolled by I have come to believe that architects themselves are really all that is the matter with Architecture . . . Well, let's start again at scratch: found a liberal society for the life of Architecture, for the lovers of good, organic Architecture. *Architecture* this time first, not architects . . . More of this later." Alas, his time was up; a few weeks later, in Phoenix, Arizona, on April 9, 1959, Frank Lloyd Wright died after a minor operation. According to the records, he was just two months short of ninety. With him, something important in America died also.

He was buried in Spring Green, at Taliesin; his coffin was carried on a farm cart. Before long, a chapel designed by Wright in his last years will be completed at Taliesin, and his remains will be transferred to this final burial place.

Spiral-ramp galleries in New York City's Guggenheim Museum. In this structure, Wright's twin concepts of plasticity of structure and continuity of space were completely fulfilled. (Photo: George Cserna)

A week before his death, Frank Lloyd Wright gave one of his regular informal talks to the Taliesin Fellowship. "What is fundamental to the architect-at-heart?" he asked. "What is it he must have? He has to have health, he has to have strength—strength of character most of all— strength of mind, strength of muscle. He has to know life, and he has to know life by studying it. And how do you proceed to study life most successfully and directly? By living it. To live the life . . . means the study primarily of Nature . . . Yours is the opportunity to shape and to determine the shape of things to come. You are the shape-hewers and the shape-knowers, or you are not architects at heart. But it takes a long time to make that kind of an architect . . ." Strength, character, life, heart: it took most of a century to complete the work of Frank Lloyd Wright; and when his work was done, Architecture had given mankind a new promise of civilization.

Taliesin, Spring Green, Wis. Here, among the hills where he was born, Wright was buried in the spring of 1959.

Prospect

ERO SAARINEN, one of the most creative architects of the generation that followed Mies and Corbu, believes that these two men, to gether with Wright, reached a certain plateau in the development of a new architecture, and that from this present plateau the ascent will soon continue, toward objectives as yet not very clearly known. Possibly so; but a good deal *is* known about the nature of the plateau on which architecture stands today, and much can be predicted from an analysis of that plateau.

The future of architecture will be shaped not only by new, creative artists, but also by certain facts to which even the most creative artist must respond. These facts have to do with technology, with political conditions, with population statistics, and the like.

The first fact—a fact of technology—is that the building frame made of straight steel or concrete members is going to continue in use because it is efficient, economical, and easy to put together. In short, the rectangular cage as refined by Mies—however limiting it may appear to those interested in a more sculptural expression—is sure to govern the shapes of most of our buildings for a great many years to come.

It is very likely that this rectangular cage will be sheathed with new materials that, in turn, will generate new patterns: for example, our preoccupation with the all-glass skin occasionally borders on the ludicrous: some architects today are actually putting up buildings sheathed with three or four layers of curtains, the inside curtain being all glass, and the additional curtains being various complicated devices designed to keep out heat, glare, and Peeping Toms. Indeed, by the time the glass wall has been made workable, it may have had so many additional skins of material attached to it that its total thickness exceeds that of the walls of Jericho. The pure, pristine glass-sheathed building will probably be with us for a long time, and fortunately so. But technology had better find more satisfactory ways of making it work.

The next fact that will govern the shape of architecture for many years to come has to do with population statistics. The suburban sprawl surrounding most American and many European cities is rapidly demonstrating the folly of horizontal planning and building. A typical American suburb has a density of only four or five families per acre; Wright's Broadacre City advocated something like one family per acre. On the other hand, the densities in new vertical apartment projects in New York and elsewhere are around 400 to 500 families per acre, and rising.

Neither one of these extremes makes any sense: the suburban sprawl has so completely engulfed every American city that few city dwellers can ever get out into open, unadulterated countryside; and the crowding within our cities is so intense that life inside the metropolis often seems close to being snuffed out completely.

The only rational solutions in the light of these facts and experiences seem to be those advocated for the past forty years by Le Corbusier and others influenced by him. Urban densities of 400 families per acre are not, in themselves, inhuman, so long as the distribution of built-on land versus park areas is handled with imagination. Corbu has demonstrated that a city of tall towers in a park is perfectly feasible without violating today's economic facts of life; the only problem is how to find the political and economic means without which such cities cannot be built.

It is, of course, remotely possible that the sort of decentralized city advocated by Frank Lloyd Wright might prove efficient in parts of the U.S.—where there is still plenty of space—though it cannot possibly work in Europe. But this presupposes two conditions that are doubtful, to say the least: first, it assumes that people don't like to live in cities; and, second, it assumes that businesses and industries can operate efficiently when cut up into smaller units. Neither one of these assumptions seems to have any basis in past or present experience; and when advocates of decentralization state, airily, that high-speed transport will overcome all difficulties by linking satellite towns to one another, they are ignoring the fact that many people like big cities not only because everything and everybody is within easy reach, but also because big cities hold a certain excitement that is intensely stimulating.

Does all this mean that the future belongs to Mies and Corbu alone? Does it mean that tomorrow's ideal cities will be assemblies of rectangular glass, steel, and concrete slabs rising out of a park landscape? Does it mean that Wright's intense effort has come to nothing?

Of course not. What is likely to happen is something suggested by the talented young American architect Paul Rudolph when he talks about the creation of "background" versus "foreground" buildings. Most of our multicellular structures—office buildings, factories, apartments, hospitals—are likely to remain "background" buildings, relatively anonymous, simple, and unaffected. These great structures will shape the spaces that, in turn, shape the city. They are like the neutral backdrops on a large stage. But within the spaces created by these "background" buildings, there will be many structures of an entirely different kind: buildings symbolizing some function of government, or some religious or communal aspirations; buildings requiring great, uninterrupted spans, like supermarkets and assembly halls; buildings for recreation and education. Many of these "foreground" buildings call for a structural system very different from Mies's cage—a much more sculptural expression, in most cases. Le Corbusier understood this very well when he demonstrated, in his plans for St. Dié and for Chandigarh, that certain symbolic buildings should be treated like huge pieces of sculpture—huge forms—carefully placed to contrast with their neutral backdrop.

And the "Search for Form," as Saarinen has called it, is on full blast. In this search, the work of Wright should suggest several exciting possibilities, and so should Corbu's excursions into plasticity. Both of these men always insisted, however, that the new forms were *significant* only if they acknowledged certain disciplines, especially the disciplines of advanced engineering. Yet, in America especially, these disciplines have lately been ignored to an alarming degree: in the name of symbolism, architects have created huge works of architectural sculpture that violate not only every known principle of engineering, but also every known functional requirement. The great Italian engineer Pier Luigi Nervi recently pointed out that there seems to be an unnatural "interest in novelty and technical daring"; that the many new sculptural roof shapes supported on only two points are "a structural absurdity which calls for sleights-of-hand in building"; and that this sort of thing amounts to "the development of ideas from the outside in"—i.e., a violation of the principles of organic architecture from Sullivan to the present.

One of the real problems is the constant demand for novelty, particularly in the U.S. Architects who do not come up with a new form every six months or so are considered "dead on their feet." Indeed, all artists, to a degree, are under the same sort of pressure—a pressure familiar enough in the area of consumer goods, where styling must satisfy the demands for new models at regular intervals to keep buyers buying and factories humming, but rarely before applied to the arts. One is reminded of some of the great works of the past—Ghiberti's doors in Florence, for example—which represent the work of a lifetime and changed the course of art decisively because they grew out of an inner conviction, an "organic" interplay between individual creative genius and the spirit of the time. By comparison, the brash, flamboyant forms presented today in the name of symbolism and greater plasticity seem to belong in the area of salesmanship and advertising, rather than architecture.

When the novelty begins to wear off, and the radical principles of engineering employed by Wright and Le Corbusier become better understood, the "foreground" buildings produced by new generations of architects will, undoubtedly, return to the fundamental disciplines of an "organic" architecture. Meanwhile, there remains one more problem: how to find architects modest enough to be content to design "background" buildings—the buildings perhaps most immediately in demand. The first decades of the modern movement had their heroes and the habit of hero worship has become deeply ingrained. Yet the time for heroes is coming to a close; the true hero of tomorrow's architecture will be the city itself, and all architecture, ultimately, will have to be subordinate to its demands. How this may be done is one of the lessons to be learned from the self-effacing life and work of Mies van der Rohe.

Indeed, it is high time that the city again became the hero of architecture, as it has been in all great periods of the past. Some years ago the British *Architectural Review* devoted an entire issue to "the mess that is man-made America." That mess was created by irresponsible exhibitionists—individualists—each trying to out-scream the next. Each was a star (so he thought), and each was some sort of hero; but in the ensuing bedlam the city went to pot. It is a fallacy to argue that this sort of bedlam is an expression of freedom. It is merely an expression of the license of the few to impose their vulgarity (or, at best, their precious egos) upon the defenseless many. A painting can exist in a vacuum—the creation of a solitary artist, to be seen and felt only by him. Most buildings cannot; they invariably impinge upon some segment of society, however small. Architecture is so powerful a medium, so potent a "persuader," that it will always be a force for something—a force for order, for chaos, or, perhaps, simply for more dreary indifference.

To create a coherent civilization—and this is its purpose—architecture must again become a force for order. Some critics have asked whether there can be freedom in architectural order. Indeed there can be; in fact, there can be no freedom *without* order, *without* a rule of law.

The three great architects who wrote so much of the story of modern architecture are its lawgivers; they created a set of physical and moral laws which architecture cannot afford to ignore. Even Wright, the freest spirit of the three, subscribed to as clear and rigid a code of architectural principles as the most disciplinarian architect of the Renaissance.

If Corbu and Mies supplied the basic functional and structural framework for tomorrow's city, Wright suggested something even more important: a way to give the city life. For though he was an implacable enemy of the city *as is*, he saw more clearly than anyone else how to make architecture come alive, how to give it what is often called "human scale." Both Mies and Corbu are monumentalists; their architecture is stirring—and why not? Man has always needed stirring buildings. But although Wright, too, built his share of monuments, he never forgot for a moment that architecture comes alive only when it becomes more than a diagram. Much of the work produced by the International Style has tended to be diagrammatic and flat; Wright's work has never been either. In a Wrightian building there was always enough detail to hold the observer's interest all the way, at a distance as well as at close quarters. There was always that subtle transition from the kind of space in which the individual would feel at home—low-ceilinged, lit at eye level, and intimate—to the dramatic, public space—high-ceilinged, lit from above, and monumental. What Wright gave to architecture was really this: a way of dignifying the individual in an architecture for a mass society. Many of these lessons Wright took from the Japanese; but regardless of where they originated, it was Wright who translated them into a modern idiom.

So, to the disciplines of function and of structure, architecture must add the discipline of individual freedom. It is not the easiest discipline to define, and it cannot be taught by means of formulas or rules of thumb. Yet it is, quite probably, the most essential discipline of the three; for if modern architecture cannot make the individual human being feel proud, it will be little more than an abstraction.

The next phase in the evolution of modern architecture would seem to be a sort of synthesis of all the concepts developed by Wright, Mies, and Corbu. The three are not nearly as far apart as they once appeared to be. Le Corbusier's concept of an organic architecture may be much more intellectual than Wright's romantic notion of the same name; but given certain cultural and temperamental differences, the two ideals now appear remarkably close. Mies—who never moved very far away from Sullivan and the early Wright—can probably find common ground with Wright in matters of principle (if not of practice). And there was, of course, never any conflict at all between Mies and Le Corbusier.

The new generation of architects which will do most of the synthesizing is now hard at work; most of its members seem dominated by Mies and Corbu—but only superficially so. In reality, the principles Wright brought into modern architecture are being rediscovered and reinterpreted—and modernized. Wright's sense of scale, his love of small-scale detail, his mastery of light and space (and the interplay of these two)—all this is beginning to intrigue the new synthesizers. But, above all, they are fascinated by the notion of continuous, plastic structures: although Wright never really built a structure that was as continuous and plastic as he knew structures could be, he recognized the fulfillment of his dream in the work of one or two younger engineers. Indeed, the only contemporary structures he was really willing to praise in his last years were the plastic concrete umbrellas by the Spanish engineer Eduardo Torroja, and the hyperbolic paraboloids by the Argentine engineer-architect Eduardo Catalano. These two men, together with Mexico's Felix Candela, Italy's Pier Luigi Nervi, Germany's Frei Otto, and others, today exert a growing influence upon the younger generation of architects. Yet what they are teaching is really the lesson of Wright—modernized, rationalized, and made practical.

Thus, Wright's influence crops up all over the place, though it is often difficult to identify as such. The more simple-minded "disciples" of the late master continue on their merry way, putting up copies of the master's somewhat old-fashioned, Victorian-looking houses without, apparently, understanding the underlying principle and its realization, which was almost in Wright's grasp when he died. Meanwhile, architects like Saarinen, Philip Johnson, and Paul Rudolph are busily synthesizing Wright's work with that of Mies and Corbu: Saarinen builds "universal spaces" à la Mies, but puts them under plastic structures of a kind imagined by Wright; Johnson is still interested in "poetic expression of structure" (again à la Mies), but the structure is becoming increasingly fluid and sculptural—a far cry from Mies's steel pilaster; and Rudolph, though influenced by everyone from Le Corbusier to Wright's Dutch admirer Willem Dudok, is really most concerned with questions of scale, and ways of establishing the scale of a building by intricacies of detail, of spatial organization, and of lighting.

Just as Wright has some simple-minded "disciples" who continue to copy every frill the great man ever doodled on a scrap of paper, so Mies and Corbu have their disciples who have stuck close to the straight and narrow path. Generally speaking, the work of these men has none of the embarrassing naïveté found in the Wrightians' labors, for neither Mies nor the early Corbu had a very *personal* style. Indeed, Mies—being concerned with the creation of a universal and anonymous vocabulary —has passed on to his followers an architectural language that can be learned with relative ease and applied successfully by almost anyone. Corbu, except in his highly personal statments of the last years, created similarly "universal" solutions in concrete, and the little Corbu slab buildings going up as part of the London County Council's housing or Japan's effort at reconstruction seem perfectly genuine and at home. But, by and large, these faithful followers of Mies and Corbu—though important as creators of "background" buildings—are simply carrying on a rich tradition, not expanding it.

Those like Saarinen, Johnson, Rudolph, and the Detroit architect Minoru Yamasaki, who are struggling with different ways of synthesizing the three great traditions passed on to them, are the more important men of the new generation. They are not innovators: it would be difficult to innovate after so overwhelming a flood of new ideas. They are the "summer-uppers," the men who are trying to find areas of agreement in the three very different idioms they have inherited from Mies, Corbu, and Wright. Their most significant work is being done in the field of "foreground" buildings; in fact, they are probably too self-important (as all artists are bound to be) to limit themselves to the creation of "background" structures. When Johnson says that the Seagram Building represents, to him, the end of modern architecture, he really means that, with Seagram completed, he personally is through designing "background" buildings. And when Yamasaki says that he uses Mies's intensely moral sense of structure as a point of reference only, he is again suggesting that the "background" buildings can be safely left to others now that Mies has designed them all for everyone to emulate.

It is a little unfortunate that the most creative talents of the new generation are leaving the vast and numerically most important field of "background" buildings to lesser men. Yet this is almost inevitable: because Mies and Corbu really solved, on paper at least, all that needs to be solved in the design of the great backdrops of future cities, the more creative minds are bound to concentrate upon those areas that still offer opportunities for experimentation, imagination, creative action—or, in any case, synthesis. The danger is, of course, that those who have chosen to concentrate upon "foreground" architecture may be too concerned with novelty for novelty's sake alone. Some of the more widely publicized "foreground" structures of the recent past suggest that this may be so; but the chances are that this new eclecticism will pass. The new generation of architects is beginning to return to the underlying disciplines of structure and function, all organically related as Corbu and Wright tried to relate them. This represents no abdication on the part of the younger architects: after all, Michelangelo was perfectly willing to follow the example of Brunelleschi's dome in Florence when he designed that of St. Peter's.

If there are to be any new Michelangelos in our time, they will have to accept the three propositions suggested above: first, that the fundamental principles of the new architecture were settled by its great law-givers; second, that the time for individual heroes is past; and, third, that the hero of the future must be the city itself. Out of this acceptance may grow a new generation of great artists, all working within a universally understood discipline, all interpreting that discipline in new ways—a new generation of Bramantes, Michelangelos and Palladios. But if the younger architects refuse to accept these three propositions and insist upon individual heroics in a mass society, the future of architecture—the future of cities—will be but a caricature of all the things that were transmitted to us by the true heroes. The alternatives are architecture or Disneyland, civilization or chaos. "What makes our dreams so daring," Le Corbusier once said, "is that they can be realized."

Index

Page references in parentheses refer to illustrations in the text